Inside Bankruptcy Law

ASPEN PUBLISHERS

Inside Bankruptcy Law

What Matters and Why

Nathalie Martin

Dickason Professor of Law
University of New Mexico

Ocean Tama

Haynes and Boone, LLP

Wolters Kluwer

Law & Business

AUSTIN   BOSTON   CHICAGO   NEW YORK   THE NETHERLANDS

Aspen Publishers
Attn: Permissions Department
76 Ninth Avenue, 7th Floor
New York, NY 10011-5201

To contact Customer Care, e-mail customer.care@aspenpublishers.com,
call 1-800-234-1660, fax 1-800-901-9075, or mail correspondence to:

Aspen Publishers
Attn: Order Department
PO Box 990
Frederick, MD 21705

Printed in the United States of America.

1 2 3 4 5 6 7 8 9 0

ISBN 978-0-7355-6829-7

Library of Congress Cataloging-in-Publication Data

Martin, Nathalie, 1961-
    Inside bankruptcy law : what matters and why / Nathalie Martin, Ocean Tama.
        p. cm.
    Includes index.
    ISBN 978-0-7355-6829-7 (pbk. : alk. paper) 1. Bankruptcy—United States. I. Tama,
Ocean, 1971- II. Title.
    KF1524.85.M37 2008
    346.7307'8—dc22
                            2008022168

About Wolters Kluwer Law & Business

Wolters Kluwer Law & Business is a leading provider of research information and workflow solutions in key specialty areas. The strengths of the individual brands of Aspen Publishers, CCH, Kluwer Law International and Loislaw are aligned within Wolters Kluwer Law & Business to provide comprehensive, in-depth solutions and expert-authored content for the legal, professional and education markets.

CCH was founded in 1913 and has served more than four generations of business professionals and their clients. The CCH products in the Wolters Kluwer Law & Business group are highly regarded electronic and print resources for legal, securities, antitrust and trade regulation, government contracting, banking, pension, payroll, employment and labor, and healthcare reimbursement and compliance professionals.

Aspen Publishers is a leading information provider for attorneys, business professionals and law students. Written by preeminent authorities, Aspen products offer analytical and practical information in a range of specialty practice areas from securities law and intellectual property to mergers and acquisitions and pension/benefits. Aspen's trusted legal education resources provide professors and students with high-quality, up-to-date and effective resources for successful instruction and study in all areas of the law.

Kluwer Law International supplies the global business community with comprehensive English-language international legal information. Legal practitioners, corporate counsel and business executives around the world rely on the Kluwer Law International journals, loose-leafs, books and electronic products for authoritative information in many areas of international legal practice.

Loislaw is a premier provider of digitized legal content to small law firm practitioners of various specializations. Loislaw provides attorneys with the ability to quickly and efficiently find the necessary legal information they need, when and where they need it, by facilitating access to primary law as well as state-specific law, records, forms and treatises.

Wolters Kluwer Law & Business, a unit of Wolters Kluwer, is headquartered in New York and Riverwoods, Illinois. Wolters Kluwer is a leading multinational publisher and information services company.

*This book is dedicated to Reva Paley,
an inspiration to all who knew her.*

Summary of Contents

PART 1. CONSUMER BANKRUPTCIES UNDER CHAPTERS 7 AND 13

PART 2. BUSINESS REORGANIZATIONS UNDER CHAPTER 11

Contents

PART 1. CONSUMER BANKRUPTCIES UNDER CHAPTERS 7 AND 13

xi

Chapter 3. Introduction to the Bankruptcy System 23

Chapter 4. The Automatic Stay 41

PART 2. BUSINESS REORGANIZATIONS UNDER CHAPTER 11

Chapter 14. Overview of CHAPTER 11 and Its Alternatives ... 161

Preface

This short book is designed to give you a succinct overview of the law of bankruptcy and creditors' rights. It is for the reader who wants a general feel for the topic, along with a bit of context, but who does not want to read a 500-page treatise on the subject. It is designed to put bankruptcy in context—in the context of society and our cultural values as a whole, and in the context of a larger body of law. It can be used by law students as a backdrop to introductory bankruptcy and creditors' rights classes, as well as in a more advanced CHAPTER 11 class. It also can be used by general practitioners as a way to become familiar with bankruptcy law.

Our book is different from most other study guides in the following ways:

- Recognizing that some people are visual learners, while others absorb abstract ideas more easily, this book presents charts, diagrams, cartoons, pictures, and other visual aids, in addition to presenting the concepts in ordinary writing. For some students and lawyers, the visual aids will make it easier and more enjoyable to understand and remember the subject matter.
- Each short chapter starts with an *Overview*. This is a very brief summary of the topics in the chapter, and can be used as an easy reference if you're looking for a specific topic or trying to put all the pieces together.
- The chapters end with *Connections,* which explain why the topics in the chapter are important in the overall context of debtor-creditor law, and how they connect with other topics in the book.
- Our book features *FAQs* (Frequently Asked Questions) and *Sidebars* that explain terminology, offer additional examples from the real world, and provide study tips.
- Key terms in this book are boldfaced, to help you learn some of the ever-important language of debtor-creditor law. Like so many areas of law, learning to speak the language will help you to understand the concepts.

Studies of learning theory suggest that if a word is repeated in different contexts, people quickly learn to understand the meaning of that word based on the context in which it is used. Thus we have attempted to use words frequently and in different contexts, so that you can master the new language with a real understanding of the concepts, not just a surface recognition of them. Most of the words in bold are bankruptcy-specific vocabulary and are highlighted to allow you to recognize them and to pay special attention to their context. Some of these are technical legal terms and others are commonly used legal jargon.

Part 1, Consumer Bankruptcies Under Chapters 7 and 13, covers general bankruptcy principles and consumer bankruptcy, mostly in the context of Chapter 7 and Chapter 13 cases. Part 2, Business Reorganizations Under Chapter 11, covers more complex business issues arising in Chapter 11 cases.

This book has been reviewed by faculty members as well as by law students. It has been edited by students who have taken the basic and advanced bankruptcy classes, as well as students who have never taken these classes. Why have we asked students to read this book? To make sure that it is understandable and useful to you, which is the ultimate test of its success.

We thank you for buying it and we hope that it is valuable for you.

Nathalie Martin
Ocean Tama
June 2008

Acknowledgments

The authors thank Stewart Paley, Sunne Preston, Chris Lopez, and Deborah Stambaugh for their tireless efforts on earlier drafts of this book. The authors also acknowledge Shawn E. Wamsley and Kevin Dilg for their fine artwork for this book.

Inside Bankruptcy Law

1

Consumer Bankruptcies Under Chapters 7 and 13

The Secured Creditor's Rights: A Brief Introduction

1

This course is the study of debt. In our society, we have devised an elaborate scheme for dealing with debt. This chapter describes two

O V E R V I E W

different kinds of debt: debt with collateral (secured debt) and debt without collateral (general debt or unsecured debt). This distinction remains critical throughout all the topics covered in the rest of this book. It is a crucial distinction not only in a formal bankruptcy proceeding, but also in ordinary debtor-creditor law, as the first two chapters illustrate.

The distinction between secured creditors and unsecured creditors is central to understanding debtor-creditor relations because, as later chapters of this book discuss in great detail, the two types of creditors are treated very differently, both inside and outside bankruptcy. Because most bankruptcy and creditors' rights laws distinguish secured creditors from unsecured creditors, it is important to understand the distinction from the beginning.

The reason secured creditors get better treatment is because secured creditors have a security agreement with the debtor that gives them contractual rights to the collateral supporting their loans. The secured creditor made a lower-risk loan than other creditors, because the secured creditor got the debtor to sign a contract giving the secured creditor collateral in exchange for the loan. So it seems only fair that the secured creditor should receive favorable treatment in bankruptcy to better reflect what the secured creditor's position would have been outside of bankruptcy.

A. TYPES OF SECURED CLAIMS OR LIENS

1. Voluntary Liens
2. Involuntary Liens

B. LIENS ATTACH TO SPECIFIC PROPERTY

Secured creditors (lenders) have **collateral** or **security** backing up their loans. Essentially, they have the right to take particular property from the borrower if the borrower doesn't repay the loan. In order to get the loan the borrower has agreed to give the lender the right to take the property if the borrower defaults on the loan. The right to take the property if the debtor doesn't pay is called a **security interest**.

Think of a mortgage on a house, which secures repayment of the loan that an ordinary American uses to buy a house. A home mortgage is the most common example of secured debt in our society, but practically any valuable possession can secure a loan. We really do mean anything, tangible or intangible — a car, a collection of tattered law books, a debt that a third party owes to the borrower, the borrower's rights under an esoteric contract (such as a musician's right to receive royalties from a song each time it gets downloaded to an iPod), or a plaintiff's rights to collect money from a lawsuit. Even a tenant's interest in a lease or a farmer's grazing rights on land can be pledged as collateral for a loan. Once you learn the legal power that a lender gets from having collateral, you'll wonder why lenders ever loan money *without* taking a security interest.

Why is collateral so important in the real world? Because a **secured lender** can take the collateral if the debt is not repaid, and thus having collateral for a loan makes it far more likely that the loan will be repaid. For this reason, business loans are often **collateralized** by tangible and intangible personal property, such as equipment, inventory, accounts receivable, and trademarks and patents. The fact that the lender can take these items from a company if the company defaults motivates the company to repay secured lenders *before* paying off other debts that are unsecured, such as utility bills and unsecured suppliers. Similarly, consumers are likely to pay their mortgages (secured by their house, on which the mortgage company can foreclose) and car payments (secured by their car, which the lender can repossess) before paying credit cards and medical bills (unsecured debts).

The philosophy and policy behind the security interest is that laws that promote the concept of a security interest (borrowers pledging collateral to secure a loan) encourage economic activity by encouraging borrowing. The easier it is for a creditor to collect a debt, the more willing a creditor is to lend money. To put it another way, the easier the mechanism for collecting debts, the cheaper the cost of borrowing money — creditors can afford to lend money at a lower interest rate when they have lower collection costs to bear. When access to capital (money) is affordable, it allows people in a society to be entrepreneurial and start businesses, which in turn creates jobs and wealth.

A lender without collateral is called an **unsecured creditor** or a **general creditor**. When a debtor defaults on an **unsecured debt**, the unsecured creditor *cannot* simply take collateral and sell it. There is no collateral to take! Instead, the unsecured creditor can endure the pain-in-the-neck of going to court, proving the debtor owes the debt, getting a judgment entered against the debtor, and then trying to collect on the judgment. This process is frequently more trouble than it's worth. And after all that, the debtor may not even have any valuable property — or at least none that the creditor can reach to pay the unsecured debt.[1]

Since secured creditors have collateral supporting their debts, a secured creditor usually has the right to simply repossess the collateral, sell it, and get paid from the proceeds. Secured creditors don't even have to involve the courts or attorneys. This is probably the biggest advantage of being a secured creditor under state law. And that's one of the reasons the legal distinction between secured creditors and unsecured creditors makes such a big difference.

In addition to the advantageous position that secured lenders have vis-à-vis unsecured lenders, banks prefer secured lending to unsecured lending because the federal government limits the percentage of unsecured loans a bank can make. This regulation prevents banks from getting themselves into trouble by making too many risky unsecured loans, on which there is no collateral to collect in the event of default.

Secured lending got a tremendous boost in the 1950s and 1960s with the advent of Article 9 of the U.C.C., because Article 9 provided the underpinning for secured financing, especially when the collateral was accounts receivable or inventory. As noted law professor Soia Mentschikoff[2] said, "Article 9 was a boon for small businessmen. Big businesses could always get loans." Those loans were usually unsecured. Karl Llewellyn once asked New York banks how they did secured lending. The answer was, "We don't do much of that sort of thing; we do unsecured loans because we deal only with people who come well-recommended."

Lending in those days was essentially an old-boys' club, and often "all in the family," because big businessmen and big bankers were frequently relatives in families like the Carnegies and the Mellons. As a result of Article 9 and the secured lending it promotes, small businesses, including those owned by minorities, women, and other underserved populations, are now treated more fairly and have a better shot at getting financing. Thus, the advent of secured lending is associated with progressive economic policy.

A. Types of Secured Claims or Liens

There are three basic kinds of **liens** that creditors hold in particular property.

(1) Voluntary Liens

First, there are **voluntary liens** (or **voluntary security interests**), which are *created by contract* between the debtor and the creditor. The debtor typically gives an Article 9 security interest or a mortgage to a secured party in order to obtain credit from the creditor. These are the most common secured creditors.

---

[1] Some assets owned by individual debtors, natural people like you and me, are "exempt" from general creditors' claims. This means the debtors get to keep certain possessions even if they do not pay their debts. Exemptions are discussed in Chapter 6 of this book.

[2] Professor Mentschikoff was the wife of Karl Llewellyn, one of the principal drafters of the U.C.C. and the father of modern commercial law.

Secured Transactions is the area of law devoted to the subject of obtaining and enforcing Article 9 security interests in personal property. The process starts with a contractual agreement by the debtor to grant the creditor a security interest in specified assets or categories of assets. The creditor must give value in exchange for the security interest and the debtor must have some rights in the property. These three things (the agreement, the value, and the rights) cause the security interest to **attach**, or become effective, as between the debtor and the secured party. Once the security interest is created and has attached, most secured parties **perfect** their security interest (usually by filing a financing statement but sometimes by possessing the collateral, among other ways), so the security interest is enforceable against third parties and the creditor can get priority over other creditors.

Voluntary Security Interests — Brief Overview	
Attachment	**Method of Perfection**
• Agreement	• Filing a financing statement
• Value	• Possession
• Rights	• Other methods under Secured Transactions law

(2) Involuntary Liens

In addition to voluntary security interests, there are **involuntary liens**.

(a) Judicial Liens

Judicial liens are created through the state court execution process described in Chapter 2. These liens are *not created by contract*. Rather, the creditor attempts to collect its debt by taking the debtor's property through the judgment, execution, and sale process, all of which occur against the debtor's will. Other involuntary judicial liens include those created by docketing a judgment in the real estate records.

(b) Statutory Liens

Finally, there are **statutory** (or common law) liens, which are also involuntary, and which are created by state statutes or by the courts — not by an adverse judgment, but by a court-created rule of law. For example, a landlord has a lien (a **landlord's lien**) in property that is left on the premises by a tenant. The landlord can sell the property and use the proceeds to pay past due rent. A **mechanics' lien** arises when a contractor remodels a house and doesn't get paid. Technically, we say the contractor is entitled to the lien because he has created a benefit on a property owner's land. Similarly, **artisans' liens** arise when an auto shop repairs a car and doesn't get paid. In that case, the auto shop can keep the car, and even sell it, if necessary, to pay the unpaid repair bill. Don't get confused by the terminology: Mechanics' liens apply to contractors and subcontractors, while artisans' liens apply to auto mechanics. Finally, there are statutes that create **tax liens**.

Some Typical Involuntary Security Interests — Brief Overview	
Name of Lien	**Typical Purpose**
• Judicial Lien	• To collect a debt by getting a judgment, executing on the judgment, and selling the debtor's property to satisfy the debt
• Real Estate Lien	• Typically filed in the real estate records to collect a judicial judgment
• Landlord Lien	• To collect unpaid rent by selling the tenant's property left on the premises
• Mechanics' Lien	• To collect unpaid contractor's bills for home improvements or building
• Artisans' Lien	• To collect unpaid bills for services, such as by auto repair shops
• Tax Lien	• To collect taxes owed

But what happens when a debtor won't pay, and doesn't have any property from which the unsecured creditor can be paid? The creditor does not get anything at all. As the saying goes, "you can't get blood from a turnip." The widely used term for this condition is that the debtor is **judgment proof**.

Of course, the creditor can technically still get a paper judgment from a court, saying that the debtor owes the money. But many times the creditor won't bother if the debtor has no money, because the paper judgment will likely be worthless, or the legal process will cost more than the paper judgment is worth. As another saying goes, such a judgment is "not worth the paper it's printed on." Perhaps "collection proof" would be a more accurate term, but lawyers frequently use the term "judgment proof" when they mean that it's not worth the effort to get a judgment.

F   A   Q

Q: Does it matter what type of lien a creditor has?

A: Outside bankruptcy, no. Liens can generally be enforced to collect on a claim, though the process is easier for voluntary liens like mortgages and Article 9 security interests, than it is for involuntary liens like landlords' liens, mechanics' liens, and artisans' liens. Once a debtor is in bankruptcy, judicial liens can be **avoided** (wiped out) if they interfere with a debtor's exemption rights. See Chapter 6. Also, if a security interest is not perfected, it can be avoided in bankruptcy. See Chapter 9, Section C.

B. Liens Attach to Specific Property

One way of thinking about liens is that they attach to something specific, or a number of specific things. They don't just float around in the air. Once the item with the lien on it is sold, the lien is usually lost on that particular property. However, to cure this problem, security agreements usually specify that the security interest is in all the borrower's property, "now owned or hereafter acquired." That way, the security interest attaches to new property, such as inventory, as soon as the borrower purchases it. This also raises the issue of **cash collateral** — the cash that a business gets when it sells inventory that was subject to a security interest. See Chapter 16 for the special rules that govern cash collateral.

SUMMARY

■ There are two kinds of creditors, those with collateral backing up their claims and those without. Those with collateral have superior collection rights both inside and outside bankruptcy, making this one of the most important distinctions in debtor-creditor law. Creditors with collateral are called secured creditors and those without are called unsecured creditors.

■ Secured creditors with certain types of collateral can repossess their collateral through self-help. All secured creditors can get their collateral back eventually, and use it to satisfy their claims.

■ Creditors with collateral backing their claims hold various types of liens in particular collateral.

■ Some liens arise when a secured creditor has a contract in which the debtor grants the creditor a voluntary security interest, usually in a written security agreement. Other creditors get their liens involuntarily, by going through the state court execution process, and others obtain liens through statutes. These are called voluntary, involuntary, and statutory liens, respectively.

CONNECTIONS

State Collection Law

Secured creditors can usually simply take collateral and sell it when a borrower defaults, whereas unsecured creditors must follow the state law collection process — filing an action in court, proving the debt, obtaining a judgment, and following the execution process — as outlined in Chapter 2.

The Automatic Stay

A secured creditor can generally get the automatic stay lifted in order to get its collateral back if it is not being paid in a bankruptcy case, as discussed in Chapter 4.

Exemptions

Voluntary secured creditors usually come out ahead of exempt property, while unsecured creditors, involuntary lien holders, and non-purchase money security interests (PMSIs) only get what's left over after exempt property is taken into account. This issue is explained in Chapter 6, Section C.

Treatment of Secured Claims in Bankruptcy

There are many detailed rules that govern the treatment of secured creditors' claims in bankruptcy generally, and in CHAPTER 7, CHAPTER 13, and CHAPTER 11 cases specifically. These are explained in Chapter 8, Chapter 12 (regarding CHAPTER 7 cases), Chapter 13 (regarding CHAPTER 13 cases) and the second half of this book (regarding CHAPTER 11 cases).

Avoiding Powers

The importance of following all the rules for becoming a secured creditor — perfecting a security interest — are highlighted in Chapter 9, Section C, which discusses how a trustee can avoid an unperfected security interest, turn the previously secured creditor into a general unsecured creditor, and get the previously encumbered property back into the estate for distribution to all the unsecured creditors to share equally.

State Collection Law

2

Even outside a formal bankruptcy system, every society needs a system for collecting debts. In the United States, our system is governed by

state law, and thus we call it the state court collection system. It is primarily a race to the courthouse. First come, first served. By the time a debtor gets so far behind on all her payments that creditors start collecting, she probably doesn't have enough money to pay all her creditors — that's why she's not paying to begin with! When there's not enough money to go around, the fastest creditor wins. That's why state court collection law is a **race of the diligent** — the most diligent creditor gets to the courthouse first and beats out rival creditors.

Most substantive and procedural areas of law focus on how to get a judgment, but this chapter describes the process of turning a judgment into money if the defendant does not pay voluntarily. The chapter also explains how different types of liens arise.

The purpose of describing state collection laws, credit reporting laws, and fraudulent transfer laws is to provide a comparison with the federal bankruptcy rules, the subject of the rest of this book. Federal bankruptcy rules change the cat-and-mouse game between debtors and creditors considerably. As you proceed, pay particular attention to the balance of power and the pressure that creditors can exert in their attempts to collect from debtors, both under the state collection laws and under bankruptcy law. And remember that a bankruptcy case freezes the race of the diligent in favor of a more collective approach to debt collection.

Keep the state court collection process in mind, because comparing how creditors are treated under state law versus bankruptcy law highlights how different the bankruptcy system is, and tells us what happens when a bankruptcy case never gets filed even though the debtor isn't paying her debts.

A. State Court Collection Process

People who do not pay their debts are subject to state laws regarding how a creditor without collateral can collect its debts.

(1) The Execution Process

Unsecured creditors do not have an interest in any particular property of the debtor. Therefore, if they're not paid back voluntarily they have to go through a long and tortuous process to collect on their debts. Most state court collection procedures focus on getting unsecured creditors paid, because most **secured creditors** don't need to go to court to get paid—they just take the property in which they have a security interest, sell it, and take the money they are owed.

Of course, an unsecured creditor can exert social pressure, or another form of **leverage**, such as offering to reduce the overall debt in exchange for prompt payment, or making telephone calls to bug the debtor. But if these types of leverage don't work, the creditor must go to court, get a judgment against the debtor, get a sheriff to execute (seize) the property, and sell the property to satisfy the judgment.

Once an unsecured creditor obtains a judgment, which can take quite a while in and of itself, the creditor cannot simply seize any of the debtor's property that it chooses. Rather, it must determine what property is "exempt" from collection efforts (discussed later in this chapter), and take a **writ package** (as it's called in many states) to the sheriff in order to direct the sheriff to **levy** or **execute** on the judgment by seizing **nonexempt property** from the debtor. The writ package is a packet of documents that tells the sheriff exactly which property can be executed upon, where it's located, and whatever else the sheriff needs to know to get the job done. The creditor's attorney should try to give very clear directions, in order to make it easy for the sheriff. Otherwise, the sheriff may execute on the wrong property or go to the wrong address, and ultimately return the judgment to the creditor **unsatisfied**.

Once the sheriff has located whatever property is available for execution, the sheriff must, in most states, **exercise dominion and control** over the property. This is necessary in order to create a **judicial lien** and thereby convert the unsecured general creditor into a secured creditor. When a sheriff exercises dominion and control over property, that gives **notice to the world** (i.e., other creditors) that this property is not available to be pledged as collateral to other creditors. This notice function prevents the debtor from tricking new creditors into extending credit supported by collateral that is already **encumbered** by a lien to someone else.

The easiest way to exercise dominion and control is to throw the property into the back of the sheriff's pickup and take it back to the sheriff's office. But if the property is too big to take, the sheriff can place big notices all over the property. Notices are usually printed on brightly colored paper, and they say something like, "The sheriff of such-and-such county has executed on this property and, as a result, will soon sell the items." This puts all potential creditors on notice that a prior creditor has a lien on the property. Depending on a state's case law, there may be other ways to exercise dominion and control over property in order to create a lien, such as changing the locks on a rented space in order to take control of the personal property inside. Regardless of the method, anyone viewing the property should be able to tell that the property has a lien on it.

In some states, the judicial lien arises as soon as the judgment creditor delivers the writ of execution to the sheriff. In these states, the lien is a secret as far as other creditors know. Thus, the statute must protect other creditors who take a security interest in the property without knowledge of the judicial lien, before the sheriff executes on the property.

However, most courts and scholars agree that there should be no secret liens. Secret liens are disfavored because they give unsecured creditors the impression that the property in question is unencumbered, and thus available to pay general unsecured creditors once they go through the state law execution process and sell it.

Once the sheriff has exercised dominion and control over this property, we say that **execution** or **levy** has occurred. This is a key moment in the state collection process, because at the moment of execution, a lien is created in the property. Before that moment, the judgment is just a piece of paper. After that moment, the property can be sold to satisfy the debt.

Selling the property at a **sheriff's sale** is the next step. Once the property is sold and the **sheriff's fees** have been paid, the **executing creditor** can satisfy its debt from the rest of the proceeds. Remember, *only execution can create a lien*. Merely having a judgment never creates a lien.

Q: What if property is sold at a sheriff's sale for less than it is worth?

A: There are no minimum prices and very often the items sell for much less than their value. Nevertheless, the executing creditor gets the proceeds and the rest of the value is lost. Items sell for below market value, generally, because sheriff's sales are not well advertised, and therefore the market is not robust enough to function optimally.

(2) Involuntary Real Estate Liens

The process of getting an involuntary lien on real property (real estate) is very different and much easier from the state court collection system for personal property. Instead of getting a judgment, bringing a writ package to the sheriff, having the sheriff exercise dominion and control in order to execute on the personal property, and selling it at a sheriff's auction, in many states all a creditor has to do is record the judgment in the real estate records. Typically, the creditor doesn't even have to file the judgment, but can file a summary or abstract of the judgment. In most states, this is done in the county recorder of deeds office.

In fact, you can usually file a judgment against a debtor *before* he or she owns real estate. Just go down to the county recorder's office, file a brief summary of the judgment under the debtor's name, and then an involuntary lien will attach to any real estate the debtor buys in that county! Any time your client wins a judgment, you should file a record of it so that your client gets an automatic lien on the other person's real estate in that county.

However, a few states do treat personal property just like real estate — you can actually get a lien on personal property simply by recording a judgment.

Repeat this 20 times:
A Judgment Is Not A Lien.

Q: Why isn't a judgment a lien? Wouldn't it be a lot easier and clearer if there were a law that automatically created a lien every time a final judgment was entered in a court of law?

A: A lien must be *in* something particular to be enforceable. It cannot just exist in the abstract. Further, notice must be given to other creditors that there is a lien on the specific property, and we need a mechanism for determining which creditor has priority over others. Of course, we could say that once a judgment is entered, all future creditors have constructive notice of the lien, and that the first judgment entered has priority over subsequent judgments. But this would require creditors to search through court records before extending credit. That would be slow and expensive, and the result would be that creditors would have to charge higher interest rates to pay for the added expense of extensive searches. Our economy is damaged when cost of capital is artificially raised. This is why Article 9 and the state court collection systems are set up as they are — to allow inexpensive access to capital.

B. State Law Exemptions

When a sheriff goes to execute on the personal property of a debtor, one of the documents (provided in the writ package, if there is one, from the creditor's attorney) asks the debtor whether any property is exempt from execution. Every state allows people to keep certain property exempt from creditors, even if they really do owe the creditor money. A typical state exemption statute allows a debtor to keep at least some of the equity in their home (so the creditor cannot sell their home and take the money), some equity in their car, some clothing, tools of their trade or profession, books, and so on.

The theory is that it would be counterproductive (not to mention inhumane) for society to allow creditors to take people's homes so that debtors become homeless, to take away their transportation to work, to take away their clothing (also needed to hold down a job), or to take away their professional equipment or tools of their trade. For one thing, most personal property is worth very little to creditors. Further, even people who don't pay their debts should be able to keep enough property to survive with some personal dignity. Finally, we don't want to create homeless, unemployed wards of the state.

Thus *individual debtors* are entitled to exemptions. *Business debtors*, at least those organized as partnerships, corporations, or LLCs, do not get exemptions, and thus have no exempt property. Thus the sheriff can execute on anything and everything that a business debtor has.[1]

State law exemptions vary incredibly from state to state. For example, in New Mexico, each person gets an exemption of $60,000 of equity in a home and $4,000 of

---

[1]This is a bit of an oversimplification since the business could be owned by a natural person as a sole proprietorship, in which case some of the property might be exempt, depending on that state's exemption law.

equity in a car. Delaware is more creditor-friendly, allowing debtors to keep no equity in their home (no **homestead exemption**), and providing little exemption for a car or any other personal property. In contrast, Texas and Florida both have unlimited homestead exemptions, allowing debtors to keep all the equity in their home, even if it's worth millions of dollars. Thus, an unpaid creditor, even a sympathetic one such as a judgment creditor who was the victim of a hit-and-run accident while the debtor was driving drunk, could not force the sale of a multi-million dollar home in Texas or Florida. But even a creditor card company could take a debtor's home in Delaware.

Whether a debtor has any exempt property is determined by the debtor's **equity** in the property, which means the amount of value in each item over and above any secured loans or liens on the property. To determine the debtor's equity, take the value of the property and subtract the amount of any secured creditor claims.

So let's say a single debtor owns a $100,000 home and owes $60,000 on the mortgage. How much equity does the debtor have in the home? If the debtor lives in a state with a $30,000 homestead exemption, will the debtor be able to keep the sheriff from selling the home to pay a debt?[2]

Sidebar

DIFFERENT STROKES FOR DIFFERENT FOLKS

States are free to choose whatever is important to their citizens in their local culture. Some choices reflect regional factors such as high or low real estate prices. Some reflect deeply held values, such as the belief that no one should be able to take your ranch or your homestead. Historically, the South and the West were settled by pioneers who were frequently debtors fleeing their New England creditors, and for this reason many southern and western states opposed national bankruptcy laws altogether. Also, some eastern states like Pennsylvania and Delaware simply have not updated their exemptions laws for a long time.

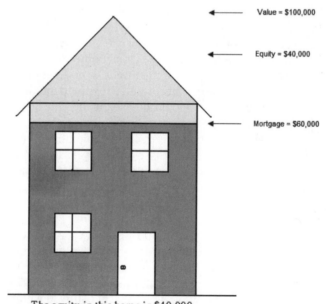

Value = $100,000

Equity = $40,000

Mortgage = $60,000

The equity in this home is $40,000

---

[2]The equity is $40,000, and because only $30,000 is exempt, the sheriff can sell this home to satisfy any debt. The debtor gets the first $30,000 from the sale, after costs of sale are paid. The executing creditor is paid next.

State exemptions never prevent a *voluntary secured* creditor from enforcing a security interest by either judicial or nonjudicial means. Only *unsecured* creditors (or at least those who do not have voluntary liens) are prevented from reaching exempt property of the debtor. One way to remember this is simply to think of the consensual security interest as being higher than the exemptions. Another way to think of it is as though the security interest is a voluntary waiver of the state exemption law. Either way, the state law exemptions don't apply when a *voluntary secured creditor* is repossessing or foreclosing.

(1) State Law Exemptions and Bankruptcy

State law exemptions protect debtors' property from creditor executions, whether there is a bankruptcy case or not. If your slant of attention is directed at bankruptcy, it's easy to forget that debtors can use state exemptions without the need for a bankruptcy.

In addition to state law exemptions, the Bankruptcy Code has its own set of exemptions, which can be used *only* in a bankruptcy case. 11 U.S.C. §522(d). However, in some states the federal bankruptcy exemptions cannot be used at all, even in a bankruptcy, leaving the debtor with *only* the state exemptions. This is because Congress allowed states to opt out of the Bankruptcy Code exemption provisions. The result is that state law exemptions are always available to everyone, both inside and outside bankruptcy, while in some states debtors can choose between state and federal exemptions in a bankruptcy case.

Remember that the main purpose of state law exemptions is to protect property from creditor executions in cases in which there is no bankruptcy case—where a creditor is executing on assets in a state court proceeding.

C. The Fair Debt Collection Practices Act and Other Regulation of Collection Activity

The **Fair Debt Collection Practices Act** (FDCPA), 15 U.S.C. §1692, was passed by Congress to curb abusive debt collection activity against consumers. The Act forbids all sorts of nasty collection tactics, including harassing debtors by phone; calling them outside the hours of 8:00 A.M. and 9:00 P.M.; causing the phone to ring continuously with intent to annoy, abuse, or harass; using threats or violence or other physical harm; using obscene or profane language; and a long list of other infractions. The Act also requires that debt collectors identify themselves to the consumer, reveal the name of the creditor on whose behalf they are collecting the debt, stop contacting the consumer at work if told to do so, and stop contacting the consumer *at all* once the consumer has requested that such contact cease.

However, the FDCPA is not as far reaching as it appears, because it does *not* apply to the original creditor, only to the collection agency hired by the creditor to collect the debt. This means that if a creditor is collecting its own debt, it is free to use aggressive, even harassing, tactics. While some *states* have adopted laws that protect debtors from harassment by creditors, the FDCPA does not forbid harassment by creditors who are collecting their own debts.

D. Fair Credit Reporting Act

The **Fair Credit Reporting Act** (FCRA), 15 U.S.C. §1682, regulates the collection, dissemination, and use of consumer credit information. The law regulates how the information that appears on a consumer's **credit report** is gathered and reported to **credit reporting agencies**. Credit reports have become a staple in the U.S. economy, providing ready information to the massive consumer credit industry about the credit risks of individual consumers. Studies show that despite the requirements of this federal law, 79% of consumer credit reports contain errors.

This law governs the behavior of the three large credit reporting agencies, Equifax, Experian, and TransUnion, as well as the creditors that provide information to credit reporting agencies and the creditors, employers, and insurance companies that rely on the reports.

The law requires that information furnishers provide only complete and accurate information to the reporting agencies, investigate disputed items when requested to do so by a consumer, and inform consumers about negative information to be sent to the reporting agencies within 30 days. Users of the reports must notify consumers when adverse action has been taken by a creditor on the basis of a report, and also tell the consumer where it got the negative information about the consumer. Reporting agencies are required to accept consumers' corrections to the report, correct the report where warranted, and provide one free credit report a year to each consumer. Consumers also are entitled to a free report when they have been denied credit based upon information in the report. The actual law is hundreds of pages long, so these are just the highlights.

E. Fraudulent Transfers Under the Uniform Fraudulent Transfers Act (UFTA)

(1) The Purpose of Fraudulent Transfer Law

Sometimes debtors conceal or transfer property away in hopes of avoiding the claims of creditors, both secured and unsecured. Perhaps the debtor has predicted financial problems and tried to conceal property that a creditor might use to satisfy the debt. Or perhaps the debtor has sold property for less than its fair market value. Perhaps the debtor never intended to pay the debt to begin with, and has put money into exempt assets with the intent to become judgment proof. The law sees through these tactics and provides some protection to creditors who have been duped. Transfers of property with actual intent to defraud creditors, and transfers for less than equivalent value that result in the debtor becoming insolvent, are reversible or **avoidable** because the law deems them **fraudulent transfers**. Creditors can usually reach such property, even though it has passed to a third party.

(2) The Elements of a Fraudulent Transfer

A **fraudulent transfer** occurs when a debtor either (1) transfers property with the actual intent to *hinder, delay,* or *defraud* a creditor, or (2) transfers property without receiving reasonably equivalent value in return, if the transfer leaves the debtor insolvent.

The first type of fraudulent transfer requires proof that the debtor was trying to defraud creditors by making the transfer. As in all cases that require proof of intent, this can be hard to prove. If intent to defraud is proven, the transfer is avoidable irrespective of whether it made the debtor insolvent.

The second type of fraudulent transfer does not require any showing that the debtor was acting fraudulently. The law simply deems transfers for less than fair value fraudulent if they leave the debtor-transferor insolvent. Typically, this type of transfer arises when the creditor sells property for far below fair market value to a relative or a friend (or just gives the property away as a gift). In this case, the property can be retrieved from the third party, even if the third party paid for it.

A full discussion of the law of fraudulent transfers is beyond the scope of this book, but here are a few highlights.

With regard to the second type of fraudulent transfer, "insolvency" is the balance sheet definition: A debtor is insolvent if liabilities exceed assets. There is also a presumption of insolvency if the debtor is generally not paying debts as they become due. UFTA §2.

A distinction is made as to which creditors can avoid the transfer. Future creditors (i.e., those who extended credit after the transfer was made) are protected only if the debtor-transferor intended to incur obligations (or should have believed that he or she would incur obligations) beyond his or her ability to repay them, or was left with assets that were unreasonably small in relation to the transaction that was entered into. UFTA §4. Present creditors, however, are protected not only in those situations but whenever the transfer is made either with the actual intent to defraud creditors, or made for less than a fair consideration. UFTA §§2, 4, and 5.

The definitions section of the UFTA, Section 1, is important. There are extensive definitions of "value" (UFTA §3) and a long explanation of when transfers are deemed made. UFTA §6.

The UFTA treats transfers to "insiders," defined as relatives, partners, and so forth (UFTA §2(7)), somewhat differently. As to present creditors, transfers to insiders for an antecedent debt are fraudulent if the insider had reason to believe that the debtor was insolvent. UFTA §5.

Sidebar

ENGLISH ORIGINS OF FRAUDULENT TRANSFER LAW

Fraudulent conveyance law has its origins in feudal England, specifically the Statute of Elizabeth. The purpose of the law is to prevent assets from being transferred away from a debtor in exchange for less than fair value, leaving a lack of funds to compensate the creditors. In the first fraudulent conveyance case on record, *In re Twyne's Case,* the English Star Chamber examined the facts surrounding such transfers to determine whether they had "signs and marks" of a fraudulent or malicious intent. Nowadays, fraudulent or malicious intent is inferred from secret transfers, continued ownership or possession of property after its alleged transfer, self-serving representations in transfer documents that the transfer was not intended to defraud creditors, transfers of substantially all assets, or transfers made while an action was pending against the transferor. In short, fraudulent conveyance law is aimed at preventing debtors from making collusive transfers to others — often friendly recipients — in an attempt to avoid their creditors. The prohibition of secret liens and fraudulent conveyances was taken very seriously in England, but its modern descendant has been watered down.

The UFTA specifies certain facts that may evidence an actual intent to defraud, including, for example, the debtor-transferor retaining possession, concealment of the transfer, a substantial transfer of all of the debtor's assets, a transfer to an insider, and so forth. UFTA §4(b). These are frequently called "badges of fraud," a term with origins in the early days of fraudulent transfer law.

When a fraudulent transfer is made, a creditor has several options. UFTA §7. The creditor may bring an action to avoid the transfer or execute on a judgment, or petition the court to enjoin the transfer or to have a receiver appointed.

A transfer made with the actual intent to defraud cannot be avoided if the transferee acted in good faith and gave fair equivalent value, nor can a transfer be avoided if a *subsequent* transferee gave value and took in good faith.

SUMMARY

■ Creditors without collateral have to use the courts to collect on unpaid debts, rather than repossessing collateral through self-help.

■ Using the court system to collect on a debt involves getting a judgment against the debtor and then getting a sheriff to locate property owned by the debtor that can be sold in order to satisfy the judgment. This process of selling assets to satisfy judgments is called executing on a judgment.

■ If the sale of the property seized by the sheriff does not fully satisfy the debt, the leftover debt is called a deficiency claim.

■ Just because a sheriff locates property owned by a debtor does not mean this property can be used to execute on a judgment and satisfy the judgment. Some property is exempt from the claims of executing creditors under the laws of most states.

■ The amount and category of property that is exempt from the claims of executing unsecured creditors varies from state to state. Many states allow the debtor to keep at least some equity in a house, a car, household goods, tools of trade, and jewelry, among other things.

■ While there are some limits on the types of acts in which a creditor can engage in order to collect its unpaid debt, harassment is allowed if the creditor is collecting its own debts. If the creditor hires a third-party collection agency to collect the debt, the collection agency cannot harass a debtor or engage in any other act forbidden by the Fair Debt Collection Practices Act, a federal law.

■ Elaborate credit histories are now kept for all people who use traditional credit in the United States, in the form of credit reports and scores. The records used to create these histories are collected and kept by three large credit reporting agencies. These agencies and the creditors that report to them are bound by the Fair Credit Reporting Act, which describes the process for clearing up errors in credit reports, among other things.

■ State debtor creditor law provides that some transfers of a debtor can be undone if the net result of the transfer hurts creditors. Known as fraudulent transfers, the transfers that can be undone include transfers of assets with actual intent to defraud creditors, and transfers for less than fair value that cause the debtor to become insolvent.

CONNECTIONS

Exemptions

We introduced the idea of exemptions in this chapter—property that is exempt from collection efforts by creditors—and it's discussed in the bankruptcy context in Chapter 6, Sections A and B.

Secured Creditors

As in bankruptcy, secured creditors are in a superior position in state collection efforts—they usually get to bypass the whole execution process because they have contractual rights to take and sell the collateral.

Unsecured Creditors

Just as unsecured creditors get worse treatment in bankruptcy, unsecured creditors have to go through the difficult, expensive, and time-consuming process required by state collection laws.

Jurisdiction

As the name reminds us, state collection actions are brought in state courts, while bankruptcy cases are always brought in federal bankruptcy court.

The Automatic Stay

One of the typical reasons for declaring bankruptcy is strategic: The debtor doesn't *really* want to declare bankruptcy, but the debtor nonetheless files a bankruptcy case in order to halt the state court collection process when an unsecured creditor is about to snatch the debtor's assets via the state law execution process.

Involuntary Bankruptcy

Remember, if a creditor doesn't like the state court collection process, or if the creditor suspects that the debtor is doing something dodgy or illegal, such as making fraudulent transfers (discussed in Chapter 9, Section B), the creditor can always attempt to force the debtor into involuntary bankruptcy, which is the subject of Chapter 10, Section F.

Introduction to the Bankruptcy System

3

There are a few different kinds of bankruptcy cases and this chapter introduces you to them. All are named after a particular chapter of the

O V E R V I E W

Bankruptcy Code. Most cases are filed under CHAPTERS 7, 13, and 11. In CHAPTER 7 cases, the debtor gives up his or her nonexempt assets and walks away from most debts. In the other two, CHAPTERS 13 and 11, the debtor pays back some creditors over time under a payment plan. These are the most common types of bankruptcy cases.

A. INTRODUCTION TO BANKRUPTCY THEORY

B. A BRIEF HISTORY OF BANKRUPTCY

C. INTRODUCTION TO THE TYPES OF BANKRUPTCY CASES

1. CHAPTER 7
2. CHAPTER 13
3. CHAPTER 12
4. CHAPTER 11
5. CHAPTER 9
6. CHAPTER 15

A. Introduction to Bankruptcy Theory

Studying bankruptcy provides a lens through which to study U.S. society as a whole. Money plays a larger role in American society than in most others. American capitalism relies heavily on spending by both consumers and businesses, and both types of spending are aided greatly by the extensive availability of credit. Our culture of spending creates people who aspire to acquire, and a large sector of our economy that makes money by extending credit.

In the area of consumer credit, harmful and extremely expensive credit products abound (such as payday loans, title loans, and high-interest-rate credit cards), particularly for those low on the socioeconomic rung. And while middle-class people take on unnecessary debt to purchase non-necessities, poorer people use expensive consumer credit to purchase necessities.

But rich or poor, we all use credit. It is the American way. How recently have you used credit, for example by charging something on a credit card or taking out a student loan? It is frequently more important to our economy that people spend money than that they be able to pay for what they buy. This in part explains why we are somewhat forgiving to those who cannot pay. As a society, we rely on spending to fuel our economy and, therefore, we need a system for addressing the problems that result when debts go unpaid. This system, of course, is provided by the federal Bankruptcy Act.

Bankruptcy laws sit at the intersection of a society's economy, values, and business culture. Professor Soia Mentschikoff used to say that if you want to know how a society deals with its failures, you should look at the society's bankruptcy laws. Societies develop commercial codes and bankruptcy laws in a manner consistent with social and business assumptions. For example, the United States, Germany, and Japan have "reorganizations" along the lines of Chapter 11 and Chapter 13. The Japanese, however, who now have a modern and very forgiving bankruptcy system, seldom use it because their society's values are different. They consider failure to repay one's debts to be highly shameful. Most European countries — and thus former colonies of European powers—have historically considered bankruptcy to be a life-long failure, although this is changing as the E.U. becomes a global economic trading powerhouse. In contrast, in the United States bankruptcy is sometimes seen as a sign of courageous, vibrant risk-taking—not such a bad thing in a capitalist society.

B. A Brief History of Bankruptcy

The word "bankrupt" likely comes from "banca rota" or "banca rupta," meaning "broken bench" in Latin and early Latin-based languages. Roman officials would literally break the workbench of an artisan who could not pay his bills. This meant he could not work anymore. And it served as a signal of shame and warning to everyone else. We may think this harsh and antiquated, but as recently as the Great Depression, when a bank foreclosed on a farm, the bank would paint the farmer's barn bright red to let the neighbors know that the farmer was bankrupt and that the bank would soon sell off his equipment and other assets. Thus, for 2,000 or more years bankruptcy has been treated as a shameful event.

Compared to the rest of the world, however, American debtors have always had it pretty good. Many American settlers were bankrupts who fled Europe's debtor prisons, and the South and West were frequently settled by pioneers who were fleeing their New England creditors. The resulting ethos of rugged individualism and the celebration of the entrepreneurial spirit supported a legal culture of tolerance toward non-payment of debts, and the idea of immigrating to the United States in pursuit of a better life and a fresh start is deeply embedded in the American dream. The relative lenience of American bankruptcy law, compared to legal notions on the European Continent, shocked some, including Alex de Tocqueville, who commented on the "strange indulgence" shown to bankrupts in the American union. He claimed that, in this respect, "the Americans differ, not only from the nations of Europe, but from all the commercial nations of our time."

Empirical studies show that the vast majority of people pay their debts. This is easy to forget when studying bankruptcy. It is also rather remarkable given the tremendous amount of consumer credit in the American economy, the lack of financial literacy in our society, and the aggressive marketing tools directed toward consumers by the credit card industry.

Even borrowers who do *not* pay their debts usually do not file a bankruptcy case. The reason for this is that formal bankruptcy, through a federal court case, is an expensive process with a lot of paperwork. Many people are simply broke, i.e., they are in **virtual bankruptcy**.

C. Introduction to the Types of Bankruptcy Cases

In the United States, all the different kinds of bankruptcy are designed to balance two things: the rights of debtors to a fresh start, and the rights of creditors to be paid. This tension is present in all aspects of the system, and all types of bankruptcy give the same general vibe: Get in trouble with your creditors and this system will help you find a way out. But if you abuse the system, you will be punished. In other words, bankruptcy is a privilege, not a right.

Bankruptcy cases in the United States follow two models. They are either " 'sell out' or 'pay out' cases."[1] In **sell out** or **liquidation** cases, also called straight bankruptcy cases, the debtor's nonexempt assets are sold and the proceeds are distributed to creditors, quickly ending the case. In **pay out** cases, the debtor promises, via a plan of repayment, to pay at least some creditors from future income over time. In the real world, particularly in a business context, there are many hybrids and permutations of these two basic models, limited only by the imagination of the business people and attorneys involved, but it is nonetheless worthwhile to understand this basic conceptual distinction.

(1) CHAPTER 7

Most cases filed in the United States are CHAPTER 7 sell out or liquidation cases, which is the simplest, quickest kind of bankruptcy. In each CHAPTER 7 case, a trustee is appointed to gather all nonexempt assets, sell them, and distribute the proceeds according to the priority scheme prescribed by the Code (discussed in detail in Chapter 7 of this book). The trustee is a **fiduciary** for all creditors and is charged with maximizing value for estate creditors. Part of the trustee's fiduciary duty is fulfilled by rooting around for free assets to distribute.

CHAPTER 7 is available to individuals as well as legal entities like corporations and limited liability companies (LLCs). A corporation or LLC filing a CHAPTER 7 case is the easiest case of all. There typically are no issues. The corporation is not entitled to exemptions because it will be dissolved or remain in limbo as an empty shell. For this reason, it does not get a discharge. Thus, the two most litigated issues in an individual CHAPTER 7 case, exemptions and dischargeability, are not at issue in a corporate CHAPTER 7 case.

Individuals file the vast majority of CHAPTER 7 cases in the United States. In these cases, the debtor turns over all nonexempt assets to a bankruptcy trustee who sells them and distributes them to creditors according to the priority scheme. Although these cases are sell out or liquidation cases, typically the debtor has no nonexempt assets. Therefore there is no sell out or liquidation. Thus, despite the sell out or liquidation classification, in such a situation nothing is sold and the debtor loses no property. That's why these are often called **no asset cases**.

What issues commonly arise in a natural person's CHAPTER 7 case?

■ The trustee could disagree with the debtor over what property is exempt and may challenge the value of the debtor's exempt property as too low, arguing that there would be assets available to creditors if the property (or some part of it) were sold.

---

[1]See Warren and Westbrook, The Law of Debtors and Creditors 121 (Aspen 2006).

- The trustee or an individual creditor might object to the debtor's discharge due to wrongdoing on the part of the debtor right before or during the bankruptcy case (if the debtor hid assets, for example, or lied on one of the disclosure forms).
- A creditor may object to the dischargeability of its particular debt.
- The United States Trustee's Office could file a substantial abuse motion in order to have the case dismissed because the debtor has income over and above his expenses and thus could afford a CHAPTER 13 plan.
- The trustee could challenge whether a CHAPTER 7 debtor should file a CHAPTER 13 instead because he or she can afford to pay a CHAPTER 13 plan rather than simply discharging most debts.

In most cases, though, there is no litigation. A CHAPTER 7 trustee administers the case within 90 days of the filing, and after 90 days the debtor obtains a discharge of most or all of the debts.

(2) CHAPTER 13

CHAPTER 13 cases are **pay out** rather than **sell out** cases. Typically, the trustee does not sell the debtor's nonexempt assets. Instead the debtor is allowed to keep them as long as the debtor is paying at least the value of these nonexempt assets to creditors over time under the plan. In effect, the debtor is buying back these assets from creditors over the course of the plan.

The idea is that the debtor will propose a repayment plan for paying creditors and will make the proposed payments for three to five years. During that time, the debtor will pay all allowed secured claims in full (as these claims are defined in Section 506 of the Code), all priority claims in full and will pay a distribution to unsecured creditors as well, assuming the debtor has sufficient disposable income to do so.

The case is administered by the CHAPTER 13 trustee who (like the CHAPTER 7 trustee) is a fiduciary for creditors, charged with creating the best possible recovery for the debtor's creditors. The trustee may do this by trying to get the debtor to contribute more of his income to the plan, by objecting to the debtor's expenses as profligate, or by encouraging the debtor to sell some nonexempt property if this is the only way the plan will work.

In a CHAPTER 13 case, commonly litigated issues include: (1) the value of the allowed secured claims (or, in some cases, the value of the underlying collateral because the debtor can sometimes pay just the value of the collateral, rather than the whole loan, to secured creditors); (2) the priority treatment of certain claims; (3) whether the debtor has contributed all of his disposable income to the plan, which is theoretically required under CHAPTER 13; and (4) the value of exempt property as that bears on the minimum distributions the debtor must pay under the plan. The CHAPTER 13 trustee plays a substantial role in the success of CHAPTER 13 cases and is often the one to object to the plan and otherwise ensure that it complies with the Code. If all of the rules contained in CHAPTER 13 of the Code are satisfied, the court approves the plan and the debtor sets out to complete the payments.

(3) CHAPTER 12

CHAPTER 12 is for family farmers and family fishermen. It is very similar to CHAPTER 13 but has slightly easier repayment rules and higher debt limits, because our society has decided that these classes of people are especially vulnerable and deserve a little extra financial protection.

(4) CHAPTER 11

CHAPTER 11 is a pay out style case, available to individuals but almost always used by business entities like corporations. Big CHAPTER 11 cases are frequently reported on the front page of the *Wall Street Journal* — just think of Kmart, Enron, WorldCom, United Airlines, and so on. In the past, Federated Department Stores (Macy's), Texaco, and many others have emerged successfully from CHAPTER 11.

CHAPTER 11 cases involve restructuring the debts and other obligations of companies that need help. The general idea, as with CHAPTER 13, is that the debtor will repay a portion of its debts over time from its future operations. Its plan must pay its priority claims in full. It also must pay all of the allowed secured claims in full, but, as in a CHAPTER 13, this does not mean that the secured creditor gets its entire claim paid in full. The debtor must pay the lesser of the value of the collateral or the amount of the loan, which define the size of the **allowed secured claim**. Thus, part of the secured creditor's claim could be unsecured, and that part would *not* necessarily be paid in full. Finally, while CHAPTER 11 does not technically require it, in most cases the debtor will pay a distribution to the unsecured creditors in its CHAPTER 11 case.

The plan approval process is different in CHAPTER 11 than in CHAPTER 13. In a CHAPTER 11 case, the debtor solicits votes from classes of creditors, for what it hopes will turn out to be a consensual CHAPTER 11 pay out plan. Creditors are placed in classes for the purpose of plan voting. They vote by class under a modified majority rule system. If all classes of creditors vote to go along with the plan, the court generally approves the plan. If there are holdouts (people who are not in favor of the plan), the court can sometimes force the creditors to accept the plan, assuming various tests are met by the plan and the debtor.

There is one huge difference between a case under CHAPTER 13 and a case under CHAPTER 11. Both are "pay out" style cases, but in a CHAPTER 13 case, there is a trustee who actively looks over and manages the plan, the plan payments, and the overall case. In a CHAPTER 11 case, there normally is no trustee in the case at all. The company that is in bankruptcy is usually run by the same people who were in management before the filing, or by some newly appointed management, but in any event by management! Some might say that the fox is guarding the henhouse. The debtor continues to run the company though it does get a different name. The debtor (in effect, its management) is now called the **debtor-in-possession**, or the DIP. The debtor-in-possession has, under the Code, all of the duties and powers of a trustee. The DIP is a fiduciary and is charged with creating the best possible distributions for creditors. The DIP, then, has many conflicting duties, to shareholders, to management, to creditors, and to employees. The primary duty, however, is to creditors.

The U.S.-style CHAPTER 11 case, in which management can stay in place, is unique in the world. You might wonder why we allow this type of thing, rather than just liquidating failing businesses as most of the world does. Keeping the company afloat and allowing it to try to stay in business is often justified on the basis that assets are usually worth more in an ongoing business and, as a result, creditors can often get more in a reorganization plan being paid over time than they could get in a liquidation. Others justify CHAPTER 11 as a way to save jobs, and to keep from disrupting communities that might otherwise be left without local industry. In any case,

CHAPTER 11's existence is controversial and some scholars have called for its abolition. Despite this, CHAPTER 11 shows no sign of becoming extinct.

This is a drastic oversimplification of CHAPTER 11, and you'll learn much more about this in Chapters 14 through 21.

(5) CHAPTER 9

CHAPTER 9 is a reorganization-style bankruptcy scheme, similar to CHAPTER 11, but for municipalities. It has been used over 70 times, but only a few times by large municipalities. The most famous cases involved the bankruptcies of Bridgeport, Connecticut, and Orange County, California.

(6) CHAPTER 15

CHAPTER 15 was added to the Code in the 2005 amendments. CHAPTER 15 is the U.S. domestic adoption of an international model law, the Model Law on Cross-Border Insolvency, promulgated by the United Nations Commission on International Trade Law (UNCITRAL) in 1997. The general purpose of CHAPTER 15, and the Model Law on which it is based, is to address insolvency cases where the debtors, assets, claimants, and other parties in interest are located in more than one country. The law has five specific objectives: (1) to promote cooperation between the U.S. courts and parties in interest and the courts and other competent authorities of foreign countries involved in cross-border insolvency cases; (2) to establish greater legal certainty for trade and investment; (3) to provide for the fair and efficient administration of cross-border insolvencies that protects the interests of all creditors and other interested entities, including the debtor; (4) to afford protection and maximization of the value of the debtor's assets; and (5) to facilitate the rescue of financially troubled businesses, thereby protecting investment and preserving employment. 11 U.S.C. §1501. Generally, a CHAPTER 15 case is ancillary to (or connected to) a primary proceeding brought in another country, typically the debtor's home country.

Sidebar

USING BANKRUPTCY TO MAINTAIN INEQUALITY?

CHAPTER 9 allows units of states, but not states, to declare bankruptcy. We doubt other countries allow local governments to do this, although the World Bank has allowed reorganizations of some developing countries unable to pay their debts. The first county to declare CHAPTER 9 bankruptcy was Orange County, California, a wealthy county that refused to pay the taxes it owed to support government services, which it saw as handouts to "outsiders" and the poor. What does *this* use of bankruptcy say about our society?

D. Bankruptcy Court Jurisdiction and the Law Bankruptcy Courts Apply

Federal bankruptcy cases are heard by federal courts, but the judges are appointed for a limited term, unlike other federal judges. This fact has caused some confusion about the authority of these courts to make various decisions.

When a bankruptcy case is filed, the bankruptcy court attempts to address all of the issues in the debtor's life. This is efficient and helpful to the debtor, but may not provide proper deference to other courts (such as a family court) or to the rights of other parties in the case (such as a creditor who would rather have a garden-variety contracts claim heard by another, perhaps more neutral, court). Some creditors may question whether a bankruptcy court has the authority to exercise jurisdiction over them at all. This section discusses limitations on the bankruptcy court's jurisdiction.

Bankruptcy law in the United States is primarily federal law rather than state law. Article I, Section 8, of the U.S. Constitution gives Congress the power to establish uniform laws on the subject of bankruptcy throughout the United States. This has been done over the years through the enactment of a federal statute, originally called the *Bankruptcy Act* and now called the *Bankruptcy Code*, or simply the *Code*. The Code is found in Title 11 of the U.S. Code. When you hear a reference to *Title 11*, this is a reference to the Bankruptcy Code. 11 U.S.C. §101 et seq.

None of this suggests that state law is unimportant when dealing with bankruptcy issues. Though federal law is supreme over state law, under the Supremacy Clause of the Constitution, there are a number of issues on which the Bankruptcy Code implicitly or explicitly incorporates state law rather than legislating its own on a particular issue. This is true when it comes to determining property rights, for example. State law determines what a person's rights are in particular property, although the Bankruptcy Code might define whether such property rights are part of a debtor's bankruptcy estate or not.

(1) General Jurisdiction over Bankruptcy Cases

The Bankruptcy Act of 1898, which governed federal law until the Bankruptcy Code was enacted in 1978, granted jurisdiction over bankruptcy matters to federal district courts, which then referred bankruptcy cases to specialized courts that had limited power. The judges of these courts, who were called referees until 1973, could only decide issues that related very directly to the administration of the bankruptcy estate's assets and not to other types of disputes arising in a more ancillary way, unless the parties (either voluntarily or involuntarily) consented to a bankruptcy court's broader jurisdiction.

When the current Code was enacted, Congress granted bankruptcy courts much greater latitude to decide cases and issues that came before them and far broader jurisdiction. Essentially, bankruptcy judges were given jurisdiction to decide all matters that a district judge could decide within the context of bankruptcy cases. However, because bankruptcy judges appointed under the Code are appointed pursuant to the powers contained in Article I of the Constitution rather than Article III, there was some question about how much of that broad grant of jurisdiction was constitutionally valid. Article I judges have lesser status than Article III judges and do not get lifetime tenure.

The Supreme Court invalidated this broad grant of jurisdiction in 1982 in *Northern Pipeline Constr. Co. v. Marathon Pipe Line Co.*, 458 U.S. 50 (1982). The bankruptcy court in the case had adjudicated a garden-variety state law contract claim involving no real bankruptcy issues. In fact, the only bankruptcy connection in the case was that one of the parties was in a CHAPTER 11 proceeding in front of the adjudicating court, and was seeking a judgment that presumably would benefit the bankruptcy estate. The nondebtor party to the contract dispute objected to the court's jurisdiction, arguing that the case had nothing to do with bankruptcy and that as a result the court had no jurisdiction to adjudicate it.

The decision was appealed several times, ultimately landing before the Supreme Court of the United States. The Supreme Court agreed with the nondebtor party, holding that the bankruptcy court had no jurisdiction to hear the contract suit, and that Congress's broad grant of jurisdiction to bankruptcy courts in Title 11 violated the separation of powers doctrine by conferring extended jurisdiction upon a court whose judges did not have a lifetime appointment and the other protections given an Article III judge.

Eventually a new system was implemented. Today bankruptcy courts can hear and make ultimate decisions about cases involving **core** bankruptcy issues (those issues that pertain directly to bankruptcy law and require an interpretation of the Bankruptcy Code), but a federal district court must review any decision that the bankruptcy court makes that is outside that core. These decisions outside the core (merely **related to** the bankruptcy case over which the bankruptcy court presides, for example, a case in which one of the parties is in bankruptcy but the litigation deals with a contract dispute) must be decided or confirmed by the district court unless the parties agree that the bankruptcy court can make final decisions in these matters.

Bankruptcy judges are adjuncts to the district court. They have no original jurisdiction. All jurisdiction vests in the district courts under 28 U.S.C. §1334, and the district courts have the power to refer core matters to the bankruptcy court under 28 U.S.C. §157(a). The district courts retain complete control over the reference, although as a practical matter, every district court in the nation has enacted a local rule that automatically refers all bankruptcy cases to the bankruptcy court.

(2) Appeals from the Bankruptcy Court

Bankruptcy courts are trial courts and are part of the federal judicial system. The bankruptcy courts hear both whole bankruptcy cases that can have many parts, as well as complaints filed within bankruptcy cases, which are called **adversary proceedings**.

Once a bankruptcy court hears an issue and enters a final order, the losing party can appeal the decision. Normally a federal district court in the jurisdiction in which the bankruptcy court sits hears this appeal. This is an odd system because you then have a trial court hearing an appeal from another trial court. To make it even odder, the appeal is coming from what is essentially a court of the same level, given that district courts have referred bankruptcy cases to their sister courts, which are not lower in status.

Because the review given by the district courts at this first level of appeal has not always been a true review but has sometimes been a rubber stamp, some circuits now offer appellants an alternative forum for the first level of appeal. These are called Bankruptcy Appellate Panels, or BAPs, and are available in the First, Sixth, Eighth, Ninth, and Tenth Circuits. Bankruptcy judges from around these circuits sit on the BAPs in groups of three. They hear cases decided by other bankruptcy judges in their circuits. In cases where courts are split on important issues, appeals cases can be brought directly from the bankruptcy courts to the federal circuit court of appeals. See 28 U.S.C. §158(d).

(3) Preemption and the Relationship Between Federal Bankruptcy Law and State Law

Throughout the federal Bankruptcy Code, the drafters refer to applicable non-bankruptcy law, by which they mean state law, as well as tribal law. But as you will see, federal law on the subject of bankruptcy law always **preempts,** or beats, state law on the same subject. In many cases, the Bankruptcy Code defers to state law in defining certain concepts. What constitutes a property interest is one thing that is defined by looking to state law, as well as the definition of fraud. There are many other areas in which the Bankruptcy Code borrows definitions, and law as well, from state law.

(4) The Court's Equity Power Under Section 105(a)

Bankruptcy courts are courts of equity, which means that throughout a bankruptcy case, the court is charged with doing what is in the best interest of everyone affected by the case, according to the spirit of the entire Bankruptcy Code. To that end, Section 105(a) states that "the court may issue any order, process, or judgment that is necessary or appropriate to carry out the provisions" of the Bankruptcy Code. The court can grant the requested relief, as long the court feels the relief promotes the purposes of the Code, and as long as the relief does not conflict directly with another provision of the Code.

F   A   Q

Q: What are the limits on a bankruptcy court's equity powers?

A: The court generally cannot enter an order that conflicts with a specific provision of the Bankruptcy Code.

(5) Sovereign Immunity of States and Tribes

Until about ten years ago, states regularly participated in bankruptcy proceedings by filing **proofs of claim,**[2] filing and responding to motions and complaints, and appearing on various issues. In 1996, however, the U.S. Supreme Court decided a case that had nothing to do with bankruptcy, but that nevertheless changed the practice of bankruptcy in drastic ways. In *Seminole Tribe v. Florida,* 517 U.S. 44 (1996), the Seminole Tribe sued Florida in federal court, over noncompliance with a state statute requiring good faith in negotiating the terms of a gaming agreement. The tribe sued the state of Florida pursuant to the Indian Commerce Clause found in Article I of the Constitution, and the state of Florida defended by saying that federal courts have limited powers over states under the Eleventh Amendment, which takes precedence over the Article I powers.

The Supreme Court ultimately held that the tribe could not sue the state of Florida in federal court because that would violate the Eleventh Amendment prohibition against suing states in federal court against their will. The Supreme Court noted that it did not believe that its ruling would affect the other Article I powers because states are not regularly sued in federal court under the other Article I powers,

---

[2]A proof of claim is a simple pleading signed by a creditor under oath, indicating how much money the debtor owes the creditor and how the debt arose.

such as bankruptcy. As it turns out, this statement proved inaccurate, as states are involved in many bankruptcy cases every year. Congress even contemplated this problem and drafted Code Section 106, which states that sovereign immunity is abrogated for many Bankruptcy Code purposes. This simply means that sovereign immunity cannot be used or alleged by states in bankruptcy proceedings because it does not apply. The constitutionality of Section 106, however, was called into question — albeit indirectly — by the *Seminole Tribe* case.

Ever since the *Seminole Tribe* case, states have been attempting to ignore bankruptcy cases and to exercise their collection rights outside of bankruptcy. Bankruptcy courts, on the other hand, have struggled to figure out which actions they may take that might affect a state, and which they may not take. In 2006, the Supreme Court provided some relief from the sovereign immunity chaos. In a 5-4 decision, the Supreme Court held in *Central Virginia Community College v. Katz*, 546 U.S. 356 (2006), that a bankruptcy court *has* jurisdiction to hear a trustee's adversary proceeding to avoid a debtor's transfer to a state agency, because states have acquiesced in subordinating whatever sovereign immunity they might otherwise have asserted in "proceedings necessary to effectuate the *in rem* jurisdiction of the bankruptcy courts."

E. Case Administration and Structure of the Code

There is a tremendous amount of paperwork required in each bankruptcy case, and a great deal of notice to creditors. There can also be many parties in interest in each case, making bankruptcy a truly multi-party proceeding. One example of a perennial party in interest is the United States Trustee. There are also various case trustees appointed by the court. Federal bankruptcy courts have their own rules, courtrooms, and clerk's offices. Bankruptcy is a legal specialty and lawyers must know the local rules and procedures, as well as the role of the various parties in interest. This section describes those procedures.

A case is initiated by filing a bankruptcy petition with the clerk's office that contains very basic information about the debtor. Once this is filed, all collection actions against the debtor are automatically stayed.

F A Q

Q: How many bankruptcy courts are there?

A: There are 90 districts and 322 judges. Some states, like California, have over 40 judges. California, Texas, and New York each have four districts.

(1) The Paperwork

Bankruptcy has always involved a lot of paperwork and a very long list of disclosures. Clients often wonder why they need to describe their assets, their liabilities, and their financial histories in such great detail. In the 2005 amendments, Congress made the process of filing for bankruptcy more arduous. First, all individual debtors must get credit counseling before filing for bankruptcy. There are some exceptions to this requirement, but it is by far easier to get the credit counseling than to be excused from getting it. 11 U.S.C. §109.

Next the debtor files his or her petition instituting the case, which contains basic information about the debtor and the debtor's assets and liabilities. This two-page petition also states that the debtor is signing his or her bankruptcy paperwork under penalty of perjury. The petition instituting the case must normally be accompanied by a filing fee, although people whose income is less than 150% of the official poverty line can have the filing fee waived. 28 U.S.C. §1930(f)(1).

When a case is filed, there are a number of forms to fill out, known as the **Official Bankruptcy Forms**. These forms include the debtor's **schedules of assets and liabilities** and **statement of financial affairs**. All the disclosures are designed to provide the trustee and the creditors with a full picture of the debtor's financial affairs. The **schedules** tell all about each and every asset (with its estimated value) and each and every debt (with the address of the creditor and the account number) of the debtor. Contingent and unliquidated debts are listed as well. The schedules also describe the debtor's income and expenses. The schedules are in essence a snapshot of the debtor's exact financial condition at the time of the bankruptcy filing (which we call the **petition**).

The **statement of financial affairs**, on the other hand, tells the story of how the debtor got into this mess in the first place. It asks the debtor to disclose the debtor's income over the past two years, and everything else that happened to the debtor financially over various periods of time. Were there fires, foreclosures, repossessions, thefts? Did the debtor close any bank accounts? Did the debtor make any payments to creditors over certain amounts, which could constitute preferences? Did the debtor give large gifts? The **statement of affairs** is not a snapshot, but a look backwards over the past two years to determine what happened to the debtor and his or her money.

The **statement of affairs** and the **schedules** are signed under oath, and it is important that they be accurately completed. If you have never seen the statement and schedules, you might ask your teacher to bring a copy to class. Soon after the filing of some or all of these documents, the clerk's office notifies all creditors listed in the debtor's bankruptcy petition about the bankruptcy. This gives the creditor an opportunity to participate in the debtor's bankruptcy case before the creditor's claim is affected in the case. See Chapter 10 for more details on these disclosure documents.

Not too long after the paperwork is completed, the debtor is required to appear at a meeting called a 341 meeting (named after Section 341 of the Code, which requires the meeting), or first meeting of creditors, where creditors can come and ask questions of the debtor. Often, none of the creditors show up because they don't get better repayment rights for attending, so they see it as a waste of time. It is an informational session only. The CHAPTER 7 trustee runs the meeting, asking the debtor pointed questions about the disclosures made in the statement of financial affairs and the schedules of assets and liabilities that each debtor has (hopefully) filed. If the paperwork has not been filed, the meeting will be rescheduled. If any creditors do attend the meeting, they also are free to ask the debtor questions.

The 2005 amendments added more paperwork for the debtor and the debtor's attorney in every bankruptcy case. The debtor must now gather and produce pay stubs, tax returns, old bills with creditors' exact addresses, checkbooks, and endless other documentation.

The new law also puts additional pressure on debtors' attorneys to verify the accuracy of all of the disclosures made by the debtor in his or her bankruptcy. A lawyer who fails to correctly transcribe the values and other information on these documents can be forced to forfeit his or her fees, or, worse yet, can be subject to sanctions. 11 U.S.C. §§526, 707(b).

(2) Some CHAPTER 7 Differences

Up to this point in the process, CHAPTER 7 and CHAPTER 13 are similar. But in a CHAPTER 7 case, the CHAPTER 7 trustee runs the 341 meeting. After the meeting, the trustee in a CHAPTER 7 case will try to find assets to distribute to creditors, as he or she is a fiduciary for the creditors and is charged with finding whatever might be available for distribution to creditors. The trustee uses the debtor's schedules of assets and liabilities, statement of financial affairs, as well as the questions that were asked at the 341 meeting, to guide his or her search for available assets. If there is nothing to distribute (what we call a **no asset case**), the case ends within three months of the filing, the debtor receives a discharge for most debts, and the case is closed.

But if there are assets to distribute, the case can go on for several months or even years, though the debtor's discharge should still take just three months, assuming no unusual problems.

(3) Some CHAPTER 13 Differences

In a CHAPTER 13 case, the 341 meeting is run by the CHAPTER 13 trustee's office. The CHAPTER 13 trustee is often a **standing trustee**, meaning that the same person is the trustee for every CHAPTER 13 case within the district. Most of the questions in a CHAPTER 13 Section 341 meeting center on income and expenses, assets, and whether the repayment plan is feasible. The 341 meeting is more detailed and takes much longer in a CHAPTER 13 case than in a CHAPTER 7 case.

After the 341 meeting, the trustee determines whether the debtor's proposed CHAPTER 13 plan meets the requirements of the Code. If it does, the trustee will allow the plan to go forward and be **confirmed** (approved) by the court. If there are problems, the trustee may object to confirmation of the plan. Either way, if the plan is not ultimately approved, the case will be dismissed. This means that the debtor will no longer be in bankruptcy and will have lost his or her filing fee. The parties will be back where they started under state law. Alternatively, the debtor might convert the CHAPTER 13 to a CHAPTER 7 case.

(4) Some CHAPTER 11 Differences

In a CHAPTER 11 case, the debtor's management acts as the trustee for creditors. The debtor is called a **debtor in possession**. In a CHAPTER 11 case, a person from the United States Trustee's Office runs the 341 meeting. The U.S. Trustee's Office is an arm of the Department of Justice, and its job is to oversee the procedures, as well as the attorneys' fees, in all cases, but particularly CHAPTER 11 cases. The U.S. Trustee is charged with ensuring that lawyers and trustees are properly using the bankruptcy system, by supervising the debtors and the trustees throughout the CHAPTER 11 process. The idea is to remove some of the administrative burden from bankruptcy judges.

The U.S. Trustee's Office is a totally different office than that of the CHAPTER 13 Trustee's Office and is staffed with entirely different people. See 28 U.S.C. §581.

(5) The Structure of the Code

One thing you should notice about the Code's structure is that its Code sections are located in mostly odd-numbered chapters. Chapter 1 contains **general provisions**, including definitions, sovereign immunity, and equity powers. These are the topics we covered in the first part of this book. These sections begin with "1," such as Section 105.

Case administration issues are covered in Chapter 3 of the Code. These sections begin with "3," for instance, Sections 341 and 362, which address case administration issues.

Code sections that begin with "5" articulate the general relationships among creditors, the debtor, and the estate. Chapter 5 contains some of the most important provisions in the Code, such as Section 507 (priorities), Section 541 (the estate), and Sections 544, 547, and 548 (the avoiding powers). Also, Chapters 1, 3, and 5 of the Code apply to all types of bankruptcy cases — CHAPTER 7, CHAPTER 13, and CHAPTER 11.

After CHAPTER 5, the Code's chapters correspond to the different kinds of bankruptcy, the most important being CHAPTER 7, CHAPTER 13, and CHAPTER 11. Thus, the 700 sections of the Code cover issues arising in a CHAPTER 7 case, the 1300 sections address CHAPTER 13 issues, and the 1100 sections cover CHAPTER 11 issues.

ELIGIBILITY FOR BANKRUPTCY

General overview of the different types of bankruptcy under the United States Code. The order of the chart mirrors the order in which we cover the material in this book. You may find it helpful to refer back to this table as you work through the rules in different chapters of the bankruptcy code.

CHAPTER	Natural Person or Corporation	Debt Levels	Income Limits	Other Eligibility Requirements	Outcome
CHAPTER 7	Natural or Corporation/ LLC	Unlimited	If income greater than median, can't have income over $100-$167 above allowed expenses. See §707(b).	Not a stock broker or commodies broker.	Usually short case (90 days) with most general unsecured debts discharged.

CHAPTER	Natural Person or Corporation	Debt Levels	Income Limits	Other Eligibility Requirements	Outcome
CHAPTER 13	Natural only	Non-contingent, liquidated, unsecured debts of $336,900 or under and secured debts of $1,010,650 or under. See §109(e).	None, but need to distribute all disposible income.	Need regular income from some source.	Debtor has 3-5 year plan and must pay according to schedule, with some debts discharged at end.
CHAPTER 11	Corporation/ LLC or Natural	Unlimited	None	None	Negotiated payment plan, some debts discharged.
CHAPTER 12	Individual or close corporation. See 11 USC §101(18).	Aggregate debts of $3,544,525 for farmers and $1,642,500 for fishermen. See §§101 (18)(A) and (19A)(A)(i).	None	Family farmer or fisherman. See §§101 (18)-(21).	Similar to Chapter 13.
CHAPTER 9	Municipality	Unlimited	None	None	Similar to Chapter 11.
CHAPTER 15	Natural or Corporation/ LLC	Unlimited	None	Need a debtor that is subject to proceeding in another jurisdiction.	Related cases in different jurisdictions administered similarly.

SUMMARY

■ We do not allow people to file for bankruptcy and discharge most of their debts to be nice. The philosophy is that relieving people of their debts allows them to get back into and contribute to the economy once again. This is considered good for our overall economy, though this theory is not without some controversy.

■ Bankruptcies fall into two general types: those in which the debtor gives up property over and above a certain value, in exchange for a fairly swift discharge of most debts, and those in which a debtor pays back some of the debts over time pursuant to a repayment plan.

■ The types of bankruptcies are named after the relevant chapters in the U.S. Code. Thus, CHAPTER 7 cases, which are quick, liquidation-style cases, involving a swift discharge in exchange for a sale of nonexempt property, are governed by the provisions found in CHAPTER 7 of Title 11 of the U.S. Code.

■ CHAPTER 7 can be used both by natural persons and by legal persons like corporations.

■ Individuals who prefer a payment plan often use CHAPTER 13, which allows the debtor to pay off secured debts (for which they would otherwise lose their secured property) and taxes and other claims over time. The CHAPTER 13 case involves agreeing to pay debts over a three- to five-year period, and thus requires a major commitment of future assets to current creditors.

■ Individuals or small business entities who wish to do a payment plan over time and who are family farmers or fishermen can use CHAPTER 12, which is similar to CHAPTER 13 but a bit more beneficial for debtors.

■ CHAPTER 11 is a type of payment plan case used most commonly by businesses. It involves a much more elaborate legal process than CHAPTERS 13 or 12, and also allows the debtor great flexibility in dealing with debts. It is much more expensive, in terms of legal fees and costs, than other types of bankruptcy.

■ There are also separate types of bankruptcy cases for municipalities (CHAPTER 9) and for cases in which the debtor, assets, or creditors are located in more than one country (CHAPTER 15).

■ Bankruptcy cases are heard by specialized bankruptcy courts, which are arms of the federal district courts. First-level bankruptcy appeals are typically heard by either panels of bankruptcy courts from other districts (BAPs) or by the regular federal district courts. The next level of appeal is heard by the regular federal circuit courts, and cases of great significance can even reach the U.S. Supreme Court.

■ Bankruptcy debtors must fill out lots of detailed paperwork. In a way, the debtor is exchanging a long list of disclosures for favorable treatment of debts.

■ In CHAPTER 7, CHAPTER 13, and CHAPTER 12 cases, a trustee oversees the case and acts as a fiduciary for the creditors. In CHAPTER 11 cases, by comparison, the debtor stays in business (if it is business) and itself acts as the fiduciary for creditors. In those cases, the debtor is a debtor-in-possession.

CONNECTIONS

Outcomes and Attributes

Refer back to this chapter, particularly the preceding chart, to compare the attributes of different types of bankruptcy as you read about the rules under CHAPTER 7, CHAPTER 13, and CHAPTER 11 cases throughout the rest of this book.

Theory and Policy

Also use this chapter to remind yourself of the theory and policies behind the intricate bankruptcy rules that are covered throughout the rest of this book.

Scope of Jurisdiction

This chapter is a good reference for understanding the scope of a bankruptcy court's jurisdiction, which is critical for filing a CHAPTER 7, CHAPTER 13, or CHAPTER 11 case.

Organization of the Code

When you need to find a provision of the Bankruptcy Code, realize that CHAPTER 1 contains definitions that apply to all types of bankruptcy cases, and CHAPTERS 3 and 5 also contain provisions that apply to all types of bankruptcy cases. Further, Code sections that begin with 7 apply to CHAPTER 7 cases, Code sections that begin with 13 apply to CHAPTER 13 cases, and Code sections that begin with 11 apply to CHAPTER 11 cases.

The Automatic Stay

4

A bankruptcy case stops most collection efforts, under a provision known as the automatic stay. In most cases, the automatic stay comes into

effect immediately upon a bankruptcy filing. Stopping collection efforts in their tracks is one of the main reasons a person files for bankruptcy, making it a valuable tool for debtors. A debtor who has filed for bankruptcy in the past, however, may not get the full benefit of the automatic stay in subsequent cases pending within the same year.

The automatic stay is a very powerful and serious part of bankruptcy law. Creditors should not ignore it or they could be fined for violating federal law. A few things are exempt from the automatic stay, meaning that some creditor collection efforts can continue. These include lawsuits by governmental bodies to protect public safety, as well as many family law proceedings.

The automatic stay is only a temporary inconvenience for some secured creditors. A secured creditor who is not being paid in a bankruptcy case can get the automatic stay lifted or removed and get its collateral back.

A. WHAT IS STAYED BY THE AUTOMATIC STAY

B. EXCEPTIONS TO THE AUTOMATIC STAY

C. MULTIPLE FILING CASES: WHEN THE AUTOMATIC STAY IS NOT SO "AUTOMATIC"

1. One Prior Dismissed Case
2. Two or More Dismissed Cases
3. Extending the 30-Day Stay Under Section 362(c)(3)
4. Obtaining a Stay Under Section 362(c)(4)

D. RELIEF FROM THE AUTOMATIC STAY

A. What Is Stayed by the Automatic Stay

A bankruptcy filing immediately changes the collection rights of almost all creditors. Non-bankruptcy state law collection procedures are an individual effort, the race of the diligent to see who can execute on valuable assets first. By comparison, bankruptcy is a collective process. Its goals include equality of distribution to creditors and providing the debtor a breathing spell from collection efforts.

The breathing spell is accomplished through the equivalent of an immediate court order or injunction, effective as soon as the debtor files his bankruptcy petition, enjoining all collection efforts against the debtor or the debtor's property, regardless of where it is located. This order imposes by law what is called the automatic stay, which is codified in Section 362 of the Bankruptcy Code. Section 362(a) outlines all of the different activities that are stayed by the bankruptcy filing. 11 U.S.C. §362.

They include any attempt to collect on a pre-petition debt, any continuing lawsuit to collect a debt, any repossession of a debtor's assets, any attempt to exercise control over property of the debtor's estate (defined very broadly, as discussed in Chapter 5 of this book), any attempt to perfect a security interest, and pretty much anything else you can think of that would allow a creditor to improve its own position against the debtor compared to other creditors.

All acts to collect from property of the estate are also stayed. The estate is the subject of the next chapter, but for our purposes here, the estate includes all property that the debtor has any interest in at all, even if the debtor does not receive the benefit until later. It includes contingent interests, like proceeds of a future lawsuit from an accident that already has happened, as well as a tax refund the debtor has a right to in the future, for a tax period that already has passed. The key question is whether the debtor has to do anything else to be entitled to the property or whether he is waiting now. See Chapter 5 for more details.

The stay continues in place until the bankruptcy proceeding is closed or terminated, or until a creditor gets the stay lifted in order to pursue its own particular debt. Section 362(a) is easy to read — check it out now.

Sidebar

A STAY OF EXCOMMUNICATION

We said all acts to collect from the debtor (such as phone calls to the debtor, letters, etc.) are stayed. One well-known case involved a creditor who was so angry after not being paid that he tried to get the debtor excommunicated from his church! The court noted in dicta (there were more obvious stay violations too, like refusing to return repossessed inventory) that trying to excommunicate someone from a church could violate the stay, if the purpose was to collect a debt. This shows how broad the stay really is!

SECTION 362(A): SCOPE OF AUTOMATIC STAY: WHAT IS STAYED?

■ Pre-petition lawsuits or administrative proceedings (§362(a)(1))
■ Enforcement of pre-petition judgment against debtor or property of estate (§362(a)(2))
■ Acts to obtain possession of or exercise control over property of the estate (§362(a)(4),(5))
■ Acts to create, perfect, or enforce a lien or security interest (§362(a)(4), and (5))
■ Any act to collect a pre-petition claim from the debtor (§362(a)(6))
■ Setoff of pre-petition debt (§362(a)(7))
■ See the statute for other actions that are stayed.

STOP

F A Q

Q: Is service of process stayed? What about garnishments? What about lawsuits by the debtor?

A: Service of process is a continuation of a collection effort and is most certainly stayed. Garnishments are also stayed, though the bank or creditor may not find out about the case in time to stop a garnishment, in which case that garnishment will be void and the money returned to the debtor or the estate. But suits *by* the debtor as plaintiff are not stayed because they are not suits *against* the debtor.

B. Exceptions to the Automatic Stay

Section 362(b) contains the exceptions to the automatic stay. Criminal suits are not stayed, nor are suits to determine or modify paternity or marital support, or to collect marital support. Actions by governmental units to enforce police powers also are not stayed. These are actions taken by state, local, federal, or tribal governments to protect the health and welfare of citizens, for example, actions taken to stop a company from polluting or to stop ongoing dangerous activity. But be careful here. Actions by governmental units merely to collect debts *are* stayed, and the line is hard to draw. Suffice it to say that *all* collection suits must stop after a bankruptcy case is filed, even if the plaintiff is a governmental body. Suits designed to stop a real danger to the public, if brought by a government body, are not stayed.

**EXCEPTIONS TO THE AUTOMATIC STAY CONTAINED IN SECTION 362(B)
(ACTIONS THAT ARE NOT STAYED)**

■ Criminal proceedings against the debtor
  (§362(b)(i))
■ Actions to establish paternity
  (§362(b)(2)(a)(i))
■ Actions to establish or modify alimony,
  maintenance, or support (§362(b)(2)(a)(i))
■ Actions to collect alimony, maintenance,
  or support (§362(b)(3))
■ Some acts to continue the perfection of a
  security interest (§362(b)(4))
■ Actions by governments to enforce their
  police or regulatory powers (to protect the
  health and welfare of citizens) but not to
  collect a money judgment. See Section
  362(b) for others.

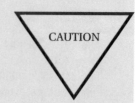

CAUTION

C. Multiple Filing Cases: When the Automatic Stay Is Not So "Automatic"

Remember that automatic stay you just learned about? Sometimes it is not so "automatic." One of the true beauties of bankruptcy has always been that once you file for it, an automatic stay goes into effect immediately, staying all collection efforts. Under the 2005 amendments, some debtors are not entitled to a full automatic stay upon the filing of a case.

F   A   Q

Q: How do creditors find out that the "automatic stay" is in place?

A: If there are past bankruptcies, the debtor's attorney will need to know if any past cases were dismissed during the year before the petition will be filed. If there are cases that have been dismissed during this one-year period, either voluntarily or involuntarily, the full stay may not go into effect under Sections 362(c)(3) and (c)(4).

(1) One Prior Dismissed Case

Section 362(c)(3) states that if the debtor has one prior dismissed case pending within a year, the debtor gets the stay for just 30 days, except as extended by the court. However, if a person files a CHAPTER 7 case that is dismissed under the means test described in Chapter 10 of this book, the subsequent CHAPTER 13 case is not affected. The debtor gets the full stay as before. However, if the first case was a CHAPTER 7, 11, or 13 case, and was dismissed for some other reason, the second case will be entitled to just a 30-day stay automatically. The debtor will need to work through the presumptions discussed below.

(2) Two or More Dismissed Cases

Section 362(c)(4) states that if the debtor has two or more dismissed cases within the year, the stay does not go into effect at all.

(3) Extending the 30-Day Stay Under Section 362(c)(3)

A request to extend the stay is made by motion. The motion will be granted if the court finds that the new case has been filed in good faith. Naturally, the motion must be filed while the stay is still in effect. Section 362(c)(3) creates a presumption that the new case was not filed in good faith in certain cases, which the debtor must then rebut. The presumption arises if:

- the debtor failed to amend the petition or other documents as required by the Code or the court, except through inadvertence or negligence; or
- the debtor failed to provide adequate protection as ordered by the court (presumably this does not refer to pre-petition adequate protection, just that ordered by the court); or
- the debtor failed to perform the plan.

Though the statute does not say this, common sense suggests that if the debtor had medical or other reasons for failing in the prior case, or if the debtor's income dropped precipitously or if some other unforeseen event caused the debtor to be unable to continue with the prior case as planned, the presumption would not arise. If no presumption arises, the debtor can get the stay extended by proving by a preponderance of evidence that the case was filed in good faith. If the presumption does arise, good faith must be proven by clear and convincing evidence, at least according to some courts.

(4) Obtaining a Stay Under Section 362(c)(4)

If the debtor has had more than one prior case pending during the past year, no stay will go into effect upon a subsequent bankruptcy case but the debtor may apply for a stay. So how does such a debtor apply for a stay? The debtor will need to file an emergency motion to stay a foreclosure or whatever the situation calls for. The prior cases create a presumption that the new case was filed in bad faith, which the debtor must now rebut. The debtor does this in much the same way as discussed above, though for a person with two prior bankruptcies, this will be harder to do. The court has a lot of flexibility in fashioning the stay, and future cases should be interesting.

The court can have the stay imposed on all or just some creditors, and can impose additional conditions or limitations as well.

D. Relief from the Automatic Stay

Sometimes creditors are able to have the automatic stay removed or lifted so that they can exercise their state court collection rights, just as if there was no bankruptcy. With some exceptions that are not important here, this right is only granted to secured creditors who can prove certain elements. These elements essentially show that the creditor that is moving to lift the stay is more entitled to the collateral than the debtor and the other creditors.

If a secured creditor can prove either (1) "cause" to lift the stay, which typically boils down to proving that its position in the collateral is at risk (what the Code calls a "lack of adequate protection"), *or* (2) that (a) the debtor has no equity in the collateral, and (b) the collateral is not necessary to an effective reorganization, the Court will lift the stay and allow the creditor to take back its collateral. In a CHAPTER 7 bankruptcy, the most common situation in which the stay will be lifted is one in which a secured creditor is **undersecured**. For example, if a secured creditor is owed $10,000 and the automobile that is the collateral is worth only $8,000, the stay will usually be lifted, and the secured party will be allowed to repossess the auto and sell it to satisfy at least part of its debt. You can probably see in this case that there is no value in the car for the estate because the debtor has no equity in the auto. 11 U.S.C. §362(d)(2). Thus it makes sense to give it back to the creditor.

At least in a CHAPTER 7 case, the car is not necessary to an effective reorganization because the case is a liquidation and there is no reorganization, so the second test is met. Because the debtor is still driving the car and it is still depreciating, and because the debtor is not making the payments on it, the first test is likely to be met as well. 11 U.S.C. §362(d)(1). The creditor's position is deteriorating, and is thus not adequately protected.

F A Q

Q: Can unsecured creditors ever get the stay lifted?

A: No, with one exception. If an unsecured creditor has a special interest in an asset, but the interest is not a security interest, sometimes the creditor can get the stay lifted to pursue the special asset. An example would be where a tort victim has a right to be paid from an insurance policy held by the debtor. In such a case, the court might find "cause" under Section 362(d)(1) to lift the stay to allow the creditor to pursue the insurance policy.

We will be discussing relief from the automatic stay in greater detail in our discussions of CHAPTER 11, where the concept is far more critical to the success of the case. A CHAPTER 7 debtor who is behind on his obligations to secured creditors, however, will find very little relief under a CHAPTER 7 case. If a CHAPTER 7 case is filed in a situation in which the mortgage is past due (or in **arrears**), the creditor will probably succeed in getting the stay lifted. If not, the case will be over in just three short months, after which time the automatic stay will disappear, leaving the creditor free to foreclose.

Again, CHAPTER 7 does not help debtors who are behind on their obligations to *secured creditors*. CHAPTER 7 involves no repayment plan and thus no time during which the debtor can make up for the past due payments. Practically speaking, a debtor who is behind on the home mortgage will not be allowed to keep the home unless the arrears are **cured** very shortly after filing. Thus, most CHAPTER 7 debtors who are homeowners are current on their mortgage and should keep it that way.

SUMMARY

■ In most cases, the filing of a bankruptcy petition or case operates as an automatic stay of all collection activity against the debtor or the debtor's assets.

■ Specific acts that are stayed include any attempt to collect on a pre-petition debt, any continuing lawsuit to collect a debt, any repossession of a debtor's assets, any attempt to exercise control over property of the debtor's estate, any attempt to perfect a security interest, and pretty much anything else you can think of that would allow a creditor to improve its own position vis-à-vis the debtor compared to other creditors.

■ Some actions are not stayed, including criminal suits, suits to determine or modify paternity or marital support, and suits to collect marital support, as well as actions by governmental units to enforce police powers. As you can see, most of these acts are not actions to collect a debt anyway.

■ If a debtor has filed a bankruptcy case that was pending during the year prior to filing the current case, the debtor may not get the full benefit of the automatic stay. This prevents abuse of the system anytime a debtor wants to freeze collection efforts.

■ Sometimes secured creditors can get the automatic stay removed or lifted, which would put the secured creditor back in the position it was in under state law, free to repossess its collateral and otherwise enforce its rights. In general, the stay can be lifted either if the collateral is diminishing in value, or if the debtor has no equity in the collateral and is not reorganizing his or her debts under CHAPTER 11, 12, or 13.

CONNECTIONS

Secured Creditors

As in other areas of bankruptcy law, secured creditors are in a superior position to fight the automatic stay. In this instance, secured creditors are frequently in a good position to get the stay lifted for cause, if they are at risk of losing their position in respect to their collateral. See Chapter 8, Section B, and Chapter 17 for more details.

The Decision to File

The automatic stay contained in Section 362 of the Bankruptcy Code is one of the main reasons debtors file for bankruptcy. As you read about Chapter 7 and Chapter 13 cases in the next nine chapters of this book, and Chapter 11 cases in the second half of this book, always remember that the automatic stay is one of the debtor's most potent weapons, and it may be enough reason, by itself, to declare bankruptcy.

The Debtor's Estate

The debtor's estate, the subject of the next chapter, is defined very broadly, which is important to remember when thinking through stay litigation issues, because you always need to be clear about exactly what property is in the estate and therefore subject to the stay.

The Fair Debt Collection Practices Act

Recall from Chapter 2, Section C, that the FDCPA does not apply to the original creditor, only to the collection agency hired to collect the debt, allowing the original creditor to engage in more harassment than an independent collection agency. Thus the automatic stay is the debtor's most potent weapon to stop all harassment from creditors, because the automatic stay stops all collection activity.

Property of the Debtor's Estate

5

The moment a debtor files for bankruptcy, pretty much all of the debtor's belongings go into the "debtor's estate." This "estate" includes almost

O V E R V I E W

all kinds of property that a debtor has any rights in. I think of the "estate" as a big bag — a bag that all the debtor's belongings go into.[1] Typically, a trustee will be in charge of the bag of belongings for the next 90 days, while the CHAPTER 7 bankruptcy case is going on. The trustee can sell everything in the bag in order to pay off the debtor's debts. But in a typical CHAPTER 7 case, many assets will come back out of the bag at the end of the three months, because they are exempt from creditor claims.

A. BREADTH OF THE ESTATE

B. LEGAL AND EQUITABLE INTERESTS IN PROPERTY

C. ADDITIONAL FUTURE INTERESTS THAT ARE PART OF THE ESTATE

D. EXCLUSIONS FROM THE DEBTOR'S ESTATE

1. Retirement Funds
2. Other Specific Exclusions

---

[1]Beyoncé might instead think of a box. In her song "Irreplaceable," as she is kicking out her ex, she tells him that everything he owns is in a box.

E. POST-PETITION ASSETS

1. CHAPTER 7 Post-Petition Assets
2. CHAPTER 13 and CHAPTER 11 Post-Petition Assets

The main thing to remember is that the debtor's estate is very broad. It includes things that you wouldn't normally think of as property. It includes money that the debtor doesn't even have now, but has a right to in the future.

For instance, the estate is broad enough to attach to the rights to lottery ticket winnings. If the debtor bought a lottery ticket and then filed for bankruptcy, the lottery ticket (along with the rights attached to the lottery ticket) goes into the bag. If this lottery ticket then wins a $2 million jackpot, the trustee will get the money to pay creditors. Therefore the creditors would get the lottery money before the debtor would (but only up to the amount the debtor owes — hopefully not all $2 million!).

A. Breadth of the Estate

When a bankruptcy case is filed, all of the debtor's property as of the filing date, wherever located, and by whomever held, goes into an estate. The estate exists for the benefit of the creditors. Virtually every possible interest of the debtor in property, whether it is a contingent interest, a partial interest, a legal interest, or an equitable interest, goes into this estate under Section 541(a). This applies to property owned or interests held *as of the filing date*. At least under CHAPTER 7, most *post-filing* assets do not go into the estate, as explained below.

Absolutely everything in which the debtor has any rights must be disclosed in the bankruptcy paperwork, and almost all assets come into the estate, at least initially. If your Code is handy, you can look at Section 541(a) now to see what goes into the debtor's estate. Section 541(a) defines a debtor's estate to include

- all of the debtor's equitable interests in property;
- all of the debtor's legal rights in property; and
- virtually all contingent property that might come into the debtor's estate in the future.

Here is a quick example. In one case, an engaged debtor had an engagement ring worth $90,000 when she filed for CHAPTER 7. Relying on cases finding that marriage is a condition precedent to ownership of an engagement ring, the court held that the debtor owned only conditional title to the ring when she filed her case, and that while this conditional title did go into her bankruptcy estate, it was worth less than the $1,000 Kansas jewelry exemption. *In re Heck*, 355 B.R. 813 (Bankr. D. Kan. 2006).

F   A   Q

Q: What about an inheritance that the debtor receives after filing?

A: If it is received within six months of the filing, it becomes part of the debtor's estate. This is an exception to the rule that the debtor needs to have *some* entitlement to an asset at the time of filing in order for it to be in the estate.

Even though it is broad, Section 541(b) does list a few things that are *excluded* from the debtor's estate (such as certain retirement plans and health insurance plans, certain trusts, and certain tax-deferred compensation plans and educational accounts). Overall, though, the estate is very broadly defined. For instance, if the debtor has an interest in a possible lawsuit, but no one has sued anyone and the debtor is not even sure that he will pursue the claim, the potential lawsuit goes into the estate and should be listed on the schedules of assets and liabilities that the debtor must file. Similarly, a lottery ticket, purchased pre-petition with pre-petition assets, belongs to the estate. If the debtor were to win, the creditors would get any nonexempt proceeds, up to the amount of the debts owed.

B. Legal and Equitable Interests in Property

Section 541(a) says that "all legal or equitable interests of the debtor in property" are included in the estate. Why does the Code use both the word "legal" and the word "equitable"?

First, a **legal interest** is one that the debtor has title to. This would include the debtor's house, if the debtor's name is on the title. If the debtor lives in the house and pays the mortgage, and the house is really his, the debtor would have *both* the **legal interest** and the **equitable interest** in the house.

A **legal interest** also includes property that is titled in the debtor's name but actually owned by someone else. An example would be where the debtor purchases a car and takes out a car loan for her brother, who is unable to qualify for the loan. The brother pays for the car and it is his, even though it is in his sister's name. If she then declares bankruptcy, she has a "legal interest" in the car and she must list the car as an asset. But the equitable interest belongs to her brother. He really owns it. In this example, the debtor's interest in the car will become part of the estate. However, the trustee will not sell the car to pay the debtor's creditors, because it really belongs to the brother.

Second, an **equitable interest** is one where the debtor *really* owns the property, even though he may not have title to it. Suppose that the debtor's mother signs her daughter's mortgage, and her name is on the title to the house, but the daughter makes all the mortgage payments. The mother would have a legal interest in the house, because her name is on the title, but the daughter has the equitable interest, because the house is really hers. An equitable interest is one that a person in fact pays for and enjoys the ownership rights of.

Let's say that the debtor is holding a bank account, in his name and his grandmother's name jointly, for the sole benefit of his grandmother. It's all her money; none of it is his. The debtor's interest in the account, though it is only a legal interest, is part of his bankruptcy estate. This asset absolutely must be listed on the debtor's bankruptcy schedules. But the trustee will not take this money to pay creditors because the debtor's interest in the bank account is solely a **legal interest**. The trustee will not take Grandma's money, because the money is really hers. But the account still must be disclosed.

The idea is that the trustee has a right to examine these items to make sure that the debtor is accurately determining whose money is in the account, and the trustee has a duty to make sure that the debtor is telling the truth.

Although everything in which the debtor has any interest of any kind must be disclosed in the paperwork that is filed to start the bankruptcy case, this does not mean that the trustee will necessarily take these assets.

By including all "legal or equitable interests of the debtor," Section 541(a)(1) defines the debtor's estate very broadly. As you can imagine, there are many quirky things one would never think about that are part of a debtor's estate. These include rights to future lawsuits for events that already have occurred; appreciation and dividends on stock accounts the debtor owns now, even though the dividends and appreciation cannot yet be collected; bonuses from work; and amounts other people owe the debtor (for anything), even pre-paid contracts and down payments. Thus there are many things in the estate that the debtor would never dream would be included, because they cannot be collected today.

A good rule of thumb is that if all the debtor has to do now is to wait for an asset or a right to future payment,[2] it is part of the estate. It goes into the bag.

C. Additional Future Interests that Are Part of the Estate

In addition to the broad definition of the estate in Section 541(a)(1), two other provisions in Section 541 state that certain property acquired *after* the filing date also goes into the estate.

First, Section 541(a)(5) says that inheritance, property settlements from a divorce, and life insurance, which would have been part of the estate if the debtor received them before the filing date, are still property of the estate if the debtor receives them within 180 days *after* the date of filing. These go in the bag.

Second, Section 541(a)(6) says that "proceeds, product, offspring, rents, or profits of or from property of the estate" are part of the estate. Thus, if the debtor owns a rental property (which normally goes into the estate), the rent from the property also goes into the estate, even though the rent is paid after the date on which the bankruptcy is filed. Similarly, if a debtor owns cattle (which is also normally part of the estate), the calves born after the bankruptcy is filed also go into the estate.

However, Section 541(a)(6) *excludes* from the estate proceeds, product, offspring, rents, or profits "from services performed by [the] debtor" after the date of filing. This section excludes the debtor's post-petition wages from the estate. Moreover, if something requires post-petition work by the debtor, it does NOT go into the estate. For example, think of a crop of corn, planted before bankruptcy is filed, but not harvested until after. The proceeds from the sale of the corn come in part from the property of the estate (the land), and in part from the labor of the debtor (harvesting the corn). Therefore, the debtor's labor should be subtracted from the sale price of the corn and excluded from the estate, but the rest of the proceeds from the sale of corn are part of the estate.

D. Exclusions from the Debtor's Estate

(1) Retirement Funds

The 2005 amendments added significant protection for the retirement funds of bankruptcy debtors. As a conceptual matter, do you think that retirement funds, earned prior to a debtor's bankruptcy filing, fall within the estate?

---

[2]Rights to proceeds of future lawsuits for events that already have occurred are unquestionably part of the debtor's estate, even though the debtor has to prosecute those to bring home the bacon.

Of course they do. They fall within the definition of pre-petition assets, and thus form part of an individual's bankruptcy estate. On the other hand, there is a strong policy reason why our society has decided to exclude retirement funds from the debtor's estate: Some retirement funds are necessary to protect a person in old age, right?

The new Code specifically excludes from the estate all employee contributions to any ERISA-qualified retirement plan, deferred compensation plan, tax-deferred annuity, or health insurance plan. §541(b)(7).

(2) Other Specific Exclusions

In addition to retirement funds, the new amendments also exclude certain educational accounts for the debtor's children and grandchildren. 11 U.S.C. §541(b)(5) & (6). This is true even if the accounts are held in the debtor's name and the debtor has a right to withdraw the funds.

Before you read on, think about what it means for an asset to be outside the debtor's estate. It means that the debtor need not use up his or her exemptions to save the asset. Rather, the asset does not come into the estate at all.

In addition to those retirement funds that are exempt from the estate, for example, those that are held in ERISA-qualified pension plans, Congress has vastly improved a bankruptcy debtor's ability to protect other retirement funds, namely those held in IRAs. IRAs are now exempt (they come into the estate but come back out as exempt property), for up to $1,095,000 per person.

No, this is not a typo. Not only can a wealthy debtor exempt up to $1,095,000 if it is in the right type of retirement account, the court can also allow a debtor to exempt more than the $1,095,000 if it deems the $1,095,000 insufficient for the debtor's retirement needs. 11 U.S.C. §522(n).

Given that over half of all people in the United States do not have a single penny in any form of retirement fund, these provisions chalk one up for rich people who take advantage of the bankruptcy system.

E. Post-Petition Assets

(1) CHAPTER 7 Post-Petition Assets

In a CHAPTER 7 case, the general rule is that property that the debtor obtains *after* the case is filed does not become part of the debtor's estate. Rather than **estate property**, this is what we think of as **fresh start property**, property that the debtor may keep as part of his or her fresh start. One very important rule is that all of the debtor's wages in a CHAPTER 7 case, earned after the case is filed, are his or hers to keep and do not become part of the debtor's estate. This is not true in a CHAPTER 11 or a CHAPTER 13 case.

However, as explained in Section C above, if a debtor *inherits* money or property, or gets a property settlement from a divorce, or gets money from a life insurance policy within six months after the bankruptcy filing, these all become part of the estate, even though they were acquired post-petition. 11 U.S.C. §541(a)(5)(A)-(C). Also, if any pre-petition asset that is part of the estate earns income, profits, rents, or other proceeds after the filing, all of those come into the estate as well, even though post-petition assets generally do not. 11 U.S.C. §541(a)(6).

F   A   Q

Q: The rule that inheritances the debtor receives within six months after the case comes into the estate seems to go against the general rule that only things the debtor has some right to at the filing are part of a CHAPTER 7 estate. Why the different rule?

A: The inheritance rule is an exception to the general rule. The policy behind the rule is that people who do not pay their debts should not get windfalls. However, it is also true that other post-petition windfalls do not get swept up in the estate, and for that there is no good explanation.

(2) CHAPTER 13 and CHAPTER 11 Post-Petition Assets

In a CHAPTER 13 or a CHAPTER 11 case, post-petition assets that are received or obtained by the debtor after the filing date *do* become part of the estate. For example, in a CHAPTER 13 case, the debtor's post-petition income not only becomes part of the estate, but is usually the money used to make plan payments. The debts ordinarily will be paid over time, from post-petition wages. Similarly, other assets the debtor obtains during the course of the bankruptcy case, such as gifts, cash, or property, also become part of the CHAPTER 13 estate and, at least in theory, must be contributed to the plan.

In a CHAPTER 11 case, post-petition assets acquired after the case is filed also become part of the estate. Because a CHAPTER 11 case is a repayment case, this makes sense and should be easy to remember. After all, the debtor in a CHAPTER 11 case usually uses its future income and profits to fund its plan.

CHAPTER 7	Estate Property Versus Fresh Start Property
Estate Property	**Fresh Start Property**
Belongings purchased before filing the bankruptcy: house, car, stereo, lottery ticket, pets, livestock, cell phone, TV, computer, furniture, sports equipment and so on	Wages earned after the bankruptcy filing date (the Code calls these "earnings from services performed . . . after the commencement of the case")
Rights to proceeds from lawsuits from events that happened before the filing date	Belongings purchased after the bankruptcy filing date
Tax refunds from the prior year, even if the debtor doesn't get the actual refund until after the filing date	Tax refunds from wages withheld after the filing date
Inheritances, divorce settlements, or life insurance proceeds from before the filing date *and* up to six months *after* the filing date (§523(a)(5)(A)-(C))	Inheritance, divorce settlements, or life insurance proceeds the debtor acquires or becomes entitled to acquire more than six months after the filing date
Rents, profits, offspring, and other proceeds from estate property	

SUMMARY

■ Filing a bankruptcy case or petition creates an estate similar to a decedent's estate.

■ The estate created consists of all of the debtor's legal and equitable interests in property of any kind, including proceeds of any property the debtor currently owns.

■ In a CHAPTER 7 case, where the debtor will not be using his or her future income to pay current creditors, future wages are not included in the bankruptcy estate.

■ In a CHAPTER 13 case, or a CHAPTER 11 case filed by an individual, the debtor's future wages do become part of the debtor's estate.

■ Most retirement funds of the debtor are completely excluded from the bankruptcy estate in both CHAPTER 7 and CHAPTER 13 cases.

■ While assets the debtor acquires after the case is filed normally do not form part of the CHAPTER 7 estate, there is an exception for anything a debtor inherits, receives from life insurance, or receives in a marital property settlement agreement, if the assets are received within 180 days after the bankruptcy case is filed.

CONNECTIONS

The Automatic Stay

Chapter 4 explains that a bankruptcy filing stays actions against the debtor. What is actually stayed, however, are actions against either the debtor or the debtor's estate. Thus stay litigation issues and the breadth of the estate are inextricably linked.

Exemptions

Understanding the debtor's estate requires that you also understand Chapter 6, (regarding exemptions) because certain property will ultimately be exempt and thus stay with the debtor rather than being used as part of the estate to pay off unsecured creditors.

Claims Against the Estate

The breadth of the estate is relevant to claims against the estate, described in Chapter 7, because determining which property is property of the estate is necessary to determining how much money can be paid out to satisfy such claims.

Post-Petition Assets Go into the Estate

In a CHAPTER 13 or CHAPTER 11 pay out case, all assets acquired after the filing, including wages, become part of the debtor's estate.

Exemptions

6

Both inside and outside bankruptcy, no debtor is required to give up *all* of his or her property, simply because he or she does not pay creditors.

OVERVIEW

Some assets can be retained by the debtor despite creditor claims. The property that the debtor gets to keep is called exempt property and the law allowing this is called exemption law. Exemption law and policy is an integral part of the debtor-creditor system, and allows debtors to move on with life, perhaps with a car, a home, clothes, and other personal belongings. Exemption policy keeps people from becoming wards of the state. In bankruptcy, some debtors can choose between the state exemption law of their state and the federal bankruptcy exemption scheme. Others are stuck with the state exemption scheme.

A. STATE VERSUS FEDERAL EXEMPTION SCHEMES

B. THE VALUATION OF EXEMPT PROPERTY

C. VOIDING INVOLUNTARY LIENS, AND NONPOSSESSORY, NON-PURCHASE-MONEY SECURITY INTERESTS THAT INTERFERE WITH AN EXEMPTION

Every bankruptcy debtor gets to keep some of his or her property, even though the debtor's creditors have not been paid. You might ask yourself, "Why have we developed a system that allows bankruptcy debtors to keep a significant amount of their property, despite a stack of unpaid bills?" The federal and state exemption schemes allow people to keep enough assets to survive, and some schemes allow much more than that. The theme of exemption law is that people who are over-indebted can still live inside, drive a car, and wear their clothes, without fear that a creditor will try to take these necessities. If we allowed creditors to take all of the debtors' possessions, it would be difficult (if not impossible) to get a fresh start.

In Chapter 7 cases, the exemptions determine which property the debtor keeps and which assets the debtor loses to the trustee for sale and distribution of the proceeds to creditors.

In Chapter 13, the debtor also generally gets to keep exempt and nonexempt assets. But the exemption calculations will be used to determine the minimum amount the debtor must distribute under the plan to unsecured creditors, because the **best interest test** requires that the debtor pay unsecured creditors at least what they would have received in a Chapter 7 case from the sale of the nonexempt assets.

Most Chapter 11 cases are business reorganizations. Because corporations and LLCs are not entitled to exemptions, the exemptions often play no part in a Chapter 11 case. If an individual were to file a Chapter 11 case, however, perhaps because the person was over the Chapter 13 debt limits, the exemptions would be used in exactly the same way in the individual Chapter 11 case that they are used in a Chapter 13 case, namely to measure the minimum amount the debtor must pay to unsecured creditors.

Most exemption schemes provide a specific item-by-item list of exactly what a debtor can and cannot keep once he or she is in bankruptcy, free from creditor claims. Because the exemptions are in specific items of property, not in just whatever items the debtor has, the debtor sometimes must choose between various items, much like ordering off a menu at a Chinese restaurant, one from category A and one from category B, and so forth.

A. State Versus Federal Exemption Schemes

All jurisdictions have state exemptions that can be used in bankruptcy as well as outside bankruptcy. In some states, such as Delaware, these are extremely minimal, allowing the debtor to keep just a few items, and almost nothing of value. Some states also allow a debtor to choose between either these state law exemptions or the federal exemption scheme contained in the Bankruptcy Code. For those debtors who get to choose between the federal and the state schemes, the choice will be made based upon the type of assets the debtor has. One scheme may be great for one person, but horrible for another.

F   A   Q

Q: Are there states in which the only choice is federal exemptions?

A: No. States either allow their residents to use only state exemptions, or they allow a debtor to choose between the state and the federal scheme. No state provides for use of only federal exemptions. This is counterintuitive because, generally, federal law preempts state law.

The federal exemptions are probably average in generosity, as compared to the various state exemptions. As you can see in Table 6.1, the main benefit the federal exemptions provide is for people who do not own a home, by allowing them to protect some other asset in lieu of a house.[1] We call this the **wildcard** or **pour-over** exemption.

State schemes rarely offer generous wildcard exemptions and thus the federal system is often better for debtors with liquid assets — cash, savings accounts, stock accounts, money market accounts, and other investments, as well as anything else that can be liquidated quickly in an established market.

Married couples may double all of the federal exemptions to get a mathematically doubled exemption limit. The most commonly used federal exemptions are listed in Table 6.1.[2]

TABLE 6.1	Commonly Used Federal Exemptions	
Description of the Asset	Amount of Asset Protection	Bankruptcy Code Section
Homestead **Personal property that the debtor uses as a residence, including a mobile home**	Up to $20,200	11 U.S.C. §522(d)(1)
Motor Vehicle **Debtor's interest in one motor vehicle**	Up to $3,225	11 U.S.C. §522(d)(2)
Household Goods **Debtor's interest in household furnishings, goods, clothing, musical instruments, etc.**	Up to $525 per item, $10,775 total value	11 U.S.C. §522(d)(3)
Jewelry **Held by the debtor or the dependent of the debtor**	Up to $1,350	11 U.S.C. §522(d)(4)
Wildcard **A debtor may use this for anything, including an additional homestead exemption if the homestead exemption is not completely used**	Up to $1,075, plus up to $10,775 of unused portion of the $20,200 homestead exemption	11 U.S.C. §522(d)(5)

---

[1]If a person does not own a home, he or she can keep over $10,000 in anything. 11 U.S.C. §522(d)(1) & (5).
[2]By law, these numbers are automatically adjusted upward for inflation and may have changed since this book was printed.

Only 16 states allow bankruptcy debtors to choose the federal exemptions. More-over, each state's own exemptions emphasize more protection for some things than others. These state exemptions can have massive benefits, or they can provide almost no relief at all. The variation between jurisdictions can be so extreme that some debtors deliberately move to a jurisdiction to get that state's exemptions.[3] An example of this is the unlimited homestead exemption in Texas and Florida. If you live in Texas or Florida and have a $10 million home with no mortgage on it, you can keep the home and file for bankruptcy. Creditors will not get any of the value of the home. In Florida, however, the state exemptions allow a person only $1,000 worth of assets other than a home. This is very difficult for non-homeowners and would not even allow people with homes to furnish them. Moreover, Florida has opted out of the federal exemption scheme and as a result, debtors in Florida can only use the state exemptions. Clearly, debtors who live in states in which they can choose their exemption scheme have more options and flexibility.

In New Mexico, for example, a debtor may choose to protect his or her assets under either the state or the federal exemption scheme. A debtor must, however, pick one scheme or the other. No jurisdiction allows a debtor to pick and choose which portions of which exemptions they would like to adopt. For example, a debtor could not use the homestead exemption from New Mexico and combine it with the federal jewelry exemption. In those states that allow a choice of exemptions, making the choice is an important strategic decision. This is also an area frequently tested on exams. The best way to tell which exemption scheme is best for a debtor is to take the debtor through both exemption sets completely, and then see which scheme allows the debtor to keep the most assets.

When working actual problems, either for clients or on exams, remember two things. First, sometimes an item is only partially exempt under a particular category but can be fully exempted by combining two categories of exemptions, such as by combining a category with part of the *wildcard* or *pour-over* exemption. Second (yes, this sounds elementary), the debtor only can use the exemption or part of the exemption for which he or she actually owns property. You cannot determine the amount of a person's exempt property merely by totaling the exemption list. No one has assets in all these categories, or in these exact amounts. In other words, if my car is worth just $500, no one is going to pay me the *other* $2,725 that the federal auto exemption would allow if I had a better car. I can only exempt $500 because that is all that I have.

One of the most interesting things about state law exemptions is how much they vary from state to state. This cannot be completely explained by the cost of living. Many eastern states just don't allow much at all, while out west at least some states are more generous. To see how much variation there is, check out the following chart:

---

[3]The new Code tries to curb this practice in Section 522(b)(3)(A).

	Arizona	California Scheme I	California Scheme II	New York	New Mexico	Texas	Florida
Homestead	$150,000 total value (regardless of whether married or single)	$50,000 for single; $75,000 for family; $125,000 if 65 or older	$17,425 (may be applied to other property)	$50,000 per person	$60,000 per person	Unlimited	Unlimited
Amount in lieu of homestead					$2,000		
Motor vehicle	$5,000 (or $10,000, if disabled)	$2,300	$2,775 (only one vehicle allowed)	$2,400	$4,000	$60,000 total various personal property	$1,000 total various personal property
Household goods	$4,000 per person for household goods; $500 for clothing	No amount specified (must be reasonable)	$450 each item (no maximum)	No amount specified	$5,000		
Tools of the trade	$2,500	$6,075	$1,750	No amount specified	$1,500		
Jewelry	$1,000	$6,075 total for household	$1,150	$35	$2,500		
Retirement funds	Up to $1,095,000 under §522(b)(3)(c)						

Examples of Variation Among State Exemption Laws[4]

To illustrate the differences among states, let's say Joe and Mary Pareja, a couple, both 40 years old, own a home worth $300,000, with a first mortgage of $100,000 and a second mortgage of $50,000. They have a stock account with $25,000 in it, $400,000 in retirement benefits, and two cars, one worth $15,000 with an $18,000 loan due and another car with a blue book value of around $4,500, with no loan. Their clothes and furniture are worth about $10,000 total, at garage sale prices. How would these debtors fare if they lived in each of the states below?

California

In California, they could keep the **upside-down** car, but would lose the car worth $4,500. They could keep all of their household goods, but would not be able to keep their house because it has $150,000 in equity and they are not allowed that much equity. They could keep all of their retirement savings under Section 522(b)(3)(c) of the Bankruptcy Code. They would lose the stock completely.

New York

In New York, the Parejas could keep the upside-down car, but would lose the car worth $4,500. They would not be able to keep their house because it has $150,000 in equity and they are only allotted $100,000 under the homestead exemption. They could keep all of their household goods, and also keep their retirement savings under Section 522(b)(3)(c) of the Bankruptcy Code. They would lose the stock.

Arizona

In Arizona, they could keep both cars because the equity in each car is under the exemption amount of $5,000. They could keep $8,000 of their household goods, but would have to sell $2,000 of them (because their total worth was $10,000). They would also be able to keep their house. They could keep all of their retirement savings under Section 522(b)(3)(c), but would lose the stock.

New Mexico

In New Mexico, the Parejas would keep the upside-down car, but lose the other car worth $4,500. They could keep half of their household goods worth $5,000, but would need to sell the other half. They would lose their house because the New Mexico exemptions allow only $120,000 per couple in equity in a house. They could keep all of their retirement savings under Section 522(b)(3)(c) of the Bankruptcy Code. They would lose the stock.

Florida

In Florida, they would lose both cars. They would lose most of their household goods, and the stock, except that they could keep $1,000 in something. However, they would be able to keep their house and all of their retirement savings under Section 522(b)(3)(c) of the Bankruptcy Code.

---

[4]These amounts will change as state law changes, and are just used as examples. Students should research current statutes to get current exemption numbers.

Texas

In Texas, the Parejas would probably be able to keep both of their cars, and their household goods. However, they would need to look at the list carefully and be sure that their personal property did not exceed $60,000. They would be able to keep their house, as well as their retirement savings under Section 522(b)(3)(c). They would likely lose the stock.

F   A   Q

Q: If a debtor has $1,000 left over from her motor vehicle exemption, can she use it to save something else?

A: No. Exemptions can be used only for the category listed. The one exception is the wildcard or pour-over exemption, for which the Code specifically provides that part of the homestead exemption, if left over, can be used for anything. Otherwise, unused exemptions go to waste.

B. The Valuation of Exempt Property

Exemptions are based on a mathematical limit on what a debtor is allowed to keep. Given the importance of valuation in determining whether a debtor can keep certain property, you might wonder who determines the value of the debtor's property. The debtor values the property initially, although the attorney may need to independently verify some of these values. The valuation numbers go directly into the schedules of assets and liabilities discussed in Chapter 3 of this book. This document is available to the public, will be scrutinized by the trustee, and may be reviewed by creditors as well.

A debtor can use many different methods of exemption valuation. Each type of property requires a different method of valuation. For the most part, homes require a recent appraisal, a study of comparable homes in the area, or some other recent approximation of home values in the area. Debtors should not rely on property tax assessments to approximate the value of their homes. Property tax valuations are almost always low. The trustee will want to know where the values on the schedules came from and obviously low numbers may draw an objection from the trustee or the debtor's creditors.

The valuation of a vehicle is much more straightforward because of the availability of book evaluations. These can be found on the National Automobile Dealers Association (NADA) website at http://www.nada.com or the Kelley Blue Book website at http://www.kbb.com, among other places. There is even a book that contains wholesale prices, equal to what a debtor might get as a trade-in price from a dealer. It's called the Black Book and is available at http://www.blackbookusa.com.

It is very easy for a debtor's attorney to plug in the year, make, model, and options of the debtor's vehicle and determine the appropriate value to use, based on one of these sources. There is, however, significant controversy over whether a debtor should use the wholesale or retail values for their valuation in a CHAPTER 7 case. Some courts have interpreted the value to be an average of the two.

When it comes to the valuation of most personal property, the debtor is given more slack. Because it would be totally inefficient to require a debtor to obtain an appraisal on all of his or her property, the court typically accepts the debtor's personal approximation of the value of his or her personal property. When calculating the value of his or her property, the debtor should use a value that reflects the item's current market price, if sold on the used goods market. This essentially means a garage sale. It is a common mistake for debtors to approximate the value of their property at what they paid for it, or significantly close to it. For example, if a debtor bought a $2,000 couch five years ago it would be difficult to sell it today at $1,500.

Most personal property should be valued at "garage sale" prices. Debtors' attorneys try their best to place as much of the debtors' property into these exemption categories. This can be visualized by characterizing each exemption as being a very large plastic bin. Each plastic bin represents one category of an exemption. For example, there will be one very large bin for cars, another for the debtor's clothing, another for the debtor's cash, and so on. The debtor's attorney's job is to place as much property in each bin as possible.

On the other hand, trustees and creditors' attorneys try their best to prevent as much of the debtor's property as possible from getting into these exemption categories. The more property they can keep out of the bins, the more goes into their clients' pockets (or in the case of trustees, their beneficiaries' pockets).

As a general rule, the federal exemptions are good for individuals with lots of cash or special items that fall outside other categories. Most states do not have wildcard provisions as large as the federal exemptions provide.

Sidebar

OVERVALUED ASSETS, GARAGE SALE PRICES, AND UNDERESTIMATED DEBTS

Despite recent concerns that numerous people are abusing the bankruptcy system, several bankruptcy judges we know suggest that people generally overvalue their assets and underestimate their liabilities. This makes psychological sense, because Americans generally underestimate how deeply they are in debt, and most Americans are financially illiterate. It also makes common sense, because people tend to value their possessions more highly than the amount of money they could sell them for at a garage sale.

C. Voiding Involuntary Liens, and Nonpossessory, Non-Purchase-Money Security Interests that Interfere with an Exemption

Under Section 522(f) of the Code, the debtor can avoid involuntary liens that interfere with or impair one of the debtor's exemptions. You may recall that a judgment lien creditor (also called an involuntary lien creditor) becomes secured by getting a judgment against the debtor and then executing on certain property. You'll also recall that the debtor is allowed to exempt certain property from execution under state law. The creditor cannot touch these items as they are exempt from state execution.

This theme continues in bankruptcy. Any property that the debtor has claimed as exempt under either the state or the federal exemption scheme cannot be impaired or interfered with by an involuntary lien. If there is a judgment lien on property in which the debtor claims an exemption, the debtor can move to have the involuntary lien avoided, which will turn the judgment lien holder back into an unsecured creditor.

If a debtor owns a home that has a voluntary mortgage lien on it, this lien will not be affected by the debtor's exemptions. Voluntary secured creditors come ahead of the debtor's exemptions in particular property. If the debtor grants a security interest to a creditor in the house or the car, this must always be satisfied first, so the exemptions are not relevant to secured creditor treatment. After the secured parties' rights, which are in first position, the exemptions come next, followed by the claims of executing creditors.

Let's look at an example outside of bankruptcy. Say that Robert owns a home worth $200,000 in New Mexico. Let's also say that the state homestead exemption is $30,000 per person. Robert also owes $150,000 on the house to the mortgage holder. Jerry Judgment Creditor obtains a $30,000 judgment against Robert and forces the sale of the home. The first creditor entitled to be paid is the mortgage holder, who either takes $150,000 or keeps its lien. The second to be paid out of the sale is Robert, who gets $30,000 for the state law exemption. Finally, though there is only $20,000 left, this goes to the judgment holder, who is paid two-thirds of its debt. This example does not take into account the costs of sale.

Let's look at another quick example, this time in a bankruptcy context. Janine owns a car that is worth $10,000. She owes $6,000 on the car to the secured party who lent her the money to buy it. Visa obtained a judgment against Janine for $5,000 and executed on the car, by having the sheriff remove it from Janine's driveway in the middle of the night. The next day, Janine filed for CHAPTER 7 bankruptcy and thereafter moved under Section 522(f) to avoid Visa's involuntary judgment lien on the car. Janine chose the federal exemptions in her bankruptcy case. Can Visa's lien be avoided and, if so, to what extent? While the Code section itself seems to suggest that if a judicial lien impairs an exemption at all, it can be avoided *in toto*, cases have held that a judicial lien that only partially impairs an exemption is only partially avoidable. In this case, the voluntary secured lender has first dibs on the car for $6,000; then the debtor's exemption must come out. Under the current federal exemptions, that leaves only $750 in value left for Visa. But that part of the lien stays in place. The lien is not avoided completely, but only to the extent that it impairs an exemption.

In addition to judicial liens, the debtor can also avoid non-purchase-money, nonpossessory security interests in certain household furnishings, household goods, wearing apparel, appliances, books, animals, crops, musical instruments, or jewelry, that are held primarily for the personal, family, or household use of the debtor or a dependent.

Although Federal Trade Commission Credit Practices Rule 16 C.F.R. §444 et seq. makes it illegal to take a non-purchase-money security interest in household goods, by making these security interests unenforceable, the provisions of Section 522(f) make it easy to wipe out the security interest once and for all, cheaply and easily. Since payday loan companies and other subprime lenders have been known to violate the FTC rule by taking a security interest in household goods, and this is an easy way to get out of such security interests, it's worth knowing about. The bankruptcy avoidance rule is also broader than the FTC rule in that it applies to clothing, appliances, books, animals, crops, musical instruments, and jewelry, in addition to household goods. All these security interests are avoidable in bankruptcy, just as in judicial liens, so long as the security interest impairs an exemption.

Remember, a purchase-money security interest (PMSI) is a security interest taken by a lender in collateral purchased with the proceeds of the loan. If you buy a car and borrow money from the dealer (or a third-party financing service) to do it, this is a purchase-money security interest. Pledging your *old* car as collateral for a new loan is *not* a PMSI.

SUMMARY

- We don't force bankruptcy debtors to give up every asset they own in order to get a bankruptcy discharge, recognizing that people need means to live after bankruptcy and need some way to get back on their feet. There is no societal benefit (in fact there is a great cost) in making people homeless or taking all of their clothes.

- The bankruptcy system allows many bankruptcy debtors around the country to choose their preferred exemption scheme: either the federal bankruptcy scheme contained in the Bankruptcy Code, or the state exemption scheme that applies to executing creditors outside of bankruptcy in that particular state. Some states, however, only allow debtors to use the state exemption scheme.

- State exemption schemes are incredibly varied, so where a debtor lives can make a huge difference in what he or she is able to keep following a bankruptcy.

- If a debtor moves shortly before he or she files for bankruptcy, that debtor may be eligible only for the exemption scheme of the prior state of residence. This is a new rule designed to keep people from moving to a new state to take advantage of a better exemption scheme.

- Typically, the exemptions allow a debtor to keep up to a certain dollar amount of equity in a certain category of assets, such as a house, a car, tools of trade, and household goods.

- Exemptions are always calculated based upon the debtor's equity in an item. For example, if a debtor owned a $300,000 house with a $280,000 mortgage on it, the debtor's equity would be $20,000. If the debtor used the federal exemptions, which allow $20,200 of equity in a house, he or she could keep the house.

- If an executing creditor obtained an involuntary lien on an asset, and that involuntary lien interfered with an exemption, the debtor might be able to avoid the lien (wipe it off the asset). The debtor can also avoid non-purchase-money, nonpossessory liens on certain assets, like household goods and tools of trade.

CONNECTIONS

CHAPTER 7

Understanding the differences between state and federal exemption law is important because CHAPTER 7 debtors give up their *nonexempt* assets to pay creditors.

CHAPTER 13

In most CHAPTER 13 cases, the debtor does not give up his or her nonexempt assets, but instead pays creditors under the plan at least what they would have gotten had the nonexempt assets been sold, in effect forcing the debtor to buy back the nonexempt assets.

State Versus Federal Exemption Schemes

Lawyers in states where the debtor can choose between state and federal exemption schemes need to work through both systems to ensure that they elect the most advantageous choice.

State Collection Law

Whether the debtor can choose between state and federal exemption law or not, exemption law will determine whether it is worthwhile to declare bankruptcy to begin with or stay in virtual bankruptcy.

Pre-Bankruptcy Planning

The exemption scheme will also determine the extent to which pre-bankruptcy planning is available and advisable.

CHAPTER 11

Most CHAPTER 11 cases are business reorganizations. Because corporations and LLCs are not entitled to exemptions, the exemptions law often plays no part.

Claims Against the Estate

7

This chapter addresses what a claim against a bankruptcy estate is and then distinguishes between different types of claims, such as **OVERVIEW** secured claims, priority claims, administrative claims, and general unsecured claims. This chapter also discusses when a claim arises, and thus when a claim can be included in a bankruptcy, as well as the protection provided to creditors who provide goods and services to the debtor during the post-petition period.

In addition to the distinction between secured and unsecured creditors, there are further distinctions between unsecured creditors. Some unsecured creditors get better treatment in the bankruptcy system than others, because we as a society believe they deserve it. For instance, creditors that are unable to spread the risk of non-payment well get special treatment. Employees of a failed business, or children needing child support, cannot spread financial risk well, whereas credit card companies can, by charging slightly higher interest rates to non-defaulting customers to make up for the money lost on customers who don't pay their credit card bills. The Bankruptcy Code priority scheme attempts to balance the needs of various creditors against one another and choose those most worthy of special treatment. It is a blatant act of social engineering, reflecting the Bankruptcy Code's roots in equity, fairness, and public policy.

Obviously, claims can be secured, in which case the creditor has the protection of its collateral, or unsecured, in which case the creditor has no collateral. Even within the category of unsecured claims, such claims can be general unsecured claims or priority unsecured claims, with priority claims being entitled to repayment ahead of general unsecured claims. Within the category of priority claims, there are further priorities, setting up an elaborate system of social engineering.

Even still, if every single asset of value in a case has been used to secure a loan, then the very highest priority claim is on top of a heap of nothing. Secured claims beat out both general unsecured claims and priority unsecured claims. Thus it is far better to be a secured creditor than a priority creditor, because secured creditors are de facto outside the priority scheme.

A. DEFINITION OF A CLAIM

B. PRIORITIES

C. TAXES

D. ADMINISTRATIVE CLAIMS UNDER CHAPTER 11

In order for an obligation of the debtor to fall within a bankruptcy and thus be eligible to be discharged by an individual debtor, or treated in the plan of a CHAPTER 11 debtor and discharged to the extent unpaid, the obligation must have matured to the level of a *claim*. The debtor always wants obligations, regardless of how tangential or uncertain, to be claims because that means he or she can discharge them in bankruptcy and will not have to pay them in full. In contrast, creditors almost always want the opposite — that an obligation of a bankruptcy debtor will *not* have matured to the level of a claim and will remain an obligation of the debtor after the bankruptcy is over.

A. Definition of a Claim

A **claim** is defined under Section 101(5) as a "right to payment, whether or not such right is reduced to judgment, liquidated, unliquidated, fixed, contingent, matured, unmatured, disputed, undisputed, legal, equitable, secured, or unsecured." 11 U.S.C. §101(5)(A). The definition also includes any "right to an equitable remedy for breach of performance, if such breach gives rise to a right to payment, whether or not such right to an equitable remedy is reduced to judgment, fixed, contingent, matured, unmatured, disputed, undisputed, secured, or unsecured." 11 U.S.C. §101(5)(B). By now, you might be getting the picture. A claim is defined in the broadest possible way under the Bankruptcy Code.

F   A   Q

Q: What is the policy reason behind defining the word "claim" in such a broad and counterintuitive way?

A: Promoting the fresh start of an individual debtor or the reorganization of a business debtor. If something qualifies as a claim, it can be discharged in a debtor's bankruptcy. If it has not yet reached the status of a claim, it will survive the case and remain an obligation of the debtor.

Claims can be discharged in any type of bankruptcy, to the extent not paid by the nonexempt assets or the plan. The question of when a claim arises is particularly important in a CHAPTER 11 case, when the debtor business is trying to use its plan of reorganization to address all of its present and future obligations. Claims can be addressed (paid in part and otherwise discharged) in a CHAPTER 11 plan, whereas rights of action that have not yet risen to the level of claims must be dealt with outside the plan, and usually must be paid in full.

Most of the time, you can tell whether a claim can be included in a bankruptcy plan (and paid a percentage distribution) by determining whether the events that led to the claim occurred pre- or post-petition. Using a simple example, assume a man is walking around in Kmart and falls down. No lawsuit has been filed. The next day, Kmart files for bankruptcy. There is no question that even though you do not know the amount, and you don't know whether Kmart is liable, the gentleman who fell down has a claim against Kmart. The action giving rise to the claim clearly occurred pre-petition, and although the claim is contingent and unliquidated, it is absolutely and unquestionably a claim in Kmart's bankruptcy. The potential tort victim would typically prefer that this *not* be a bankruptcy claim, because then he could be paid in full from the reorganized debtor at a later time, after the claim is adjudicated. Kmart, on the other hand, would prefer that it *be* a claim, so that it can be discharged in connection with its bankruptcy case.

Let's try a trickier example. You own a business and plan to file for CHAPTER 11 or any other type of bankruptcy. Let's assume your mother guaranteed one of your debts. Pursuant to Section 502(e)(1)(B), your mother has a contingent claim for reimbursement or contribution based on her guarantee of your debt. There is a chance in this particular scenario that your mother will never have to pay your debt. Regardless of this, however, your mother holds a contingent claim in your bankruptcy assuming you file right now. She has a claim even though you don't know if she'll ever have to pay. Your mother is one of your creditors because she holds a claim in your case.

Some of the toughest cases, in terms of deciding what obligations constitute claims in a bankruptcy, and can thus be included in a CHAPTER 11 plan, involve future tort claims. But before getting to those, make sure you understand why a debtor cares about this. The debtor is hoping to include as many claims or obligations as possible in its bankruptcy, so that when it emerges from bankruptcy those obligations have been included in the bankruptcy plan and otherwise discharged.

Now consider the situations involving asbestos companies and A.H. Robins, the manufacturer of the Dalkon Shield, a faulty IUD birth control device that caused many women to suffer injuries. If A.H. Robins went into CHAPTER 11 to reorganize its affairs, its CHAPTER 11 case would be of little use if, after the case was filed, more claimants continued to surface claiming they were damaged by the Dalkon Shield. Given the extremely broad definition of claim in the Bankruptcy Code, many courts have found that if a debtor's pre-petition conduct led to the injury, regardless of when the injury is manifest, the resulting injuries, both current and future, constitute claims in the debtor's bankruptcy. Under what's known as the **conduct test,** these claims are pre-petition claims because the injuries resulted from the debtor's pre-petition conduct.

The law in the area of future claims has developed over time and courts have used several different tests to define the outer limits of a bankruptcy claim. Some courts use a test based on when a claim arises under state law to determine whether a claim has arisen pre-petition. One of these tests requires that the claimant and debtor must have had a pre-petition contract or privity from which the claim arises for a resulting claim to be a pre-petition claim. This is called the **relationship test**. Under this test, a claim by an operator of a forklift manufactured pre-petition but purchased by the claimant's employer post-petition was not considered a pre-petition claim. Using the same test, a claim by the EPA for environmental clean-up costs that would not be incurred until after confirmation (in other words, would be incurred post-petition, even though the contamination started pre-petition) was held to be a pre-petition claim based on the relationship between the environmental regulating agencies and the parties subject to the regulation.

Another test the courts sometimes use to determine whether a claim is a pre- or post-petition claim is called the **fair contemplation test**. This test does not require that there be a pre-petition relationship between the debtor and the claimant, but instead that the pre-petition interaction between the two be within the fair contemplation of the parties at the time of the bankruptcy.

For example, in *Piper Aircraft*, the issue was whether a claim for a defective aircraft sold pre-petition was discharged in Piper's bankruptcy, when the defect causing a resulting plane crash did not even happen until long after the bankruptcy case was over. *In re Piper Aircraft*, 244 F.3d 1289 (11th Cir. 2001). The court held that a claim arises when the conduct giving rise to the alleged liability occurred. The court adopted a hybrid of the conduct test and the relationship test, finding that in order for a claim to fit within Section 101(5), the events that caused the injury must occur pre-petition and must create some sort of relationship between the claimant and the debtor's product. The court further elaborated that this relationship must be with an identifiable claimant or group of claimants and that the basis for the claim must be the debtor's pre-petition conduct in designing, manufacturing, and selling the allegedly defective or dangerous product. In *Piper*, the court therefore found that the claim could not have been discharged in Piper's bankruptcy because there was no identifiable group of claimants, because it was impossible to predict at the time of confirmation of the plan who the future claimants (purchasers of these aircraft and their passengers) would be. In other words, there was no way to know not only who these parties would be, but which planes would crash. The claimants were not ascertainable or identifiable at the time of Piper Aircraft's bankruptcy.

In *Johns-Manville*, the landmark asbestos case, the court came to the opposite conclusion, holding that asbestos claims were pre-petition claims because the asbestos causing the injuries was manufactured pre-petition, even though some of the individuals who later suffered from melanoma and asbestosis did not have any symptoms at the time of the Manville bankruptcy. *In re Joint Eastern and Southern Dist. Asbestos Litigation*, 129 B.R. 710 (Bankr. E.D.N.Y. 1991). This clearly stretches the notion of what constitutes a claim, but is an excellent example of how far courts are willing to go to fit claims within a Chapter 11 plan. In many other asbestos cases, courts have controversially found that a person who comes down with melanoma or asbestosis years after one of the asbestos companies files for bankruptcy has lost his or her ability to object to the debtor's bankruptcy. The court found these to be pre-petition claims because the debtor created a channeling trust in its Chapter 11 plan, from which future claimants could recover part of their claims. None of these claims are ever paid in full, and these future claimants are provided due process in the Chapter 11 case through a future claimant's representative. Whether this constitutes real due process or not is a question with which courts have struggled.

Congress enacted Section 524(g) to deal explicitly with future asbestos claims. This provision of the Bankruptcy Code provides that a court may enjoin future claimants from pursuing the assets of a debtor who has already been through bankruptcy, as long as the debtor forms a trust pursuant to its plan of reorganization that assumes the liabilities of the debtor for these personal injury, wrongful death, or property damage actions resulting from the manufacturer of asbestos. The debtor must also fund this part of the plan with some of the equity in the debtor company and fulfill certain other obligations as well. See 11 U.S.C. §524(g).

B. Priorities

The previous section discussed when an obligation becomes a claim for bankruptcy purposes. This one distinguishes between general unsecured claims and priority unsecured claims. Despite the Bankruptcy Code's emphasis on equality of treatment, some claims are paid ahead of other claims, even among unsecured creditors. This is true in all types of bankruptcy. This is accomplished through the Bankruptcy Code's priority scheme, which is set out in Section 507(a). If you have your Code handy, look at Section 507(a) now.

As a society, we believe that some creditor claims are more important than others. We purposely give preference to those we feel need preference, as well as some who have simply asked for special treatment. While the claims that have priority under Section 507 are intended to be those debts that society places the most value on and that society wants to pay the most, some creditors found their way into the section merely by successfully lobbying Congress.

Priorities are important in every type of bankruptcy case. In a CHAPTER 7 liquidation, Section 507 tells the trustee which creditors to pay first out of the proceeds of any sales. In a CHAPTER 13 liquidation, priority claims under Section 507(a) must be paid in full under the CHAPTER 13 plan. In a CHAPTER 11 liquidation, all priority claims must be paid in full under the plan, but most must actually be paid much earlier, shortly after the court approves the reorganization plan.

The way that Section 507 works is that each category of claim that is entitled to special priority is listed in the section in the order of priority that the claims are paid. Thus, since domestic support obligations are in 507(a)(1), they come ahead of recent taxes, which are found in 507(a)(8). Employee wage claims, which are found in 507(a)(3), come ahead of taxes but behind domestic support obligations. Priority claims in higher categories must be paid in full before the next category of priority claim gets anything at all.

Note that Section 507(a) applies to unsecured claims. Secured claims are not included because secured parties are protected by their collateral, at least up to the value of the collateral. Secured creditors may be able to get back their collateral, or, if the trustee sells it, will be paid first out of the proceeds. In effect, property encumbered by a security interest or lien is not available to pay unsecured creditors, except to the extent that the debtor has equity in the property over and above the value of the security interest.

Unsecured claims entitled to priority are called **priority claims**. As described above, Section 507(a) ranks these special types of unsecured claims, and provides that they are paid ahead of other unsecured claims that are not entitled to priority. Unsecured claims not entitled to priority are called **general unsecured claims** or just **general** claims.

Many non-lawyers and lawyers alike are shocked to hear that out of all the claims entitled to priority under Section 507(a) — which include claims for child support and alimony; wages owed to employees of the debtor; customer deposits (up to a limited amount); as well as income taxes, property taxes, and withholding taxes (within certain periods) — the trustees and their attorneys who work on the post-petition case are first in line to be paid. Unfair and self-serving? Perhaps, but how many trustees and attorneys would participate in the administration of bankruptcy cases if they could not get paid for their services? However, the *debtor's* attorney in a CHAPTER 7 case is NOT a priority creditor.

Sidebar

POLITICAL REALITY

Like all legislation, the Bankruptcy Code is a product of pragmatic political considerations and Machiavellian compromises. In this case, the 2005 amendments to Section 507 were sold to the public with the promise that domestic support obligations, such as child support, would get first priority. However, when the final legislation was passed, it looked essentially like this:

§507(1) Priorities:
(a) The following expenses and claims have priority in the following order:
(A) Domestic support obligations.
(B) Domestic support obligations assigned to a government unit.
(C) Trustees "shall be paid before payment of claims under subparagraphs (A) and (B)."

Thus, under Section 507(a)(1)(C), the trustee leapfrogs ahead of child support, so that the trustee's own fees, as well as his or her attorneys' fees, still come first. Funny how that is not how the statute is ordered. The third thing mentioned is actually first — one way to compromise, presumably.

The priorities can be summed up as follows (but also take a look at Section 507(a) yourself):

- Domestic support obligations, as defined in Sections 507(a)(1)(A) and (B), except that the trustee, under Section 507(a)(1)(C), will be paid first for administering the assets that are used to pay the domestic support obligations in (A) and (B). 11 U.S.C. §507(a)(1).
- Administrative expenses under Section 503(b), which include all of the trustee's costs of creating and preserving the estate, such as costs of sale, insurance on estate assets, and paying the electricity bills to protect a house that is part of the estate. Section 506(b) includes the trustee's fees, and the trustee's attorneys' fees, too. It also covers the claims of any other creditor who creates value for the estate creditors, such as post-petition rent due to a landlord or electric bills owed to a utility company. 11 U.S.C. §507(a)(2).
- Expenses incurred by creditors during the *gap period* that arises between the filing of an involuntary petition and the court's entry of the order for relief. This applies only in involuntary cases, which are extremely rare, making this a little-used priority. 11 U.S.C. §507(a)(3).
- Up to $10,950 per employee for back wages incurred by an employee of the debtor during the 180 days prior to the filing. The same rules apply to independent contractors who work for the debtor for at least 75% of their time. 11 U.S.C. §507(a)(4).
- Another $10,950 per employee for contributions into employee benefit plans arising during the 180 days prior to the filing. 11 U.S.C. §507(a)(5).
- Grain sellers and fishermen, under certain circumstances. 11 U.S.C. §507(a)(6).
- Deposits, paid by individuals to the debtor, up to $2,425. 11 U.S.C. §507(a)(7).
- Taxes of various kinds, including income tax due during approximately the three years prior to the filing, property tax due within approximately one year of the filing, withholding taxes, certain excise and employment taxes, and a few others. Normally, penalties on taxes do not get special priority, and in fact

are even paid after general unsecured claims because they are subordinated under Section 726(a)(4). One thing to keep in mind about taxes: All are contained in the same priority category, Section 507(a)(8). This means if there is not enough to pay them all, they do not get paid in the order listed in the statute. Rather, they share the proceeds equally, based on the percentage of their claim, pro rata. 11 U.S.C. §507(a)(8). There is more information on tax claims below.

■ FDIC deposits promised by the debtor. 11 U.S.C. §507(a)(9).

■ DWI claims for death or personal injury. 11 U.S.C. §507(a)(10).

The priority scheme goes against the basic principle of equality of distribution underlying the Code, but it is in line with the tradition of social policy and equity that also undergird the Code. For instance, we as a society believe that child support payments should have priority over other claims. Likewise, we believe tax claims should have priority. However, some claimants, like fishermen and the grain sellers, may simply have organized excellent lobbying efforts in Washington, D.C. — another tradition in our democracy. In any event, the list above tells you how estate funds get distributed after secured creditors have been paid.

C. Taxes

Tax treatment is tricky and requires a bit more explanation, which applies here as well as in the context of CHAPTER 11. The following common types of taxes, if unsecured (there has been no lien created by the taxing authorities yet), are pre-petition eighth priority taxes of the government:

■ Income taxes for tax years ending on or before the date of filing the bankruptcy petition, for which a return is due (including extensions) within three years of the filing of the bankruptcy petition.

■ Income taxes assessed within 240 days before the date of filing the petition. This 240-day period is increased by any time, plus 30 days, during which an offer in compromise with respect to these taxes was pending, that was made within 240 days after the assessment.

■ Income taxes that were not assessed before the petition date, but were assessable as of the petition date, unless these taxes were still assessable solely because no return, a late return (within two years of the filing of the bankruptcy petition), or a fraudulent return was filed.

■ Withholding taxes for which the debtor is liable in any capacity.

■ Employer's share of employment taxes on wages, salaries, or commissions (including vacation, severance, and sick leave pay) paid as priority claims under 11 U.S.C. §507(a)(3) or for which a return is due within three years of the filing of the bankruptcy petition, including a return for which an extension of the filing date was obtained.

The Code's impenetrable after-before language is hard to work with, but a time-line helps. Take income taxes as an example. First, mark on a timeline the filing date, then work backward and mark the date exactly three years prior to the filing. Then find all the dates upon which tax returns came due during that three-year period. For individuals, you'll be marking off April 15 for each of the years within the three-year period, unless an extension was requested. If it was, use the extension dates. The taxes owed on those dates get priority.

D. Administrative Claims Under Chapter 11

The difference between pre-petition claims and post-petition claims (as we discussed in Section A of this chapter) becomes preeminent when determining what claims constitute administrative expenses in a Chapter 11 case. In general, obligations incurred post-petition must be paid in full, including those claims we call **administrative priority claims** or **administrative priority expenses**. Administrative expenses are among the very highest priority claims among the general unsecured creditors. They are paid ahead of all other priority claims, including wage claims, tax claims, claims resulting from marital settlement agreements, and so on, as well as all general unsecured claims. Pursuant to Sections 503(b) and 507(a), second priority administrative claims include many claims that arose during the post-petition period, including fees for the debtor's attorneys, accountants, other professionals, and for the unsecured creditors' committee's professionals. See 11 U.S.C. §§503(b), 507(a).

Administrative claims entitled to priority pursuant to Sections 503(b) and 507(a)(2) also include all post-petition claims for goods and services rendered to the debtor or the debtor's estate during the Chapter 11 case. This continues the theme that was previously discussed, that once a bankruptcy is filed, the debtor is fully responsible for all obligations incurred post-petition. This concept is easy to understand when dealing with suppliers who supply goods to the debtor post-petition, as well as utilities, which provide services to the debtor post-petition. All of these claims are **first priority administrative claims** (see Sections 503(b) and 507(a)(2)), and must be paid either in the regular course of the debtor's business or in full upon the effective date of the debtor's Chapter 11 plan. In other words, these claims must be paid in 100-cent dollars. The reasons for this are quite clear. People providing post-petition goods and services to a Chapter 11 debtor must be assured of payment to encourage them to participate in the reorganization process. 11 U.S.C. §503(b). Moreover, the debtor is responsible for all expenses it incurs after the case is filed, none of which can be paid at discounted rates.

In the second half of this book, you will learn about the Chapter 11 debtor's right to assume or reject executory contracts and unexpired leases (see Chapter 19). If the debtor rejects an executory contract or unexpired lease (meaning the debtor decides not to comply with it), normally the resulting claim becomes a general unsecured claim and is paid along with other general unsecured creditors. 11 U.S.C. §502(g). If the debtor instead decides to assume the executory contract or unexpired lease, the assumed contract becomes a post-petition obligation and all of the obligations due under the contract (irrespective of the fact that the contract was originally entered into pre-petition) become first priority administrative expenses in the debtor's bankruptcy. 11 U.S.C. §503(b). Because the decision to assume affects not only the potential distribution to all general unsecured creditors but also to priority claimants, the debtor must obtain court approval to assume a contract or lease. 11 U.S.C. §365(a). The court pays particular attention to any claim the debtor incurs post-petition to ensure that taking on these obligations does not unfairly interfere with the rights of other creditors.

SUMMARY

- Filing for bankruptcy helps a debtor to discharge or stretch out payments on debts, but for the most part, the bankruptcy case only helps with debts that arose before the bankruptcy case was filed. Debts arising after the filing still have to be satisfied in full without regard to the bankruptcy filing.

- A right to be paid by a bankruptcy debtor, even if it is still contingent, is called a bankruptcy claim.

- When a claim arises is important to determining whether that claim can be discharged in bankruptcy or whether it will continue to be an obligation of a debtor after the case is over.

- Some bankruptcy claims, and the people who hold them (claimants) get special treatment under the Bankruptcy Code because we think they are poor risk spreaders, worthy of better treatment, or both.

- Special treatment is given to some creditors under the Code's priority scheme. A few of the types of claims entitled to special treatment are alimony and child support claims, claims for wages, certain tax claims, and claims for those who administer and work for the bankruptcy estate.

CONNECTIONS

Different Types of Claims
Bankruptcy claims come in a variety of types. They are discussed in even more detail in Chapters 15 and 19, in the context of business reorganization plans under Chapter 11.

Secured Creditor Treatment
Secured creditor treatment is covered in the next chapter. For now, suffice it to say that secured claims beat out both general unsecured claims and priority unsecured claims, and therefore it is still far better to be a secured creditor than a priority creditor. Secured creditors are essentially outside the priority scheme.

Assumption or Rejection of Executory Contracts and Unexpired Leases
Normally, the claim from a rejected executory contract or unexpired lease becomes a general unsecured claim, whereas the obligations from an assumed executory contract or unexpired lease become post-petition obligations that are treated as first priority administrative expenses, even though the contract was entered into pre-petition. A debtor's right to assume or reject executory contracts and unexpired leases is explained in Chapter 19, Section A.

People Whose Contracts Are Rejected Are Allowed to File a Late Proof of Claim

Creditors are supposed to file a proof of claim by a certain bar date. However, even if that date has passed at the time a contract is rejected, Section 502(g) extends the bar date for filing those types of claims until 30 days after the contract is rejected by the debtor. Thus the party left holding the bag when a contract is rejected by a bankruptcy debtor can still file a claim.

Treatment of Secured Claims

8

Special rules apply to creditors holding collateral at the time the debtor files for bankruptcy. This builds on the secured creditor versus unsecured

OVERVIEW

creditor distinction made in Chapter 1. The general rule here is that a secured party is only secured up to the value of his or her collateral. This means that if a creditor does not have quite enough collateral to cover his or her debt, the creditor will have a claim that is secured for part of the debt (up to the value of the collateral) but unsecured for the part that has no collateral (the unsecured part). In this situation, the claim is **bifurcated**.

Thus there is a lot of practical importance for lenders to have not only collateral, but also *enough* collateral, because the more collateral a creditor has, the more likely it is to recover a claim in full, with interest and fees.

A. SECURED CREDIT IN GENERAL

1. A Recap of Secured Creditor Remedies Outside Bankruptcy
2. Secured Creditor Treatment in Bankruptcy

B. SECURITY IS PROTECTION

C. UNDERSECURED AND OVERSECURED CREDITORS

1. How Big Is Happy's Claim Today?
2. Assume Collateral Is Worth $130,000. Now How Big Is Carol's Claim Today?
3. If the Case Goes on for Seven More Months, What Will the Claim Be?

The theme within bankruptcy is similar to what happens to the creditor outside bankruptcy. Remember that once the collateral is sold, the creditor must resort to the state court collection process to get the rest of the money, just like any other unsecured creditor.

If the creditor has more than enough collateral to cover its debt, it will get to collect interest and attorneys' fees while in bankruptcy, as long as the security agreement so provides. If there is not enough collateral to cover the debt, no interest or attorneys' fees arise during the bankruptcy case.

In the last chapter, we looked at the distinction between unsecured creditors with priority and unsecured creditors without priority. Another distinction is that between the treatment of secured versus unsecured, or general, creditors. We discussed how secured creditors' rights differ from unsecured creditors' rights under state law in Chapters 1 and 2. The theme of providing more favorable treatment to secured creditors continues under bankruptcy law.

A. Secured Credit in General

By now you know that secured creditors are those who have liens on certain property, real or personal, of the debtor. Liens arise under state law, not under bankruptcy law, but the Bankruptcy Code recognizes them as property interests of the person holding the lien. The liens may arise as a result of

1. the judicial process in which a creditor gets a judgment, executes on the judgment, and has the sheriff levy on certain property of the debtor;
2. statutory or common law liens, which dictate that a lien arises because of the relationship of the parties (e.g., the lien that a landlord has on the personal property of the tenant that is on the premises); or
3. a voluntary act of the debtor (i.e., the debtor grants to a creditor a security interest in some of his or her property by creating a mortgage on real property or an Article 9 security interest on some of his or her personal property).

Secured claims are property interests. This is important because bankruptcy law reveres property rights, while at times thumbing its nose at contract rights. See Chapter 19 (on rejection of executory contracts in Chapter 11 materials). By revering property rights in bankruptcy, we recognize that it is constitutionally impermissible under the Fifth Amendment to take away someone's property without due process of law. This fact results in a long list of protections provided to secured creditors in bankruptcy. One could summarize them by saying that the debtor must provide the secured party with **adequate protection** of the secured party's position in its collateral. In other words, the debtor cannot harm the secured party's position in its collateral.

If the debtor is using property and causing it to depreciate, this could mean the debtor must compensate the secured creditor for this use. It also may mean, as we saw in Chapter 4, that the debtor may have to give the property back to the secured party. The main thing to keep in mind is that the creditor's property interest cannot be impaired by the debtor.

F A Q

Q: But bankruptcy does impair a secured creditor's collection rights, for example, through the automatic stay. Does this mean some impairment is permissible?

A: Not in theory. True, the secured party is going to be delayed in its collection efforts by any bankruptcy, but the Code attempts to compensate the secured party for this delay in most situations through the payment of present value interest, or at least to keep the delay to a minimum. Moreover, if a secured party has enough collateral to cover its debt, it will continue to get interest during the delay. Thus, in theory, the secured party is no worse off financially. Reality can be quite different, but this is the rationale behind the treatment rules.

To be a voluntary secured creditor in a bankruptcy case, a creditor must comply with either Article 9 of the Uniform Commercial Code, which is state law, or with state real estate law. When the secured party is taking a security interest in personal property, Article 9 requires that the debtor grant the secured party a security interest in certain property, in order to secure repayment of the loan. This process is similar to granting a bank a mortgage on your home to secure your repayment of the loan. Usually, to be a secured creditor in a bankruptcy, the creditor also must do something to **perfect** this security interest. Because the rules regarding secured creditor treatment in bankruptcy are most commonly used with respect to voluntary Article 9 security interests, the rest of this discussion focuses on those kinds of security interests.

(1) A Recap of Secured Creditor Remedies Outside Bankruptcy

When an Article 9 secured creditor's borrower is not in default and not in bankruptcy, the borrower pays the loan as promised and eventually the creditor releases its security interest on the collateral and the debtor owns the property **free and clear**. If the borrower does not pay the loan on time, the loan instead goes into default, and if the collateral value is less than the debt, the secured creditor has the right to repossess its collateral, sell the collateral to pay down the loan, and then pursue the debtor for a **deficiency judgment**, the part of the loan that was not paid off from the sale of the collateral. The creditor is of course an unsecured creditor for this deficiency judgment because the collateral is already gone. There is no longer any collateral to cover the part of the loan that is still unpaid. If the creditor wants to get a judgment for this remaining debt, it will need to execute on other property of the debtor in order to be paid, just as any unsecured creditor would. We covered this material in more detail in Chapter 2.

(2) Secured Creditor Treatment in Bankruptcy

This state law theme of being paid upon default up to the value of the collateral, but not in excess of the value of the collateral, continues into the bankruptcy process. In a CHAPTER 7 case, if the debtor is a business and the business is now out of business, the secured party can get the automatic stay lifted, in order to gain the right to repossess and sell its collateral in the same way it would repossess and sell outside bankruptcy.

If the debtor is an individual CHAPTER 7 debtor, a number of things could happen. First, the debtor may just keep paying the loan and the creditor will not be affected by the bankruptcy. The debtor could also reaffirm the debt or redeem the collateral, something you'll learn more about in Chapter 12 of this book. Alternatively, if the debtor is in default (behind on the payments), the secured creditor may get the stay lifted and again gain the right to repossess and sell the collateral. If this happens, the creditor is limited in its recovery to the value of its collateral. Once the creditor has sold the collateral, the deficiency claim becomes an unsecured claim in the bankruptcy and in most CHAPTER 7 cases, the unsecured claim is simply discharged. This assumes there are no assets to distribute to creditors, which is often though not always the case. Thus the secured creditor in a CHAPTER 7 liquidation case can only be paid as much as his or her collateral is worth, unless there also is a distribution for unsecured creditors.

In a CHAPTER 13 or a CHAPTER 11 case, the secured party frequently gets paid over time under the debtor's plan. Other chapters of this book cover this subject in detail (see Chapters 13 and 15). The state law theme of being paid whatever can be realized from the collateral, and being an unsecured creditor for the rest, is continued for the most part in CHAPTER 13 and CHAPTER 11, though typically the collateral is never sold. As you will see, in both a CHAPTER 11 and a CHAPTER 13 case, the amount a secured creditor is paid is usually tied to the value of its collateral, not the amount it is owed. The debtor usually must pay the lesser of the loan amount or the value of the collateral. Home mortgages are one exception. Those generally must be paid in full, even if the home is worth less than the amount of the lender's loan. A new exception created by the 2005 amendments makes it necessary to pay the whole debt on any purchase-money auto loan incurred within two and a half years of the bankruptcy filing, as well as any purchase-money loans[1] incurred on anything else within one year of the bankruptcy filing. See 11 U.S.C. §1325 (the sentence at the very end of the section, with no number or letter on it).

In any event, it is far better to be a secured creditor (as compared to an unsecured creditor), and also much better to be fully (as compared to only partially) secured.

Sidebar

THE INFAMOUS "HANGING PARAGRAPH"

The provision in bankruptcy reform that limits the ability to strip down autos with loans taken out within 910 days of the petition is found at the very end of Section 1325(a). In some Codes, it is attached to 1325(a)(9), though paragraph (9) has nothing to do with this. Congress actually added this clause without numbering it, an embarrassing oversight that makes it impossible to cite the provision. Most attorneys and judges cite the provision like this: 11 U.S.C. §1325 (hanging paragraph at end of section).

---

[1]A purchase-money loan is simply a loan in which the lent money is used to purchase the collateral. Try to picture a loan that qualifies and one that does not. One that does not would be any loan where the debtor uses something he or she already owns to secure a new loan.

B. Security is Protection

Being a secured creditor in a bankruptcy — or outside a bankruptcy for that matter — is far better than the alternative. It means having a much better chance of being paid and a great deal of leverage over the debtor. It obviously beats being a general or unsecured creditor, with no collateral from which to be paid if there is a default or a bankruptcy. Just because one is secured, however, does not mean the creditor is fully secured.

Moreover, cases can drag on for some time. This is particularly true in a CHAPTER 11 case. If the collateral value is high enough, the creditor can continue to charge interest during this delay and also collect reasonable attorneys' fees.

C. Undersecured and Oversecured Creditors

The creditor whose claim is bigger than the value of its collateral is called an **undersecured creditor**. Conversely, a creditor whose collateral value more than covers the amount due on its loan to the debtor is an **oversecured creditor**. The two are treated quite differently in bankruptcy. The oversecured creditor gets extra benefits not available to either undersecured or unsecured creditors, including interest that continues to accrue at the contract rate after the bankruptcy case has been filed.

The debtor and the secured creditor are usually parties to a written loan contract that provides that interest will accrue at a certain interest rate and also that attorneys' fees will be charged to the debtor if the loan goes into default and the creditor has to hire an attorney to help collect the loan. The oversecured creditor can also recover attorneys' fees if the creditor must go to court to enforce its right to be paid. Essentially, the oversecured creditor's claim can grow during the case, just as it would if there was no bankruptcy (through the continuing accrual of interest and fees), whereas the unsecured claim and the undersecured claim do not increase during the case. They stay the same size. The way that secured claims are calculated is covered in Section 506 of the Code. Special rights granted to creditors that are oversecured are spelled out in Section 506(b).

Another thing about secured claims is that if they are undersecured, the claim ends up being split, for bankruptcy treatment purposes, into two parts. The part that is covered by the value of the collateral is treated as secured, and the part that is not covered is treated as unsecured. We call this **bifurcation**. The practical result is that the secured claim is really only as large as the value of the collateral. This concept is explained in Section 506(a). The secured creditor's claim is allowed in the amount of the value of the collateral, for the purposes of payment in bankruptcy. Whatever is left over of the claim is an unsecured claim.

We noted above that the secured creditor's claim continues to accrue interest and attorneys' fees at the contract rate, if it is oversecured. Section 506(b) makes it clear, however, that such post-petition interest and fees can accrue only for as long as there is still value left in the collateral. As we've discussed, any value in the collateral over and above the total secured creditor claims is called **equity**. In other words, once the claim equals the value of the collateral (remember that the claim continues to increase during the case for the oversecured creditor), all the fees and interest cease to accrue. They do not become part of an unsecured claim either. Due to the timing issues, this can make for some tricky calculations.

Q: So is this why creditors ask for so much collateral, sometimes as much as twice the amount of their debt?

A: There are many reasons why creditors want to always have collateral worth more than their debt, and this rule is one of them. The main reason, however, has nothing to do with bankruptcy. Creditors know that if they have to sell the collateral in satisfaction of their debt, they are likely to get less than full value for the collateral. They expect some shrinkage, so to speak, so they plan ahead and make sure they have plenty of collateral. Also, sometimes collateral values can go down more quickly than originally predicted and cause a creditor to become undersecured.

To illustrate how these calculations work, suppose that Carol Maroll owes $110,000 on an equipment loan from Happy Finance Co. The loan earns interest at 12% per annum. She has fallen on rough times and is eight months behind on her interest-only payments of $1,200 a month. She thinks the equipment securing the loan is worth about $100,000. Happy Finance has spent $5,000 trying to repossess the equipment, which Carol was able to resist by putting up a big fight. Happy Finance is looking to repossess these goods, and Carol has decided to file a CHAPTER 7 bankruptcy today. All of these amounts accrued prior to the bankruptcy.

(1) How Big Is Happy's Claim Today?

Well, if Happy's claim was for a debt of $120,000 in principal and interest, and $5,000 in legal fees allowed under the contract, all accruing pre-petition, and if the debt was collateralized by equipment worth $100,000, Happy would be undersecured and could not collect any more than the value of Happy's collateral, meaning just $100,000. Thus the secured part of the claim would be for $100,000. Happy's claim would be bifurcated, meaning that Happy also would have an unsecured claim, valued at $25,000.

(2) Assume Collateral Is Worth $130,000. Now How Big Is Carol's Claim Today?

If the collateral was worth $130,000, Happy's whole claim going into bankruptcy would be secured. There would be no unsecured claim. The claim would be for $110,000 for the pre-petition claim, plus $9,600 for the pre-petition interests, and $5,000 for the fees, for a total of $124,600.

(3) If the Case Goes on for Seven More Months, What Will the Claim Be?

Interest is accruing post-petition at the rate of $1,200 a month. Seven months after the case was filed, interest in the amount of $1,200 × 7, or $8,400, would theoretically accrue based strictly on the math. Because Section 506(a) allows only the secured claim to grow until the claim reaches the value of the collateral, however, not all of this interest would be allowed in the allowed secured claim. After the pre-petition claim of $124,600 is accounted for, there is just $5,400 extra equity in the collateral. This means that the total allowed claim, seven months out, and for time immemorial into the future, is just $130,000. Would the other $3,000 be an allowed unsecured claim? No. Section 506(a) provides that for the post-petition period, this additional interest just fails to accrue at all.

SUMMARY

- Secured claims are backed up by collateral; unsecured claims are not. This does not mean, however, that every time a creditor gets a dime of collateral, it acquires all of the benefits of secured creditor treatment for its whole debt regardless of size.

- A secured claim is secured only up to the value of the collateral, as a general rule. There are, however, many exceptions.

- A creditor with collateral worth less than its debt is undersecured. A creditor with collateral worth more than its debt is oversecured. Undersecured claims are bifurcated into two parts, the secured part, which is measured by the value of the collateral, and the unsecured part, which is the part left over once the collateral is sold (or what would be left over *if* the collateral were sold).

- The deficiency claim is treated just like any other secured claim. It gets no special treatment, at least as a general rule, just because it was once part of a claim secured by collateral. There are important exceptions to this rule, however, as described in Chapters 12 and 13.

- Unsecured claims and undersecured claims do not accrue interest, or, for the most part, attorneys' fees, even if the contract creating the debt provides for interest and fees.

- Secured claims can accrue interest and attorneys' fees as provided for in the contract but only up to the value of the collateral. At that time, all interest and fees stop accruing. They do not become part of an unsecured claim.

CONNECTIONS

State Law Collection Efforts

In bankruptcy, a secured creditor is only secured up to the value of its collateral. However, if you think about it, this is really the position in which the creditor finds itself when a borrower defaults outside of bankruptcy — the creditor is really only protected to cover as much of the loan as the collateral is worth.

If the value of the collateral was insufficient to repay the loan, the creditor would have to resort to the state law collection procedures covered in Chapter 2.

Interest and Attorneys' Fees

The creditor gets to collect interest and attorneys' fees while in bankruptcy if the collateral more than covers the debt and the original loan agreement contains a provision allowing for interest and attorneys' fees. But if there is not enough collateral to cover the debt, no interest or attorneys' fees arise during the bankruptcy case.

CHAPTER 11

The principles governing the treatment of secured creditors apply with most fervor in CHAPTER 11 cases, but these issues also apply to CHAPTER 13 cases. They are discussed in those contexts in Chapters 13 and 15.

Adequate Protection

Whenever you're thinking about the position of secured creditors in bankruptcy, think of the value of their collateral, the value of the equity in the collateral, and whether the secured creditors are adequately protected. See Chapter 17 for a discussion of how this works in the business context.

Automatic Stay

Stay litigation, one of the most frequently litigated areas of the Bankruptcy Code, also involves the issue of the value of secured creditors' collateral and whether the secured creditor is adequately protected. In general, if a secured creditor can show that it is not adequately protected, it can get the automatic stay lifted. Chapter 17, Section C focuses on this issue.

Secured Creditor Treatment in CHAPTERS 7 and 13

The particular treatment of a secured creditor in bankruptcy is treated in more detail in Chapter 12 and 13. This treatment varies quite a bit in these two different types of cases, as well as in the less common types of cases for individual debtors, cases filed under CHAPTERS 11 and 12.

The Avoiding Powers

9

The bankruptcy law is designed to distribute the debtor's assets among the creditors according to the scheme laid out in the Bankruptcy Code. The whole point is that all the rules we've been talking about in this book — the automatic stay, the estate, the exclusions, the exemptions, the priorities, the treatment of secured creditors — make bankruptcy relatively fair to competing creditors. But the debtor might, intentionally or unintentionally, frustrate the whole scheme by transferring property, right before declaring bankruptcy, to favored creditors or co-conspirators. Although some transfers on the eve of bankruptcy are perfectly proper, others impede equal treatment among creditors and thus can be **avoided** — undone — by a trustee or a debtor-in-possession.

O V E R V I E W

A. PREFERENTIAL TRANSFERS

    1. Preferential Payments and Transfers in Consumer Bankruptcy Cases
    2. Defenses to Preferential Transfer Accusations

B. FRAUDULENT TRANSFERS

C. UNPERFECTED SECURITY INTERESTS

The avoiding powers give trustees and debtors-in-possession almost magical powers to bring certain property that has been transferred away prior to a debtor's bankruptcy back into the debtor's estate. In this chapter, we'll focus on the three main avoiding powers, which play an important role in most CHAPTER 11 cases, and some CHAPTER 7 and CHAPTER 13 cases as well.

The three most commonly avoided types of transfers are **preferential transfers**, **fraudulent transfers**, and **transfers of unperfected security interests** — those that were not perfected at the time a bankruptcy case was filed. When the debtor makes one of these impermissible transfers on the eve of declaring bankruptcy (the actual time limits are set by the Code), the trustee or debtor-in-possession can avoid the transfer, and thereby bring the property or its value back into the debtor's estate for the benefit of all creditors.

Avoidance of impermissible transfers softens the transition between the pre-petition period, during which some creditors may have improved their position by convincing the debtor to pay them first or by using the state court collection processes to coerce payment, and the actual bankruptcy period.

Some transfers can be avoided or undone because a creditor has executed on property immediately before the bankruptcy, thus greatly improving his or her position vis-à-vis the debtor's assets. Other transfers can be avoided where the debtor simply transferred property or payments to a creditor, either to keep creditors from taking action, or just because the debtor wanted to pay one creditor over another. Sometimes the debtor gives away property, or sells it for less than it is worth, to avoid having to give it to creditors.

These transfers of property are subject to avoidance if certain elements are met. Note that a "transfer" in these cases includes not only the payment of money or the transfer of property, but also the creation of a security interest. For example, if a debtor gives a mortgage on a house, or gives a security interest in a car in order to secure a loan, these constitute "transfers" that could potentially be undone under the avoidance powers.

Avoidance actions must be brought by **adversary proceeding**. An adversary proceeding is a complaint or lawsuit within a bankruptcy case. Remember that a bankruptcy case is a multiparty proceeding and it does not necessarily involve litigation. If the debtor wants something specific from one creditor or a creditor wants something from the debtor, the debtor or creditor files a complaint within the big bankruptcy case, which the other party answers. There is discovery and all the other things you associate with a lawsuit in this separate case, and it proceeds within the big case on its own schedule.

A. Preferential Transfers

What is a "preferential transfer"? Suppose you don't have enough money to pay all of your bills. You might pay the electric company first, because you are already a month behind and afraid you will get your electricity cut off. You also might pay your mortgage or your rent, because you don't want to be evicted. But you might not pay your vet's bill for shots she gave your dog, or the dentist's bill, because you know they will not do anything except send a new bill next month, perhaps tacking on an interest charge. And you may decide that paying off your entire credit card balance is your lowest priority, because the credit card company won't complain if you carry a balance.

The payments you make are all preferential transfers, because you have paid some creditors in *preference* over others. In fact, the creditors who did NOT get paid may be happy, because now they can charge you more interest, and make a bigger profit off the money you owe them. But then, suppose that you declare bankruptcy. Now, all of a sudden, the creditors who did not get paid are upset, because they might not get paid at all.

For instance, say Jeff has five credit cards, and he's struggling to make all the payments. But one of them is his favorite card, because he's had it the longest and they have forgiven him twice for making late payments when they could have charged him a late fee but didn't. The balance on Jeff's favorite card is down to $1,000. So Jeff pays that off, and then declares bankruptcy the next week, erasing his debts to the other four credit card companies. As you can see, Jeff's *other* credit card companies would be upset, because they would want their fair share of the $1,000. From their point of view, all five credit cards should split $1,000. Further, if Jeff had declared bankruptcy before making the final payment (and his credit cards were his only debts), all five credit card companies would get to split the $1,000, under the principle that all creditors are treated equally in bankruptcy. In this case, Jeff's bankruptcy trustee could *avoid* Jeff's *preferential transfer* to his favorite credit card, get the money back, and distribute the $1,000 to all five credit cards on a pro rata basis. See Section 547. That's what avoidance powers are all about.

Section 547(b) contains the elements of an avoidable preferential transfer, and requires a transfer of property of the debtor on account of an antecedent debt, made within 90 days before the filing (or one year for transfers to insiders such as family members), while the debtor was insolvent, that gives the creditor more money than the creditor would have gotten in a CHAPTER 7 liquidation. This last element means that if a bank lends money and takes a security interest for the new debt, the grant of the security interest does NOT constitute a preferential transfer because in a CHAPTER 7 case, the bank would recover from the collateral and be no better or worse off as a result of the transfer.

Now we need to elaborate just a bit on some of the elements of a preference. These elements are set forth in Section 547(b):

1. to or for the benefit of a creditor;
2. for or on account of an antecedent debt;
3. made while the debtor was insolvent;
4. made on or within 90 days of the filing of the bankruptcy petition; and
5. enabled the creditor to receive more than it would receive if the debtor's assets were liquidated as of the date of its bankruptcy filing.

The transfer must be to a creditor or, alternatively, it can just benefit a creditor indirectly. It must be for or on account of an **antecedent debt**. An antecedent debt is one that is old or past due. We are not talking here about this month's electricity bill, just past due debts, that had been ignored until now. That is what makes it preferential to pay it now. A choice is being made to pick this one over another when paying past due debts, not just paying all the regular or monthly bills.

The next element is insolvency. Although the trustee has the burden of proof on each of the five elements referenced above, there is a presumption of the debtor's insolvency during the 90-day preference period. This presumption is sensible because it would be somewhat rare for a person to be solvent if they were in bank-ruptcy. Still, this is just a presumption and can be rebutted. Note that neither the purpose of the transfer or the "state of mind" of either party (creditor or debtor) is relevant. Instead, the focus is on the effect that the transfer had on the debtor's estate.

F   A   Q

Q: Why is insolvency required in order for a transfer to be a preference?

A: Because at the time of insolvency, even if it precedes the bankruptcy filing, the policy of equality of treatment among creditors kicks in. Further, if the debtor is not insolvent at the time of a purportedly preferential transfer, there is no harm to other creditors because the remaining property should be sufficient to cover all creditors' claims.

The transfer must be made within 90 days of the bankruptcy case. This period is expanded to one year for insiders, such as family members, shareholders, or partners (see Bankruptcy Code Section 547(b)(4)(B)), on the theory that insiders are more connected to the debtor and thus more likely to be preferred, and also that they could have waited to be paid until the other creditors were taken care of first.

The last element is key. The transfer must have allowed the creditor to get more than it would have received in a Chapter 7 liquidation case. If the debtor is paying down secured debt (especially fully secured debt), the secured creditor would have been paid in full in a Chapter 7 case, so these payments are not preferences. If the creditor is undersecured, there could be a preference, but not if the creditor is fully secured.

Above we talked about how granting a security interest to a lender is a classic preference, as it is an interest in property. This is particularly true if the debtor is granting a security interest to the creditor to secure a prior or antecedent debt. For example, maybe the debtor has not paid a creditor for some time and the creditor insists on securing the past due debt. This grant of a security interest is a classic preference.

Sometimes, perhaps in most cases, a secured lender is taking a security interest in exchange for new lending, for example, a lender who is providing working capital for a business, secured by existing debtor assets. Normally, this would not be a preference because the loan is being granted simultaneously with the taking of the security interest and not in connection with an antecedent debt. If a secured lender is doing this type of loan, the lender must be very careful to perfect its security interest promptly. If the lender perfects its security interest later, this act of perfecting could be considered a preference because by then the loan could be considered antecedent. We sometimes call this a delay that creates an antecedency. It also creates, unfortunately for the creditor, an avoidable preferential transfer.

The creditor need not perfect the same day as it lends, however, Section 547(e)(2) of the Bankruptcy Code provides that the transfer of a lien (including a voluntary security interest) is deemed to have been made at the time of the loan if the lien is perfected within 30 days. (This was 10 days, before the 2005 amendments.) Conversely, if perfection is delayed for more than 30 days, the transfer is deemed to have been made at the time of perfection. This means if the perfection occurs after the thirtieth day, the trustee or debtor-in-possession can avoid the security interest and turn the lender into an unsecured lender for the whole loan.

(1) Preferential Payments and Transfers in Consumer Bankruptcy Cases

In CHAPTER 7 and 13 cases, preferential transfers can be avoided, but this often makes less difference than it does in a CHAPTER 11 case. This is because payments made during the preference period tend to be smaller and thus have less of an impact on other creditors.

At times, however, preferences do play an important part in a consumer bankruptcy. For instance, transfers to insiders can be avoided for a full year, rather than the usual 90 days for other transfers. **Insider** is defined in Section 101(31) of the Code to include family members.

(2) Defenses to Preferential Transfer Accusations

In some situations, the preferential transfer elements are all met, but the payee can assert a defense that will prevent the trustee from recovering the allegedly preferential transfer.

(a) Ordinary Course of Business Defense

The most common defense to a preferential transfer, and the most litigated, is the ordinary course of business defense. The Code states, in so many words, that paying your monthly bills in the ordinary course of your affairs — your rent or mortgage, satellite TV, cell phone, internet, gas and electric, car payment, and credit cards — does not constitute a preferential transfer. 11 U.S.C. §547(c)(2). Payments of regular monthly bills are the quintessential ordinary course payments, though other payments sometimes qualify as well. In a sense, most of these debts are antecedent or old. Think about it — the mortgage may have been taken out a long time ago.

The key is that the bill that is being challenged is being paid off regularly, and is not past due. That makes the payment *ordinary*. On the other hand, payments on past due bills are always preferential. Hence, even if an underlying debt is technically *antecedent*, regular payments that are not past due *cannot* be avoided, whereas payments made on an account that is past due *can* be avoided. Most of the time, this defense is used in a business context. The defense can only be asserted if the payments are made within the ordinary course of business between the parties, or alternatively, within the ordinary course within the industry. §547(c)(2)(A) and (B).

(b) The New Value Exception

Another exception to avoidable preferential transfers is the new value exception. §547(c)(3). This exception allows a creditor who has extended new credit, after receiving a preferential payment, to deduct the amount of the new credit from the preferential payment received. Let's say Solar Power Company makes a preferential

Sidebar

NO PAYMENTS TO FAMILY MEMBERS TO AVOID PAYING CREDITORS

Payments to family members are avoidable for a full year because a family member is more likely to be aware of the debtor's failing financial condition and thus he or she knows of the increased risk of loaning the debtor money, and is also more likely to be preferred by the debtor when it comes to choosing which creditor to pay first. Sometimes we may even question the motivation of the so-called loan, because it's possible that Mom really intended to give her debtor-child a gift, right?

payment of $1,000 to a supplier of solar panels. (Assume the money was paid three weeks before declaring bankruptcy, while Solar Power Company was insolvent, and the account was past due.) After the supplier received the payment, the supplier shipped $500 worth of solar panels to Solar Power Company, extending *new* credit. The new value exception nets out these amounts. The result is that the supplier only has to return $500 to the bankruptcy estate, which is the amount that was paid toward the antecedent debt, rather than the full $1,000.

Was it still worth it for the supplier to ship the last $500 of solar panels? Yes, because the supplier would have to either pay back the $1,000, or pay back $500 and ship $500 of supplies. At least under the second scenario, the supplier ends up with the profits from the sale of $500 of solar panels.

Note that the policy behind the exception is to encourage businesses to continue to deal with distressed companies by extending credit, knowing that they will get some protection against having to return preferential payments they receive. This also makes sense because the solar panels in the example above will now become part of the bankruptcy estate (and can be sold to pay other creditors).

Nonetheless, the law of avoiding preferential transfers does not seem fair *at all* to the one who received the transfer and is then forced to return the money to the trustee. After all, this supplier was owed $1,000! Why should it have to give back the money just because the customer always paid late? There is no satisfying answer, except that the principle of equitable treatment among creditors is being upheld.

(c) The Substantially Contemporaneous Exchange for New Value Exception

The **substantially contemporaneous exchange for new value** exception, found in Section 547(c)(1), is almost superfluous because it restates one of the elements of preferential transfer law. A preference is only a preference if it is a payment made on account of an antecedent debt. If a payment is made contemporaneously with receipt of goods or services, then, by definition, such payment is not a payment made on account of an antecedent debt.

The real reason why the exception appears in the Code is that the exchange need not be precisely contemporaneous, but can be just *substantially contemporaneous*. Thus you could have a substantially contemporaneous exchange for new value even though the debtor did not hand over a payment at the very moment that the supplier provided the goods or services. Emphasize the word *substantially* and you'll get the picture.

B. Fraudulent Transfers

All states have laws allowing harmed creditors to undo fraudulent transfers. Most of these laws allow a harmed creditor to reverse a fraudulent transfer for a period of six years after the transfer is made. The Bankruptcy Code adopts these state laws in Section 544(b)(1), which allows the trustee to attack a transfer by the debtor as fraudulent if there is a creditor with an unsecured claim at the time the petition is filed who had the right to avoid the transfer under state fraudulent transfer law.

In addition to pursuing the rights of creditors under state fraudulent transfer laws, the trustee's (or the debtor-in-possession's) avoidance powers include a federal version of fraudulent transfer law. Section 548 of the Bankruptcy Code allows the trustee or the debtor-in-possession to set aside a fraudulent transfer made by the debtor, while the debtor was insolvent or that caused the debtor to become insolvent, within one year prior to the debtor's bankruptcy filing. Like state law, Section 548 allows transfers to be avoided for both **actual fraud** (transfers made with actual intent to hinder, delay, or defraud creditors) as well as **constructive fraud** (transfers for less than fair value that leave the debtor insolvent). Once a transfer has been avoided, the person who received the transfer (the transferee), either directly or indirectly, is liable to the trustee for return of the transferred property or its value. 11 U.S.C. §550. Further, making a fraudulent transfer prior to a bankruptcy could cause a CHAPTER 7 debtor to lose his or her entire bankruptcy discharge. See 11 U.S.C. §727(a)(2).

But how does the trustee get the fraudulently transferred asset back? Well, sometimes the item transferred is a house. In that case, the avoidance action for the fraudulent transfer brings the house back into the debtor's estate, where it will be sold to pay back the unsecured creditors. But if money or a boat, or any tangible or intangible property that can disappear, has been fraudulently transferred and is now gone, the trustee (essentially the estate) will get a money judgment against the person who received the transfer, to be collected from another of that person's assets. At that point, we are back to the execution process discussed in Chapter 2. Or the recipient of the fraudulent transfer might be judgment proof, in which case the estate is out of luck for now.

Now let's review an example of a transfer for less than equivalent value. Let's say Rhonda needs to fix the transmission in her car, so she sells her brand new DVD entertainment center, which she bought for $5,000, to her friend for $1,000. The friend is trying to help Rhonda fix her car, and does not even really want the entertainment center. If Rhonda then declares bankruptcy, her trustee can probably avoid the transfer and bring the system back into the estate for sale and distribution of the proceeds to Rhonda's other creditors.

> ## Sidebar
>
> ### INNOCENT INTENTIONS AREN'T ENOUGH
>
> The policy of Section 548 is clear. A debtor cannot give away property or sell it for less than it is worth if doing so will harm his or her creditors by taking away an asset that they could have used to satisfy their claims. It is easy to see why we unwind a debtor's transfer when the transfer was made to purposely avoid the claims of creditors. But in some instances, sales for less than fair value appear to be innocent, yet the Code allows these transfers to be unwound as well.

What does it mean to avoid the transfer? It means that the friend will have to give back the entertainment center (or the equivalent — the $1,000 cash) and will be stuck with a bankruptcy claim against Rhonda. Wow! This really makes you wonder about garage sale deals that are too good to be true.

The conclusion above assumes two things that might not be true: first, that the system is worth more than $1,000, and second, that the system would not have been exempt in Rhonda's bankruptcy. If either of these assumptions turns out to be false, the trustee cannot avoid this transfer.

C. Unperfected Security Interests

Section 544(a) gives the trustee "strong-arm powers" to avoid unperfected security interests. When this happens, the previously secured creditor is turned into a general unsecured creditor. The security interest is, in essence, returned to the estate. The property is then unencumbered and its value can be distributed to unsecured creditors.

F	A	Q

Q: How do you "perfect" a security interest?

A: Usually by filing a financing statement in the Secretary of State's office in the state in which the debtor was organized. There are some other ways (such as possessing the collateral or exercising control over the collateral), but a full discussion of those issues is better left to Secured Transactions. The filing system enables lenders to search, before lending money, under the borrower's name for prior security interests granted by that borrower. If the lender finds that the borrower has granted security interests, the borrower can examine the financing statement and see the description of collateral listed to determine if the present collateral was previously encumbered. This gives the lender the information it needs to determine whether the collateral the borrower is offering to secure the loan is available, and to what extent it is already encumbered.

Under the law of Secured Transactions, a secured creditor with a perfected security interest has priority over one that has not perfected. The judgment lien creditor also has priority over the unperfected voluntary security interest.

Outside bankruptcy, the fact that a secured party has failed to perfect its interest does not wipe out the interest completely. Rather, the secured party still has the rights of a secured party as against the debtor and can repossess its collateral and sell it to realize on the creditor's claim. This is true, assuming no senior lienholder's rights are impaired.

The priority themes from Article 9 of the Uniform Commercial Code are continued in the Bankruptcy Code, though the avoidance powers go a step further and allow the trustee to wipe out the unperfected security interest entirely rather than letting it linger around in its low priority state.

Why undo unperfected security interests? Isn't that a bit hyper-technical? Well, although it sounds technical, the law hates secret liens and fears that they could mislead creditors into thinking the debtor has more unencumbered assets from which to pay creditors than the debtor actually has. After all, *unperfected* security interests have not been recorded in the Secretary of State's office, since no financing statement has been filed. Consequently, other lenders have no way to search for them — they can do a search of the Secretary of State's records, but unperfected security interests won't show up.

So the policies here are obvious and sensible, but the Code reaches the right result in a roundabout way. Following the rules of Article 9, the Code gives the trustee the rights of a **hypothetical judgment lien creditor**. 11 U.S.C. §544(a). Since lien creditors beat out unperfected security interests under Article 9, this means that the trustee can beat out an unperfected security interest. We call these avoidance powers the trustee's **strong-arm powers**.

To simplify, it is enough just to remember that the trustee has the right to avoid unperfected security interests under Section 544(a), and leave the hypothetical lien creditor status out of it.

The bottom line is that the trustee can void unperfected security interests. There is one important exception to this rule, however. For example, a creditor who grants a loan and receives a purchase-money security interest in exchange for the loan has 20 days within which to perfect its security interest and still be first in priority under Article 9, with respect to collateral that his or her loan allowed the creditor to buy. The Bankruptcy Code avoidance powers are consistent with this 20-day grace period. Section 546(b) of the Code protects the holders of PMSIs for the 20-day period. Thus, even if a PMSI was unperfected as of the debtor's bankruptcy filing, the trustee could not avoid the security interest. In fact, the creditor is still permitted to perfect this security interest during the 30 days, despite the automatic stay. See 11 U.S.C. §362(b)(3).

After this chapter, we move out of the bankruptcy principles that apply in all cases and discuss the specifics of CHAPTER 7 cases.

SUMMARY

■ One important bankruptcy policy is equality of treatment among creditors during the bankruptcy case. In reality, the filing happens at a particular moment in time, so equal treatment occurs at that moment, even though the debtor may have been preparing to file for some time.

■ Sometimes the debtor pays some creditors prior to the case but not others. There is nothing wrong with this per se, but the Bankruptcy Code will sometimes undo transfers of property that impair the equality principle, using several tools unique to bankruptcy law, which are known as the trustee's avoiding powers.

■ The avoiding powers undo preferential payments and transfers, as well as those made to hinder, delay, or defraud creditors, and those made for less than fair value.

■ The avoiding powers also allow the trustee to avoid security interests that are not properly perfected. The idea here is that a failure to perfect a security interest could result in unsecured creditors and other secured lenders not knowing about the hidden security interest and perhaps lending on the strength of assets that appeared unencumbered at the time.

CONNECTIONS

The Estate

The avoiding powers apply in all types of bankruptcy cases, to all property that would come into the estate. Hence, as you think about issues surrounding the debtor's estate, which we discussed in Chapter 5, it's worth remembering the avoiding powers as a possible way to enlarge the estate.

Confirmation of a CHAPTER 11 Plan

The avoiding powers are especially important in CHAPTER 11 cases, because they can be a good source of revenue with which to fund a plan. Thus the avoiding powers are linked to feasibility and confirmation issues in CHAPTER 11 cases, which we discuss in Chapter 15, Section A and Section E.

Bankruptcy Policy and Theory

The avoiding powers promote equality by returning property transferred preferentially for less than fair value, and security interests, to the debtor's estate. Although we saw exceptions to this theme in our discussion of claims and priorities in Chapter 7 of this book, a major theme of bankruptcy law is equality of treatment among creditors. This theme was discussed throughout Chapter 3 and Chapter 4.

The State Law Execution Process

Where a fraudulent transfer has occurred, and the item transferred has disappeared, the trustee must resort to state law to obtain a judgment against the transferee and then collect the value of the lost asset through the execution process described in Chapter 2.

Judgment Proof Transferees

The transferee may be judgment proof, the concept described in Chapter 1, in which case there's not much the estate can do at this time.

The Anatomy of a CHAPTER 7 Case

This chapter describes the procedures for filing a CHAPTER 7 case, including the means test, which was one of the major additions that the 2005

OVERVIEW

amendments brought to the Bankruptcy Code. Some of the tests and procedures in this chapter apply to all bankruptcy cases (such as CHAPTER 13 and CHAPTER 11 cases), whereas some of the information is unique to CHAPTER 7 cases. This chapter also covers the bankruptcy discharge, the primary reason for filing a CHAPTER 7 case, and involuntary bankruptcy, in which creditors force a debtor into bankruptcy.

F. TRYING TO BEAT THE MEANS TEST

G. INVOLUNTARY BANKRUPTCY

A. The Debtor's Financial Information

Before filing any bankruptcy, there are questions about the debtor's past and current financial life that you, as the lawyer, must help your client answer. This information will help you determine which chapter works best for a particular debtor, or whether the person needs a bankruptcy at all. Unfortunately, empirical evidence shows that when debtors who are having financial difficulties consult a bankruptcy attorney, they usually end up filing for bankruptcy, whether it is appropriate for them or not. You don't want to be the kind of attorney who automatically puts all your clients into bankruptcy. Where appropriate, you want to offer advice about *not* filing for bankruptcy.

However, once you decide bankruptcy is the right decision for your client, you will need to look at past credit card statements and other records of debts due, past tax returns, past pay stubs, and bank and investment statements. You'll also ask your client a long list of questions designed to help you formulate the best plan of action.

F   A   Q

Q: Are lawyers allowed to help clients move their money before bankruptcy to help them keep as much as possible? For example, may lawyers encourage clients to put their money into a protected retirement account?

A: **Pre-bankruptcy planning has** always been part of the process of advising a bankruptcy debtor. It is controversial because it looks bad when people try to game the system. It is also uncertain — while many cases have held that some pre-bankruptcy planning is appropriate, in other cases debtors have lost their bankruptcy discharge for doing too much pre-bankruptcy planning (discussed in Chapter 11, Section C). Also, the 2005 amendments limit the ability to move to a new state to take advantage of a better exemptions scheme. 11 U.S.C. §§522(b)(3)(A)(o) and (p). Still, the short answer is that lawyers can advise clients to do pre-bankruptcy planning, but they also must explain the risks, so the client can make an informed decision about what to do.

The forms to fill out when a case is filed are known as the **Official Bankruptcy Forms**. Official Form B1, called a **voluntary petition,** initiates the case. The voluntary petition contains very basic information, such as the debtor's name, address, the last four digits of his or her social security number, information about the number of creditors, debts, and property, and whether, during the 180-day period before the filing date, the debtor has lived, maintained a residence or business, or had assets in the district where the petition is being filed. This gives the debtor the right to file in that district.

The petition is accompanied by a certificate proving that the debtor has attended pre-bankruptcy credit counseling, copies of the debtor's most recent federal tax return and pay stubs, an analysis of the means test (discussed below), and, in community property states, a statement of the name and address of any non-debtor spouse.

In addition to the basic petition, the debtor must also file **schedules of assets and liabilities** (Official Forms B6 (A through J)) and a **statement of financial affairs** (Official Form B7) either with the petition or within 15 days thereafter. The **statements and schedules** (as they are sometimes called for short) are designed to provide the trustee and others with a full picture of the debtor's financial affairs. These documents are very long and complex. They require the debtor to disclose all interests that he or she may have in any property, including property that will be exempted; all of his or her obligations, including **contingent debts** and **unliquidated debts** (see Chapter 7 of this book); what the debtor claims as exempt property; how the debtor plans to treat his or her secured creditors in bankruptcy; and so on. The **statements and schedules** are signed under oath, and it is important that they are accurate.

B. Mandatory Credit Counseling Courses

The 2005 amendments make it harder and slower for consumers to file a Chapter 7 case, get rid of most of their debts, and start fresh.

The first provision in the 2005 amendments that limits consumer access to Chapter 7 is the requirement that every individual debtor receive a **credit briefing** before being allowed to file bankruptcy. 11 U.S.C. §109(h). Most people call this pre-bankruptcy credit counseling, but that makes it sound more substantive than it really is. All that is really required is that the debtor go to an approved credit counselor and receive information about opportunities for credit counseling, a budget analysis, an analysis of the debtor's financial condition, an analysis of the factors that caused the financial condition, and help developing a plan of action for dealing with the debt without incurring negative amortization of debt.

There are exceptions to the pre-bankruptcy credit counseling requirement for people who are disabled or incapacitated, or on active military duty in a combat zone. 11 U.S.C. §109(h)(4). There also is an exception for "exigent circumstances." 11 U.S.C. §109(h)(3). Even so, the requirement keeps many debtors out of bankruptcy. *In re Davenport*, 2005 WL 3292700 (Bankr. M.D. Fla. 2005); *In re Hubbard*, 333 B.R. 377 (Bankr. S.D. Tex. 2005). Sometimes even a foreclosure is not enough to constitute "exigent circumstances," making it advisable for most debtors just to get the counseling rather than trying to get out of it. *In re LaPorta*, 332 B.R. 879 (Bankr. D. Minn. 2005). Otherwise the attorney needs to go to court to get a court order excusing the debtor from the requirement, which is more trouble than it is worth.

Sidebar

THE POLICY DEBATE: WERE DEBTORS ABUSING THE SYSTEM?

Credit card companies and other consumer credit companies successfully lobbied Congress by building a bipartisan consensus that consumer access to Chapter 7 should be curtailed to prevent purported debtor abuse of the system. But virtually all bankruptcy scholars disagreed that there was substantial debtor abuse. Regardless of who was right, the 2005 amendments reflect the perception that the system was being abused, and they make it harder on debtors and debtors' attorneys.

Although the credit counseling requirement sounds like a good idea, it's not as helpful as it sounds. Many credit counselors have been unscrupulous, acting as nonprofits while funneling profits to for-profit entities and actually damaging debtors' credit. Further, the timing of the counseling is off—it comes at a point when the debtor's finances have already spun out of control and the debtor is on the steps of the court house, ready to declare bankruptcy. At this stage, it is too late to help! It also costs money and takes time, thereby preventing some impoverished debtors from being able to declare bankruptcy at all. The post-bankruptcy debt management course, described below, holds more promise for actually improving the lives of ordinary Americans.

The new law also requires individual debtors, under either CHAPTER 7 or CHAPTER 13, to take a post-filing "debt management course . . . designed to assist debtors in understanding personal financial management." 11 U.S.C. §111. According to the instructions distributed by the U.S. Trustee's Office, which is required to administer the debtor education requirements, the course (which some people call the *second course*) must cover at least three areas of instruction: budget development, money management, and the wise use of consumer credit.

C. The Means Test

(1) Introduction

Another provision in the 2005 amendments that limits access to CHAPTER 7 is the "means test," added by Congress to push consumers into CHAPTER 13 bankruptcies instead of CHAPTER 7. Essentially, if a consumer[1] would have enough **disposable income** to pay off a good portion of his or her debts, the consumer is ineligible for CHAPTER 7. The debtor's **monthly income** minus necessary **monthly expenses** equals the debtor's **disposable income**. If the disposable income is less than the portion of debts specified in the means test, the consumer's case can be dismissed, or converted to a CHAPTER 13 or CHAPTER 11 case.

(2) Summary

One way to think through the means test is in terms of thresholds. If a debtor's disposable income is below $100 a month, the debtor *always* passes the means test. Conversely, if the debtor's income is above the median income (if the debtor's disposable income is above $167 a month), the debtor *never* passes the means test.

In the middle, if the debtor's disposable income is between $100 and $167 per month, compare the debtor's disposable income to 25% of the debtor's non-priority unsecured debt. If the debtor's disposable income is below the 25%, the debtor passes. If the debtor's disposable income is above the 25%, the debtor fails.

---

[1]The means test applies only to debtors with primarily consumer debts, not business debts.

Table 10.1	Basic Overview of Means Test Results

Monthly Disposable Income	Outcome of Means Test
("Current Monthly Income" minus Projected Monthly Expenses)	
Below $100 per month	Debtor always passes.
Between $100 and $167 per month	To pass, debtor's disposable income must be less than 25% of nonpriority unsecured debts.
Above $167	Debtor always fails (if above median income).

(3) A Look at the Details of the Section 707(b) Means Test

Now let's walk through the details to see how the means test actually works.[2] Section 707(b) uses the word "abuse," and provides that if the debtor flunks the means test, a court *must presume* that an "abuse" exists. §707(b)(2). Then the court must either dismiss the case or convert it to a CHAPTER 13 or a CHAPTER 11 case.

The idea is that if the debtor has enough money to pay off a good portion of her debts, she should pay them off under CHAPTER 13 instead of getting them discharged under CHAPTER 7. So how do we calculate whether the debtor has enough money to pay off a good portion of her debts? That's what the means test is all about. The formula is described below:

Step One — Compare the Debtor's Income to the Median Income for the Debtor's State

Compare the debtor's "current monthly income," defined in Section 101(10A), to a baseline "median family income," defined in Section 101(39A). If the debtor's income is *less than* the median family income, the debtor passes the means test!

To make this comparison, calculate the debtor's **current monthly income,** which is the debtor's average monthly revenue from all sources for the past six months. We know it is a little silly to call this *current monthly income,* since it is not current, not monthly, and not limited to just income (it includes gifts), but that is what the test requires.

Just add up all[3] the money the debtor has received during the past six months, including income, gifts, child support, and alimony. Include the debtor's spouse's income, even if the spouse is not jointly filing for bankruptcy, unless the two are separated or living separate and apart (except if they are merely living separately to evade this provision). 11 U.S.C. §707(b)(7)(B)(i)(I) and (II).

---

[2]By the way, **Form B22A** has the means test calculation for a CHAPTER 7 case. It refers to **expenses** as **deductions**. The terms are interchangeable.

[3]Some money is excluded from current monthly income: social security benefits, and payments to victims of war crimes, crimes against humanity, and international terrorism. 11 U.S.C. §101(10A)(B).

Next, divide the money from the past six months by six, to get a monthly average. The result is the debtor's "current monthly income."

Then go to http://www.usdoj.gov/ust/eo/bapcpa/meanstesting.htm to find the *median family income* for your state. For example, as of June 2007, the median income for one person was $53,553 in Connecticut, $44,499 in California, $42,896 in New York, and $29,299 in Mississippi. Where you live makes a big difference!

If the debtor's current monthly income is below the median family income in the debtor's state, the debtor passes the means test.[4]

Step Two — The Debtor's Projected Monthly Income

Now pretend that the debtor's **current monthly income,** calculated in Step One above, will stay the same for the next five years. Five years is 60 months, so multiply the current monthly income by 60, and the result is the debtor's **projected monthly income**. It makes sense to use five years as the measuring period for the means test, because this is the likely length of a Chapter 13 plan.[5]

Step Three — The Debtor's Projected Monthly Expenses for the Next Five Years

Now you need to calculate the debtor's **projected monthly expenses** for the next five years. All you need to do is add up all the allowed expenses, listed below.

The purpose of this part of the calculation is to find an expense number that fairly estimates the debtor's necessary monthly expenses. What expenses are "necessary"? Courts and the Code use the phrase "reasonably necessary for the maintenance or support of the debtor or his dependents." It's a factual question for the court to determine on an *ad hoc* basis.

a. Personal Expenses Set by the IRS National Standards. Go to http://www.usdoj.gov/ust/eo/bapcpa/meanstesting.htm, and look at the National Standards for Allowable Living Expenses (excluding Alaska and Hawaii) chart. This chart lists the allowable expense for Food, Housekeeping Supplies, Apparel & Services (Clothing), Personal Care Products & Services, and Miscellaneous. These are national standards,[6] unrelated to the debtor's actual expenses. This is essentially an allowance.

All you need to do is find the allowable expense on this chart.[7]

The allowable personal expense from this chart is subtracted from projected monthly income.

---

[4]The good news is that most debtors in the real world will pass this first step and therefore pass the whole means test. Empirical data show that only a small percentage of Chapter 7 filers have income that is greater than the median family income in their state.

[5]Chapter 7 debtors who fail the means test have their cases converted to Chapter 13 and are required to do a five-year repayment plan.

[6]Hawaii and Alaska have higher allowances, because personal expenses are so much higher in those states.

[7]In addition, if the debtor's actual expenses exceed the IRS set expenses, you can add up to 5% for the debtor's actual Food and Clothing expenses. This 5% is listed at the bottom of the chart, so you don't even have to do the math.

b. Housing and Utility Expenses Set by Local Standards. Using the same website, look at the chart for Housing and Utility Expenses. Unlike the cost of food and clothing, the cost of housing and utilities varies tremendously depending on where you live. For instance, housing in San Francisco or New York City is a lot more expensive than housing in Albuquerque, Omaha, or Pittsburgh. That's why these are local rather than national standards.

Find the state and county where the debtor lives. The chart gives the **Housing and Utility Expense**, which is subtracted from **projected monthly income**. Again, this is an allowance. The debtor can deduct the whole amount even if he or she does not spend that much.[8]

c. Other Necessary Expenses Set by the IRS. In addition to the **personal expenses** and **housing and utility expenses** described in subsections a and b above, the IRS allows specific categories of **Other Necessary Expenses**. Each category has its own line on Form B22A. These categories are federal, state, and local taxes, such as income taxes, self-employment taxes, social security taxes, and Medicare taxes; mandatory payroll deductions, such as mandatory retirement contributions, union dues, and uniform costs; life insurance; court-ordered payments, such as spousal or child support payments; education for employment or for a physically or mentally challenged child; childcare; health care (actual health care costs, but NOT health care costs reimbursed by health insurance or by a health savings account — those are listed elsewhere on Form B22A); and telecommunications, such as cell phones and internet services.

Each category here is the average of the debtor's *actual* monthly expenses. The total of these Other Necessary Expenses is subtracted from the **projected monthly income**.

d. Transportation Expenses Set by Region and Metropolitan Area. Using the same website, look at the chart for **Transportation Costs**, listed by region and metropolitan area. There are two numbers: the cost of operating a car or paying for public transportation; and the cost of buying or owning a car.

If the debtor does not own a car, she only gets to subtract the cost of paying for public transportation. But if the debtor owns a car, she gets to subtract *both* the operating costs *and* the cost of owning the car.

Find the region where the debtor lives, and determine whether the debtor owns a car or uses public transportation, and you'll have the Transportation Costs that the debtor is allowed to subtract from her **projected monthly income**.

e. Actual Expenses for Continued Care and Support of Elderly, Chronically Ill, or Disabled Members of the Debtor's Household and Immediate Family; Actual Costs of the Debtor's Children's Education; Health Insurance, Disability Insurance, and Health Savings Account Expenses; and Continued Charitable Contributions. Section 707(b)(2)(A)(ii)(II) and (IV), and Form B22A, allow the *actual* monthly expenses incurred in each of these categories to be subtracted from the debtor's projected monthly income.

However, the education expense, which, for example, would apply to private school tuition, is capped at $1,500 per child per year, *and* the debtor must detail

---

[8]Note that Section 707(b)(2)(A)(ii)(V) allows a debtor to use actual home energy costs if the actual expense is greater than the allowance. But the debtor must demonstrate that the actual expense is reasonable and necessary.

why this expense is not already accounted for in the other categories listed in Section 707(b).

Also note that that any charitable contributions must be rooted in the debtor's pre-bankruptcy past, because Section 707(b)(1) exempts only charitable contributions that the debtor "has made, or continues to make." It follows that debtors cannot "get religion" after filing, in order to reduce their monthly expenses. The grey area, of course, relates to debtors who start making charitable contributions a few weeks before filing bankruptcy. (This concern is addressed by the court's discretion under the **Two Hurdles** explained below — the Bad Faith Test and the Totality of Circumstances Test.)

f. Administrative Expenses. Section 707(b)(2)(A)(ii)(III) allows the debtor to subtract the *actual* administrative expenses that she would have to pay if she were in a Chapter 13 plan. Using the same website, find the chart that lists the percentage charged in the judicial district where the debtor is filing. This is typically between 5% and 10% of the Chapter 13 monthly payment.

Once you have the percentage that is charged in your district, multiply that by the projected average monthly Chapter 13 plan payment (to get this payment amount, pretend the debtor was going to file Chapter 13, and calculate what her monthly payments would be under Chapter 13).

The result is the average monthly administrative expense, which is subtracted from projected monthly income.

g. Payments on Secured Debts and Priority Claims (Including Child Support and Alimony) Under Sections 707(b)(2)(A)(iii) and (iv), the debtor's projected expenses include payments on secured debts and priority claims. This includes all scheduled payments, all payments to cure arrearages, and any required lump sum payments during the next five years. Simply add up all the payments due during the next five years, and you'll have the total projected expenses for secured debts and priority claims. Divide the five-year total by 60 months, and you'll have an **average monthly payment** for secured debt, which is subtracted from **projected monthly income**.[9]

---

[9]As of this writing, there is a split of authority regarding how to treat payments on secured debt — as an *allowance*, or an *actual* expense. On the one hand, a plain reading of Section 707(b) suggests that ALL the expenses listed above can be deducted from the debtor's income. On the other hand, some expenses are listed twice: Child support and spousal support are listed in "Other Necessary Expenses," but they are also "Priority Claims"; "Housing and Utilities" are listed as allowed expenses, but a mortgage is also a "Housing Payment" and a "Secured Debt"; and the cost of owning a car is a set expense under "Transportation Expenses," but a car loan is also a "Secured Debt."

Form B22A takes the position that no double dipping is allowed. Every time an expense is listed twice, Form B22A requires the debtor to subtract the actual expense from the allowance. If the actual expense is bigger, the allowance is listed as zero. Then, later in the form, where the actual expense is required to be listed, the entire actual expense can be listed. The result is that if an actual mortgage payment or car payment is bigger than the set expense, the debtor gets the benefit of the larger, actual amount.

h. Catch-All Additional Expense Claims. Form B22A also allows a debtor to claim any additional monthly expenses that "are required for the health and welfare of you and your family." Although not expressly authorized in Section 707(b), it appears that courts are following Form B22A and allowing some additional expenses.

i. Add Items a Through h, and You Get Projected Monthly Expenses. Finally, it is time to add up the expenses listed in items a through h. These are the debtor's projected monthly expenses (or deductions). Again, we're trying to compare apples to apples, so double check to make sure that all the expenses are *monthly* expenses.

Step Four — Find the Debtor's Monthly Disposable Income

Now subtract the debtor's projected monthly expenses (Step Three) from the debtor's projected monthly income (Step Two). This is the **monthly disposable income**, a very important number for the means test.

Step Five — Find the 60-Month (Five-Year) Disposable Income

Multiply the monthly disposable income (Step Four) by 60 months, and you'll get the debtor's **60-Month Disposable Income** — the total disposable income that the debtor will have over the next five years.

Step Six — Evaluate the Results

Recall that the whole point of the means test calculation is to figure out whether the debtor has the "means" to pay off a worthwhile portion of her debts over the next five years. But how much is a *worthwhile* portion? Unsurprisingly, the Code's answer requires several more steps. Yikes!

Table 10.2	Means Test Results for All Incomes		
Five-Year Disposable Income (a.k.a. income available to pay debts) Explained in Step Five	**Monthly Disposable Income (five-year disposable income/60) Explained in Step Four**	**Compare with Nonpriority Unsecured Claims (e.g., credit card debt) Explained in Step Six**	**Outcome**
$10,000 (See paragraph **a** below for a more detailed explanation.)	$167	Doesn't matter — based on high disposable income.	Debtor can pay worthwhile portion of debt. Fails means test, cannot file CHAPTER 7.
		Low debt (under $24,000), debtor fails means test and is ineligible to file a CHAPTER 7 bankruptcy.	

| Between $6,000-10,000 (See paragraph **b** below for a more detailed explanation.) | Between $100-167 | Between $24,000 and $40,000 nonpriority unsecured debt, the outcome depends on the ratio. To pass means test and be eligible to file Chapter 7 bankruptcy, 25% of debt must be greater than five-year income (notice the perverse incentive, only those with high debt will pass means test at this step and be eligible for Chapter 7!). High debt (over $40,000), debtor passes means test and may be eligible to file a Chapter 7 bankruptcy. | |
| $6,000 (See paragraph **c** below for a more detailed explanation.) | $100 | Doesn't matter— based on low disposable income. | Debtor unable to pay worthwhile portion of debt, passes means test, may be eligible to file a Chapter 7 bankruptcy. |

a. Five-Year Disposable Income Greater Than $10,000. If the debtor has enough disposable income to pay more than $10,000 of her debts over the next five years, the Code provides that the debtor should pay her debts in Chapter 13 rather than Chapter 7. §707(b)(2)(B)(iv)(II). Therefore, if the 60-month disposable income (Step Five) is greater than $10,000, the debtor fails the means test and is ineligible for bankruptcy under Chapter 7.

This is the same as saying that if the debtor has more than $167 per month of disposable income (Step Four), the debtor should go into Chapter 13 (or be denied bankruptcy) ($167 per month, multiplied by 60 months, equals approximately $10,000 over five years).

b. Five-Year Disposable Income Between $6,000 and $10,000. If the debtor's 60-month disposable income (Step Five) is *more than* $6,000 *and* the debtor's 60-month disposable income is *greater than* 25% of the debtor's nonpriority unsecured claims, the debtor is ineligible for Chapter 7 bankruptcy.

To evaluate this test, multiply the debtor's nonpriority unsecured claims by .25. Compare that to the debtor's 60-month disposable income (Step Five). If Step Five is larger, the debtor flunks the means test. But if Step Five is smaller, the debtor passes the means test.

This is the same as saying that if the debtor has more than $100 per month in disposable income ($100 per month times 60 months equals $6,000) *and* the debtor's disposable income is greater than 25% of the debtor's nonpriority unsecured claims, the debtor is denied access to Chapter 7 and forced into Chapter 13 (or out of bankruptcy altogether).

c. Five-Year Disposable Income Less Than $6,000. Finally, if the debtor's 60-month disposable income is less than $6,000, the debtor passes the means test, no matter what!

This is the same as saying that if the debtor's disposable income is less than $100 per month, the debtor automatically passes the means test.

Table 10.3	Total Disposable Income Between $6,000 and $10,000	
Nonpriority Unsecured Claims	**Multiplied by 25%**	**Outcome**
$24,000	$6,000	Fails means test, ineligible for bankruptcy under CHAPTER 7, case converted to CHAPTER 13 or debtor out of bankruptcy altogether.
Between $24,000-40,000	Between $6,000-10,000	If total disposable income is greater than 25% of claims, debtor fails means test and CHAPTER 7 is denied.
		If total disposable income is less than 25% of claims, debtor passes the means test and CHAPTER 7 is okay.
$40,000	$10,000	Passes means test, debtor is eligible for CHAPTER 7.

D. The Means Test's Narrow, Rebuttable Presumption

The Code is set up so that if the debtor's income, after calculating the means test, is above the prescribed thresholds (above $10,000, or above $6,000 and 25% of nonpriority unsecured claims), there is a **rebuttable presumption** of "abuse." Further, recall that "abuse" means the debtor is denied his or her discharge under CHAPTER 7, and the case can be converted to CHAPTER 13 or 11.

Thus there is a narrow exception that allows the debtor to rebut the presumption of abuse by showing "special circumstances." What are special circumstances? The Code gives as examples "a serious medical condition" or an "order to active duty in the Armed Forces," which decrease the debtor's disposable income under the means test below the prescribed threshold and "for which there is no reasonable alternative." 11 U.S.C. §707(b)(2)(B)(i).

This provision gives some discretion to bankruptcy judges. For example, a rural couple with $95,000 in annual income wanted to file CHAPTER 7, but their disposable income under the means test was initially about $315 per month.[10] (Remember, disposable income above $167 per month results in automatic failure of the means test, and anything over $100 per month could result in failing the means test if the 25% of debtor's nonpriority unsecured debts are less than $6,000.)

But what about our rural couple? Well, they commuted 40 miles and 70 miles, respectively, to work every day on country roads with lots of deer. So they claimed

---

[10]See *In re Batzkiel*, 349 B.R. 581 (Bankr. N.D. Iowa 2006).

an extra $219 per month in necessary expenses. Part of this they allocated for extra gas and extra replacement tires. Remarkably, a large portion was for the operating expenses associated with keeping a backup car ready for whenever either of them hit a deer with their regular car. When the regular car was in the auto shop, they would drive the backup car to work. They explained to the judge that they had hit three deer in 2006, and seven deer altogether in recent years. The judge agreed that these "special circumstances" warranted an increase in monthly expenses and rebutted the presumption of abuse. Serendipitously, the $219 in additional expenses changed the means test result, bringing the couple's disposable income down to $96 per month—just below the $100 threshold, giving them an automatic pass!

E. Two More Hurdles

Now assume a debtor passes the means test, or flunks the means test but then rebuts the presumption of "abuse." The debtor is home free, right? Well, almost, but not quite.

(1) Bad Faith

The court is required to consider whether the debtor filed for Chapter 7 in bad faith. This returns some of the Bankruptcy Court's traditional, equitable power to weed out bad apples. 11 U.S.C. §707(b)(3)(A).

(2) Totality of the Circumstances

The court must also consider whether the debtor's overall financial situation demonstrates abuse. 11 U.S.C. §707(b)(3)(B). Again, this restores some of the court's discretion and equitable power, although it seems redundant after the mechanical means test has been used to evaluate the debtor's entire financial situation.

F. Trying to Beat the Means Test

In reality, the Bad Faith and Totality of the Circumstances tests will rarely be used, now that the means test sets the general standard. So why do we bother with them? Because a debtor (or a debtor's attorney) who plans carefully before filing for bankruptcy can employ various strategies to beat the means test.

For instance, the debtor could take on more secured debt by buying a more expensive house or car. Suppose the debtor drives by a car lot with a big sign claiming "No Credit? No Problem," and buys a new BMW on the spot, three weeks before declaring bankruptcy. The new car loan would decrease the debtor's disposable income, because payments on secured debt get subtracted from the debtor's monthly income.

Another strategy for beating the means test is to take on more unsecured debt, simply by shopping with a credit card, in order to increase the 25% of nonpriority unsecured debt. Or let's say the debtor brashly stops making mortgage and car payments before declaring bankruptcy, because under the means test payments required to cure arrearages on secured debt get subtracted as necessary expenses, thereby lowering the debtor's disposable income. Notice that these incentives are all perverse.

More simply, suppose a debtor just quits her job, waits six months, and then declares bankruptcy? She would have zero current monthly income, and by definition would fall below the median family income. Or what if a debtor who has been unemployed for six months (and thus has zero current monthly income) declares bankruptcy right *before* starting a job that will pay $100,000 a year, which would provide enough disposable income to repay more than 25% of his general unsecured nonpriority debt?[11]

This is where the two Section 707(b)(3) tests kick in. These two hurdles give the court power to weed out debtors who try to game the system by taking advantage of the mechanical nature of the means test. So even though these additional mechanisms will likely be seldom used, they are not completely toothless.

G. Involuntary Bankruptcy

While in many countries around the world, bankruptcy is something that is forced upon a debtor, in the United States the vast majority of all bankruptcy cases filed are voluntary cases, instituted by the debtor. This is true of cases filed under all chapters of the Code.

If creditors wish to force a debtor into bankruptcy, it is generally required that there be three creditors[12] holding noncontingent, undisputed claims of at least $13,475 each. 11 U.S.C. §303(b)(1).

Further, under Section 303(b)(1), none of the petitioning creditors' claims can be the subject of a bona fide dispute. This is designed to keep people from throwing other people into bankruptcy just because the two parties have a disagreement about whether a debt is due, or how much is due.

Moreover, the court must find that the debtor is "generally not paying debts as they come due," a test that has proven elusive to pin down. 11 U.S.C. §303(i). Does it mean that the debtor is generally not paying most of its debts, 50% of its debts, or perhaps merely failing to pay the long-term debts? What if the debtor is paying all debts but one, but the one not being paid is 400 times the size of all the others?

If the creditors fail to meet this test, and the case is dismissed, the petitioning creditors are liable for all the debtor's damages, including loss of reputation and business, which can be quite substantial. On the other hand, creditors sometimes get frustrated with that system and decide to try the bankruptcy route. Involuntary bankruptcy works best for creditors who want information and think the debtor is hiding things. The bankruptcy case, if it sticks, will require the debtor to file all of the disclosures. Everything the debtor and the other creditors have done recently will come out into the open.

---

[11]See *In re Pak*, 343 B.R. 239 (Bankr. N.D. Cal. 2006).
[12]If the debtor has fewer than 12 total creditors — a test rarely met by any debtor — just one creditor who meets the dollar and other eligibility requirements can file the petition for involuntary bankruptcy.

SUMMARY

■ Debtors are required to make a tremendous number of disclosures on their way to the bankruptcy discharge. They essentially must disclose every one of their debts or potential debts, as well as everything they have, and everything they had or lost (even to gambling) during the past two years.

■ Some financial matters from longer than two years before the filing date must also be disclosed. Debtors also must disclose payments to creditors during certain periods, suits to which they have been a party, past spouses in some states — the list goes on.

■ The primary disclosure documents are called the schedule of assets and liabilities and the statement of financial affairs.

■ Since 2005, debtors also must pass a means test to determine if they are eligible for CHAPTER 7. If they theoretically have too much money left over at the end of the month, based on an odd and complex formula, they may be ineligible for CHAPTER 7 because they could theoretically afford to pay back a substantial portion of their debts in a CHAPTER 13 bankruptcy.

■ The goal of the means test is to see if a debtor has enough money at the end of the month, after deducting expenses from income, to repay a substantial portion of his or her debt.

■ If so, filing a CHAPTER 7, which does not involve a payment plan, would constitute an abuse of the bankruptcy system.

■ The actual means test, as set out in the Code, does not use real current income. It uses an average of *past* income and other money received to determine if the debtor can afford to pay creditors in the *future*. It also uses artificial expenses rather than real ones. The primary effect of the means test has been to discourage filing, because of the burdensome paperwork and calculations it requires.

■ All consumer debtors (with very limited exceptions) also must complete consumer credit counseling before they are eligible to file a personal bankruptcy case.

CONNECTIONS

The Discharge

Next up is the bankruptcy discharge and its exceptions, as well as grounds for denying a discharge. In other words, this chapter described how you file, and the next one describes what you get once you file.

Virtual Bankruptcy

In light of the cumbersome process and voluminous paperwork involved in filing a bankruptcy case, it may well be cheaper and easier to remain in virtual bankruptcy (a concept presented in Chapter 2), particularly if the debtor is judgment proof anyway (discussed in Chapter 1).

Negotiating with Creditors

Another alternative to filing for bankruptcy is to negotiate with creditors and try to work out a payment plan. Here, a debtor who has fallen behind on paying her bills can negotiate "in the shadow of the law" — with her right to declare bankruptcy looming in the background as an implicit threat if the creditors are unwilling to be reasonable.

Asking the Right Questions

An attorney preparing to file a bankruptcy petition on behalf of a client must ask the right questions so that all the paperwork is accurate. Otherwise, the client may lose his discharge for lack of good faith. This is particularly important when it comes to listing all the debtor's assets, which are easy to miss, because the debtor's estate is defined so broadly that it includes nearly all of the debtor's assets, tangible and intangible, and nearly all the debtor's future rights that have any monetary value.

The Discharge

11

Frequently the primary and often the only reason that a debtor files a bankruptcy petition is because he or she wants to be discharged from

OVERVIEW

debts. In most cases, the discharge is pretty much automatic. As you would suspect, though, it isn't that simple in all cases. There are exceptions to the dischargeability of debts. This chapter deals with debts that are not dischargeable, as well as some of the reasons to deny a debtor's entire discharge. These limitations on discharge, combined with the steps a debtor may take to voluntarily limit his or her discharge, narrow the benefits of a bankruptcy for some debtors. The ways in which a debtor voluntarily waives a portion of the discharge are described in the next chapter.

The bankruptcy discharge frees the debtor from the legal obligation to pay discharged debts and creditors are forever barred from collecting those discharged debts, because Section 524(a)(2) contains a permanent injunction against collection.

3. Objections to Discharge Based upon Fraud in the Fiduciary Capacity, Embezzlement, or Larceny
4. Forgetting or Simply Failing to List a Creditor on the Bankruptcy Paperwork
5. Domestic Support Obligations and Property Settlements
6. Intentional Torts and Debts Arising from Driving Under the Influence of Alcohol
7. Student Loans

C. OBJECTIONS TO THE DEBTOR'S GENERAL DISCHARGE

1. A Knowing and Fraudulent False Oath in or in Connection with a Bankruptcy Case
2. Inexplicable Loss of Money
3. Concealment, Loss, Destruction, Falsification, or Mutilation of Records, or a Failure to Keep Records
4. Transfers Made with Intent to Hinder, Delay, or Defraud Creditors
5. Prior Discharge Within the Past Eight Years

A. The Bankruptcy Discharge: The Reason for the Case

Now we are changing the subject from the anatomy of a CHAPTER 7 case to the discharge that CHAPTER 7 debtors enjoy. In so doing, we are moving from the highly technical into the most philosophical of bankruptcy subjects: the reason to grant a bankruptcy discharge in the first place.

(1) The Policy Behind Discharge for Individual Debtors

In *Local Loan v. Hunt*, 292 U.S. 234 (1934), the U.S. Supreme Court explained the policy behind this incredibly important aspect of bankruptcy law:

> One of the primary purposes of the bankruptcy act is to "relieve the honest debtor from the weight of oppressive indebtedness, and permit him to start afresh free from the obligations and responsibilities consequent upon business misfortunes." This purpose of the act has been again and again emphasized by the courts as being of public as well as private interest, in that it gives to the honest but unfortunate debtor . . . a new opportunity in life and a clear field for future effort, unhampered by the pressure and discouragement of preexisting debt.

Id. at 244. This policy is a uniquely American phenomenon. Note the emphasis in this landmark case on a "clear field for future effort." The theory is that American capitalism is best served by making sure that people are motivated to make money, and free to spend money and fuel the economy in the future.

Q: Doesn't the idea of a broad bankruptcy discharge encourage overspending and personal irresponsibility?

A: Some might say yes, but even if they're right, the economic benefits to society of encouraging more spending and fueling the economy might outweigh these concerns. There is also a powerful argument that when Americans overspend with credit cards, the last thing on their mind is a bankruptcy discharge (if they are even aware of the intricacies of bankruptcy law at all). Our financial literacy is so poor, and advertisers (particularly those in the consumer credit industry) use such effective psychological techniques, that we doubt that bankruptcy law can be blamed for Americans' overconsumption.

The discharge is handled differently in CHAPTER 7 than in CHAPTER 13. In a CHAPTER 7 case, the discharge happens more or less automatically, at the end of the case. This takes about 90 days from the date of the filing. The discharge is dependent upon the debtor surrendering all of his or her nonexempt property to the trustee, if there is any, and also being completely honest in the bankruptcy paperwork, among other things.

In a CHAPTER 13 case, as well as a CHAPTER 12, the debtor proposes a plan for repaying many of his or her debts over time. In most cases, at least some debts will remain unpaid after the payment plan is completed and those debts will be discharged after all the plan payments are made. The debtor does not, however, receive a discharge until the plan is complete. However, Section 1328(b) does allow a CHAPTER 13 debtor to obtain a discharge even without completing a plan, where the debtor has met with circumstances for which she should not be held accountable, has paid creditors at least as much as they would receive in a CHAPTER 7, and modification of the plan is not practicable. These facts could result in a CHAPTER 7-style discharge, but, if secured property was not yet paid for, could also result in loss of that property. 11 U.S.C. §1328(b).

(2) The Scope of the Discharge

Various bankruptcy provisions limit the scope of the debtor's discharge, all of which are discussed below and in later chapters.

(a) Only Pre-Petition Debts Are Discharged

For the most part, only debts that arose prior to the bankruptcy are discharged, as bankruptcy is only designed to clear up the debtor's pre-filing obligations. This makes sense. The debtor will list all of his or her pre-filing debts in the **schedules of assets and liabilities** and the **statement of affairs**. The creditors who are listed in this paperwork will receive notice of the bankruptcy case

Sidebar

WAITING FOR A DISCHARGE

In **pay out cases,** it takes at least several years to obtain a discharge (three to five years for a CHAPTER 13 case, and the time of the useful life of the collateral for a CHAPTER 11). If the plan is never finished, the payments are essentially lost—they are sunk costs that cannot be recovered. In a CHAPTER 11, most debts are discharged upon confirmation or approval of the plan, not upon completion of all plan payments. In the case of an individual debtor, the debtor does not receive a CHAPTER 11 discharge until the plan payments are completed, much like a CHAPTER 13 or CHAPTER 12 discharge.

and thus are provided due process in the case. The debtor is expected to pay any debts that arise after the filing, just like a person who is not in bankruptcy. Naturally, these post-petition creditors will not be listed on the bankruptcy paperwork and will not receive notice of the case.

For instance, assume that a debtor files a CHAPTER 7 case in the morning and in the afternoon takes out a new car loan. Will the new car loan be discharged? Absolutely not. The auto lender will probably have a security interest on it that will allow the creditor to take the car back if the payments are not made. Moreover, the debtor will owe the entire debt, not just the secured part, because the car was purchased after the filing. This is a post-filing debt, for which the debtor is liable and upon which the filing has no impact whatsoever.

The rule that a bankruptcy discharge applies only to pre-petition claims is modified slightly in CHAPTER 13 and CHAPTER 11 cases. As a result, some post-petition debts are sometimes included in the discharge in these other types of cases. In a CHAPTER 11 case, the confirmation order discharges all pre-confirmation debts, some of which will be incurred during the case. See 11 U.S.C. §1141(d). In a CHAPTER 13 case, all debts dealt with in the plan are discharged. While most of those are pre-bankruptcy claims, it is possible that some will be from the post-petition period. See 11 U.S.C. §1305.

(b) Only Claims Are Discharged

To be discharged, a debt must have risen to the legal level of a **claim**, as that word is described in Section 101(5). The definition of a claim is broad, however, and most things that you might think are not yet claims, and should not be listed on the bankruptcy paperwork, probably are claims. Thus, as we discussed in Chapter 7 of this book, most of these things can be discharged in bankruptcy.

For example, if the debtor was in a car accident and it is not even clear whose fault it was, and no suit has been filed, the debtor should list the other party to the accident in his or her bankruptcy schedules. If it turns out, long after the bankruptcy case is over, that the debtor is liable for the accident in a negligence suit, the debt would be discharged in the bankruptcy even if the debt was never liquidated, as long as the potential creditor was listed on the bankruptcy paperwork, and as long as there was no distribution in the case. The timing of this situation confuses students, who often disbelieve that this debt would be discharged. It would be discharged, however, given the broad definition of claim found in Section 101(5).

Drawing by Kevin Dilg.

(c) Not All Debtors Get a Discharge

In addition, as you'll see in greater detail shortly, some individual debtors are not entitled to a discharge at all. Thinking back to *Local Loan v. Hunt*, remember that bankruptcy discharges are for honest but unfortunate debtors. The right to a discharge comes with obligations on the part of the debtor: to be honest in the case, to turn over nonexempt assets rather than trying to hide them, and to disclose absolutely everything that the bankruptcy paperwork requires. These obligations are not to be taken lightly. Failure to comply will result in denial of the entire discharge.

Corporations, partnerships, and limited liability companies do not get a discharge in CHAPTER 7. Thinking back once again to *Local Loan v. Hunt*, individual debtors (meaning people) need a discharge to continue their lives, unhampered by past debt and hopefully in better financial health in the future. Artificial or legal entities, such as corporations, partnerships, and limited liability companies do not need a discharge in a CHAPTER 7. They can just disappear. They do not have lives to continue into the future and can instead just be dissolved. Thus, in outlining all of the reasons why a debtor might be denied a general CHAPTER 7 discharge, Section 727(a)(1) provides that the debtor shall not obtain a discharge if "the debtor is not an individual."

> **S i d e b a r**
>
> **DENIAL OF DISCHARGE**
>
> Hiding assets and lying in the case are obvious reasons to deny a debtor a discharge, but a discharge can also be denied for less obvious behavior, such as making a fraudulent transfer right before the case, not keeping records, or losing money without explanation.

(d) Some Debts Are Not Entitled to Discharge

A debtor can receive a general discharge, but still be left with some debts after the bankruptcy. Some of these debts are excluded from discharge because society has decided these are the types of debts that people should be obligated to pay no matter what. See 11 U.S.C. §523(a). Nondischargeable debts include alimony and child support, debts for some taxes, debts from criminal restitution claims, debts arising while driving under the influence of alcohol or drugs, and student loans. Likewise, debts incurred by fraud, debts for luxury goods purchased within 90 days of the filing, certain property settlement debts owed to spouses, debts neither listed nor scheduled in the bankruptcy paperwork, debts for fraud or defalcation while acting in a fiduciary capacity, and debts arising from embezzlement or larceny are all nondischargeable. Moreover, these types of debts are not discharged under CHAPTER 7, CHAPTER 13, CHAPTER 12, or CHAPTER 11.

For cash advances and credit card charges incurred shortly before filing for bankruptcy, as described in Section 523(a)(2)(C), there is a presumption that such debts are nondischargeable on the basis of fraud, but the presumption can be rebutted. The idea is that it's not right to rack up a lot of credit card charges and then declare bankruptcy to get rid of them.

In addition, under Section 524(c), a debtor can choose to waive his or her discharge of a particular debt by reaffirming that debt. **Reaffirmation** involves promising to pay back a debt that would otherwise be discharged in bankruptcy through a formal court-supervised process. Both secured and unsecured debts can be reaffirmed, though it is usually not advisable to reaffirm unsecured debts. In some jurisdictions, even secured debts should not be reaffirmed, as we will discuss further in Chapter 13 of this book.

Finally, the debtor can simply choose to voluntarily repay any debt that would otherwise be discharged in bankruptcy, without entering the formal reaffirmation process. See 11 U.S.C. §524(f). This is not unfair preferential treatment, and is not frowned upon in the Code. In many situations, it is preferable to formal reaffirmation.

> ## F   A   Q
>
> **Q: Why would a debtor pay debts that he or she is not legally required to pay?**
>
> A: He or she may want to make good on a promise or to keep property that is subject to a security interest.

B. Debts that Are Not Discharged Under Section 523(a)

The Bankruptcy Code is policy-driven law. As discussed in the prior chapter, the Code gives debtors a "fresh start" through a broad discharge of various debts and obligations. Section 523 contains exceptions to the discharge, based on countervailing policy considerations designed to protect the interests of certain creditors. While the bulk of the Code gives the debtor an opportunity to erase or discharge most debts, Section 523 contains the exceptions. While this section lists almost 20 categories of specific debts that are nondischargeable, we discuss only the most common exceptions here.

Try not to confuse the issue discussed here (**nondischargeability**, and the exceptions to discharge for particular debts), with **objections to the debtor's general discharge**, a phrase that refers to the process of objecting to a debtor's entire bankruptcy discharge, which is the subject of the second part of this chapter.

In order for many of these debts to be found nondischargeable, the creditor must institute an adversary proceeding and get the court to order the debt nondischargeable. This is true in all situations in which the chart below says the creditor must *object*. Remember that an adversary proceeding is a separate lawsuit within the bankruptcy case.

(1) Taxes

Sections 523(a)(1)(A)-(C) makes virtually all taxes that are entitled to priority under Section 507(a) nondischargeable. This is true under all chapters and cases filed under the Bankruptcy Code. The key to determining whether taxes are entitled to priority and are thus nondischargeable is determining what type of taxes they are and when a return was due for them.

Since all priority taxes are nondischargeable in a CHAPTER 7 case, a debtor with major recent tax problems will rarely gain much relief in a CHAPTER 7. While the same taxes are also nondischargeable in a CHAPTER 13 case, CHAPTER 13 provides important tax relief because taxes can be satisfied over the life of the plan. Further, once a CHAPTER 13 case is filed, taxes stop accruing interest, which can be a powerful incentive to file a CHAPTER 13. Taxes also are not entitled to present value interest in a CHAPTER 13 case.

In a CHAPTER 7 case, if the debtor's taxes are large and recent, filing a bankruptcy case will provide little help. Similarly, if a debtor wants to file a CHAPTER 7 because he or she is behind on the mortgage, the case won't accomplish much.

Nondischargeable Debts		
Category of Debt	Code Section	Which Party Claims Exception?
Taxes	523(a)(1)(A)-(C)	Automatic
Fraud — actual	523(a)(2)(A)	Creditor must object and prove the elements of fraud
Fraud — false financial statement	523(a)(2)(B)	Creditor must object and prove three elements
Fraud — presumption for charging luxury goods or taking cash advances	523(a)(2)(C)	Creditor must object, debtor may overcome presumption
Fraud in fiduciary capacity, embezzlement, or larceny	523(a)(4)	Creditor must object and prove the elements
Debts neither listed nor scheduled	523(a)(3)	Automatic
Domestic support obligations and property settlements	523(a)(5) and (15)	Automatic
Intentional torts	523(a)(6) and (9)	Creditor must object and prove the elements
Student loans	523(a)(8)	Debtor must request and prove undue hardship exception

(2) Objections to Discharge Based upon Fraud

Under Section 523(a)(2), a debtor who obtains credit through fraudulent means is not permitted to discharge the resulting debt. The goals of Congress in drafting the three fraud-based exceptions to discharge include protecting the defrauded creditor and not rewarding fraudulent behavior on the part of the debtor.

(a) Actual Fraud

Section 523(a)(2)(A) makes debts obtained through actual fraud nondischargeable. Actual fraud is proven by establishing the elements of common law fraud, which requires the objecting creditor to prove actual intent to defraud. One example of such a test for actual fraud requires that the objecting creditor prove these six elements: (1) the debtor made a representation; (2) the representation was false; (3) the debtor knew it was false at the time it was made; (4) the representation was made with the intent to deceive the creditor; (5) the creditor actually and justifiably relied upon the representation; and (6) the creditor sustained a loss or was damaged as a proximate result of the false representation. See *Fowler Bros. v. Young (In re Young)*, 91 F.3d 1367, 1373 (10th Cir. 1996). This exception to the dischargeability of debts is known as the actual fraud exception to discharge.

(b) Fraud Based upon the Use of a False Financial Statement

Section 523(a)(2)(B) makes debts obtained through the use of a false financial statement nondischargeable. You might wonder why a situation like that would require its own separate test, as this still sounds like fraud and could be covered under the provisions of Section 523(a)(2)(A) discussed above. The reason for this separate provision is that debtors fill out financial statements to get loans all the time, and in some cases, the creditors help them fill out the forms. The debtors do not always understand the forms and the creditors do not always rely on the information contained in them. To deal with these special cases, Congress came up with a different rule.

To establish nondischargeability under this subsection, there must be a writing pertaining to the debtor's financial condition and the writing must be materially false, meaning the document must not only be erroneous, but must also be substantially inaccurate. In essence, the false information must bear upon an "important or substantial truth." *First Interstate Bank v. Greene*, 96 B.R. 279, 283 (B.A.P. 9th Cir. 1989). Finally, and perhaps most important, the creditor must rely on the false or inaccurate information to its detriment. Thus there are three essential elements to this exception to discharge: (1) there must be a writing pertaining to the debtor's financial condition; (2) the writing must contain a *material* misrepresentation; and (3) the creditor must rely on the misrepresentation in the writing to its detriment.

(c) A Presumption of Fraud for Charging Luxury Goods or Taking Cash Advances

Section 523(a)(2)(C) states that debt incurred within 90 days of the bankruptcy filing to buy luxury goods or services under an open-ended plan (which includes a credit card) is presumed to be nondischargeable on the basis of fraud. This is sometimes called the **presumptive fraud** section. The theory behind this fraud-based objection to discharge is that a debtor who goes out and loads up on luxury goods right before filing for bankruptcy was or should have been aware of his or her dire financial condition, and probably had no intention of paying back the debt. As a result, the debtor should be required to pay the debt back after the bankruptcy is completed.

The phrase "luxury goods or services" is not defined in the Bankruptcy Code but basically means goods not necessary to support the debtor or the debtor's dependents. As you can well imagine, interpreting this phrase involves much discretion on the part of the judge. Is a computer a luxury good? Does it depend on what you do for a living? How about food, or a vasectomy? What about a new suit or underwear?

Section 523(a)(2)(C) also presumes that all cash advances aggregating more than $825 from a single creditor within the 70 days prior to a bankruptcy filing are nondischargeable on the basis of fraud, under the same logic: The debtor took the cash with full knowledge of his or her financial condition and with no intention of paying the debt back. Note that balance transfers (meaning transfers from one credit card to another), which credit card companies sometimes characterize as cash advances in their own bookkeeping, do not constitute cash advances for the purposes of this section.

An important limitation on this objection to discharge is that no creditor can object under this section unless it is owed more than $550 total "for luxury goods or services" or $825 for cash advances. Thus, if the debtor charges $450 for a Coach bag during the 90 days prior to her bankruptcy filing, and then gets a cash advance from a different creditor of $400 to pay her mortgage, either creditor could rely on the *actual fraud* exception (the one discussed earlier), but neither could use this *presumptive fraud* section, because neither creditor is owed enough for luxury goods or services.

On the other hand, if the debtor charges $400 to his or her MasterCard for designer jeans, and then charges another $440 to the same card for jewelry, Master-Card could rely on the luxury goods exception. Remember also that the debtor can rebut the presumption of fraud under this section, by proving that he or she did not contemplate bankruptcy at the time of the charges, or by proving that the goods are not luxury goods.

(3) Objections to Discharge Based upon Fraud in the Fiduciary Capacity, Embezzlement, or Larceny

Section 523(a)(4) augments 523(a)(2)(A) by not discharging debts incurred "for fraud or defalcation while acting in a fiduciary capacity, embezzlement, or larceny." The fraud referred to in this section is different from that covered in Section 523(a). It deals not with garden-variety actual fraud or the debtor's purchases of luxury goods or services, but instead with fraud within a fiduciary relationship. It makes nondischargeable debts arising from fraud in the context of a unique position of trust and power. Another debt not discharged in bankruptcy is one resulting from larceny.

(4) Forgetting or Simply Failing to List a Creditor on the Bankruptcy Paperwork

Just as Section 523 seeks to prevent debtors who commit fraud from reaping the benefits of a fresh start, on the other side of the coin the section also seeks to protect creditors that don't receive notice. Specifically, the debtor's bankruptcy petition and accompanying documents, and the notices that are sent based upon the information contained in these documents, are designed to put all creditors on notice that a bankruptcy has been filed. This notice serves many practical purposes, as well as satisfying the notice required by the Constitution of the United States.

Practically speaking, the notice tells creditors who receive it to stop all collection activity pursuant to Section 362(a), informs them to file a proof of claim if there are assets to distribute in the case, and informs them of the deadline to object to the dischargeability of their debt or to the debtor's entire discharge. By providing these deadlines and this general notice of the case, the creditor also receives the procedural due process required by the Constitution when a person's property (or their right to recover their debt) is taken away (a "taking" under the Fifth Amendment).

Unlike the actual fraud exception, there is no mental intent requirement under Section 523(a)(3). Whether the debtor purposely sought to leave a creditor off his or her schedules or whether the

Sidebar

LIST IT OR LOSE IT

Win or lose, object or not, the creditor has received all the due process necessary by law if it has been listed on the petition and has received notice of the debtor's bankruptcy filing. On the other hand, Section 523(a)(3) provides that debts that are not listed on the schedules of assets and liabilities ("neither listed nor scheduled," in the words of the statute) are not dischargeable. The practical result of such an omission is that the unlisted debt will not be discharged by the bankruptcy.

debtor just forgot, if the creditor and the debt are not on the schedules, that debt will not be discharged—it's like a form of strict liability. One way a debtor can get around this requirement is by proving the creditor had notice or actual knowledge of the bankruptcy case and, with this knowledge, could have filed a proof of claim. Another way is to prove that the case was a no-asset case, and that the lack of notice was harmless error. But it is unclear whether either of these arguments will prevail after the new notice requirements of the 2005 amendments.

(5) Domestic Support Obligations and Property Settlements

Domestic support obligations flowing from a divorce are defined in the Bankruptcy Code as any debt that accrues before, on, or after the filing of the bankruptcy petition, including interest due under non-bankruptcy law, owed to a spouse, former spouse, child of the debtor, or such child's parent, legal guardian, or responsible relative. Some of these terms remain undefined in the Code, but the clear intent of Congress is to broaden the possible holders of domestic support obligations, to include non-married parents of a child of the debtor, as well as various responsible persons and legal guardians.

Debts that fall into the category of a domestic support obligation *are not* dischargeable in a bankruptcy of any kind. 11 U.S.C. §523(a)(5). Domestic support obligations covered include those for alimony, maintenance, and child support, as established in a divorce decree, a separation agreement, a property settlement agreement, or a court order. The claims covered by the definition include child support owed to governmental entities, because in many states child support is paid through the state attorney general's office. 11 U.S.C. §101(14A).

The 2005 amendments made property settlement obligations arising out of a marital settlement agreement nondischargeable as well.[1]

FAMILY LAW AND BANKRUPTCY: A TRAP FOR THE UNWARY

The new Code creates a huge pitfall for family law attorneys. Most marital settlement agreements split the debts between the parties. Agreeing to pay a debt in such an agreement is part of a property settlement, and property settlements are now nondischargeable. Thus the person making that promise will be stuck with those debts, post-bankruptcy, even if they are just credit card debts. Thus, if bankruptcy is contemplated, it is best to not split the debts in the marital settlement agreement.

(6) Intentional Torts and Debts Arising from Driving Under the Influence of Alcohol

Debts for intentional torts, such as battery, assault, and so forth, as well as debts for judgments resulting from driving while under the influence of alcohol, are nondischargeable. See Sections 523(a)(6) and (9). These sections are expressions by Congress that a debtor will not be excused from liability for behavior, whether intentional or not, that society abhors.

---

[1]The distinction between support and property settlements is important in determining which state court actions are stayed by a bankruptcy filing. Actions to determine or collect alimony, maintenance, or support are not stayed at all under Section 362(b). Actions to either establish or collect a domestic support obligation *are* stayed. Practically speaking, if you are not sure you are talking about support, it is safest to request relief from the automatic stay before proceeding against the debtor in state court.

(7) Student Loans

Student loan obligations are nondischargeable except in rare situations. Although a student loan is a general unsecured debt, Congress made student loans non-dischargeable based on the fear that students would receive the benefit of an education and then file for bankruptcy to erase their student loans. This exception to the discharge is designed to ensure that more funds will be available to educate future generations of students, on the theory that current students are essentially repaying their loans into a fund for the future.

While generally disallowing the discharge of student loans, Congress also recognized that in some situations it might be necessary to allow student loans to be discharged. Section 523(a)(8) provides that student loans may be discharged if the debtor has suffered undue hardship. Unfortunately, the Bankruptcy Code does not define undue hardship, so courts have developed different interpretations of the undue hardship test. Thus the Second Circuit's test requires that the debtor prove three things: (1) that the student cannot meet her current expenses; (2) that this financial condition is likely to endure; and (3) that the student has made an effort to pay back the loan in issue. *Brunner v. New York State Higher Education Services Corp.*, 831 F.2d 395 (2d Cir. 1987). However, other courts have developed longer, more complex tests. See *In re D'Ettore*, 106 B.R. 715 (Bankr. M.D. Fla. 1989). Indicia of undue hardship include very serious permanent disabilities, inability to find work, and other permanent problems. The test is extremely difficult to meet in most districts, which is what Congress intended.

Unlike most objections to the dischargeability of a debt, which are instituted by creditors, the debtor requests that the student loans be discharged by way of filing a complaint in an adversary proceeding. Thus the debtor has the burden of proving that he or she meets the undue hardship standard, whereas normally the creditor has the burden of proving that the debt is nondischargeable.

C. Objections to the Debtor's General Discharge

Like Section 523(a), Section 727 is used to impair the debtor's discharge. Compared to the limited objections reviewed in the first half of this chapter, which pertain to objections to the dischargeability of just one debt, the rest of this chapter discusses a far greater threat to the debtor's entire bankruptcy case, namely objections to the debtor's *general discharge*.

While some of the Section 523 objections are for bad deeds, such as fraud or intentional torts, many simply protect debts that we as a society want to protect. No bad deed is required. By comparison, Section 727 almost always requires a very bad act, such as hiding assets, lying in the bankruptcy case, or destroying business records.

Because it is easy to confuse the two sections, we call objections to the discharge of a particular debt **objections to dischargeability**, and call objections to the general discharge **objections to discharge**. If an objection to discharge is successful, *none* of the debtor's debts get discharged. From the debtor's standpoint, the entire case is a waste. Indeed, the debtor will be worse off because all of the debtor's nonexempt property will be gone and the debtor will still owe all of the debts that weren't paid by the trustee.

Section 727(a) contains more than ten grounds for denying a general discharge, of which we will discuss only the five most common grounds.

(1) A Knowing and Fraudulent False Oath in or in Connection with a Bankruptcy Case

Section 727(a)(4) contains one of the commonly used objections to discharge. Under this section, a discharge can be denied if a debtor makes a "knowing and fraudulent false oath in or in connection with the case." The creditor objecting to discharge must prove that the false oath was made in the case, not prior to the case or in some other capacity. This objection goes to the very heart of the honesty and disclosure requirements. The false oath requirement refers to a statement made under oath, most commonly either in the written bankruptcy disclosure documents (the petition, the statement of affairs, or the schedules of assets and liabilities), or at the creditors' meeting or another bankruptcy court hearing or deposition.

The statement must be false, of course, and the debtor must make it knowing that it is false. The additional requirement that the oath be fraudulent essentially imposes a materiality requirement. Thus the creditor must prove that the debtor made (1) a false oath, (2) knowingly, (3) that is material enough to be fraudulent, and (4) that was made in, or in connection with, the case.

(2) Inexplicable Loss of Money

Another ground for denial of a discharge is that the debtor has failed to explain satisfactorily a "loss of assets or deficiency of assets to meet the debtor's liabilities." See 11 U.S.C. §727(a)(5). In essence, this means that the debtor has failed to explain what happened to income or property that he or she had before the financial trouble began. In one case, where $90,000 went missing, the debtor claimed to have spent it on "wine, women, and song." *In re Bahre*, 23 B.R. 460 (Bankr. D. Conn. 1982).

In another case, a person simply lost $20,000. Though he was a big spender and said he carried huge amounts of cash, the court found denial of a discharge justified, given that he had no explanation for where the $20,000 went. *In re Reed*, 700 F.2d 986 (5th Cir. 1983).

(3) Concealment, Loss, Destruction, Falsification, or Mutilation of Records, or a Failure to Keep Records

Section 727(a)(3) makes it grounds for denial of a general discharge to destroy, mutilate, conceal, falsify, or even lose financial records.

F   A   Q

Q: It is easy to see why a bankruptcy debtor cannot receive a discharge if he or she destroys or hides records. But why should people be punished for merely losing their records?

A: The justification for this rule is that every bankruptcy trustee has a right to examine the financial records of his or her debtor, which can only be done if these records are kept and available. There is also a suspicion that if people do not safeguard these records, for whatever reason, they may be trying to hide something.

In one infamous case, a debtor who lacked candor in the court's eyes claimed that the rubbish man must have taken all his business records, which he was storing in the garage near his trashcan. *In re Harron*, 31 B.R. 466 (Bankr. D. Conn. 1983).

Section 727(a)(3) also provides that a failure to *keep* records can be a ground for denying a discharge. A court is most likely to deny a discharge based upon a failure to keep records when there is evidence that the failure was intentional and in contemplation of bankruptcy. Courts have held that the record-keeping requirement essentially applies only to business people, and not to the average consumer. The Code itself does not say this but courts have interpreted the section in this way, perhaps in recognition that average people are not always organized.

(4) Transfers Made with Intent to Hinder, Delay, or Defraud Creditors

In the state law chapters of this book, you learned that people are not necessarily free to transfer (or give away) their assets, particularly if doing so will make them insolvent or if they are giving away assets in order to avoid creditor claims. You learned that a transfer could be a fraudulent transfer and could be avoidable or reversible if the debtor intended to hinder, delay, or defraud creditors, or even if there was no such intent but the debtor transferred an asset to another person for less than equivalent or fair value. Outright gifts can be undone in this way, as can sales for less than the market value of the item sold.

Fraudulent transfer law stands in odd juxtaposition with another area of debtor-creditor law, namely **pre-bankruptcy planning**. Pre-bankruptcy planning is the process by which a person who is contemplating bankruptcy determines whether he or she is holding assets in a way that takes best advantage of the exemptions allowed under the Bankruptcy Code. For example, let's say that Amara lives in Iowa, where she is allowed (both inside and outside bankruptcy) to exempt all the equity or value in a home of any value. Iowa does not allow a person to keep any cash from the reach of creditors, however, and Amara has a bank account with $30,000 in it. Amara decides to use the $30,000 in cash to pay down her home mortgage. Now the $30,000 has been converted to home equity, which is exempt. One result of this transaction is that the debtor does not lose the $30,000. The other result is that creditors do not get the $30,000 in her later bankruptcy. On its face, this example seems to be a clear fraudulent transfer, since Amara obviously had the actual intent to deprive her creditors of the $30,000. Confusingly, the legislative history of the Bankruptcy Code seems to allow a reasonable amount of pre-bankruptcy planning. In fact, the legislative history says: "As under current law, the debtor will be permitted to convert nonexempt property into exempt property before filing a bankruptcy petition. The practice is not fraudulent as to creditors, and permits the debtor to make full use of the exemptions to which he is entitled under the law." H.R. Rep. No. 595, 95th Cong., 1st Sess. 361 (1977). Some courts have found, however, that the phrase "as under current law," means that if the debtor intends to hinder, delay, or defraud creditors through the transfer, the transfer can be undone despite this language in the legislative history.

In addition to these conflicting signals in these two related areas of the law, a third area of the law makes pre-bankruptcy planning, or at least pre-bankruptcy fraudulent transfers, a ground for denial of a global discharge. Section 727(a)(2) states that a debtor can be denied a general discharge if he or she transfers property of the estate, within a year prior to the filing or after the filing, "with intent to hinder, delay or defraud a creditor or officer of the court." This is a very serious punishment. Having a transfer reversed or avoided is one thing. Losing one's entire bankruptcy discharge is quite another. Some courts continue to hold that pre-bankruptcy planning is acceptable if it is within reason, while others deny an entire bankruptcy discharge for relatively small transfers done in the spirit of pre-bank-ruptcy planning.

Some scholars suggest that what matters most is the size of the transfer, giving rise to the saying, "when a pig becomes a hog, it must be slaughtered."

For example, in one case, the court denied a discharge for transfers of $700,000 made by a doctor who admitted that he transferred the assets to keep them from creditors (*In re Tveten*, 848 F.2d 871 (8th Cir. 1988)). The same court let the discharge go through for a farmer who transferred $31,000 for essentially the same reasons (*In re Hanson*, 848 F.2d 866 (8th Cir. 1988)). Yet another doctor was allowed his discharge after transferring $400,000 (*In re Johnson*, 880 F.2d 78 (8th Cir. 1989)). These cases highlight the uncertainty about how much pre-bankruptcy planning a debtor can get away with.

(5) Prior Discharge Within the Past Eight Years

You'll often hear people say that you can only file for bankruptcy once every seven years. Actually, under the biblical sabbatical or jubilation, one could discharge one's debts once every seven years. But after the 2005 amendments, the new Code provides one discharge every eight years, even less often than in biblical times! However, one can *file* for bankruptcy as often as one likes, but if the filer received a discharge during the prior eight years, the filer cannot receive another one. Since the discharge is usually the purpose of the case, the common lore is more or less true.

The eight-year bar to a discharge is the *only* ground for denial of a global dis-charge that does not involve a bad deed. There are no lies, no hidden assets, no evil intentions required. Congress decided that bankruptcy was something one could only avail oneself of once in a while.

The eight-year rule has an interesting effect. Some lenders, especially used car dealers and small high-interest lenders, jump at the chance to lend to someone who has just filed a bankruptcy petition because they know the debtor cannot get another discharge for eight years.

SUMMARY

■ The whole point of filing a bankruptcy case for most debtors is to get a discharge of past debts. Under bankruptcy policy and theory, honest debtors are entitled to this relief.

■ Some kinds of debts do not get discharged in any type of bankruptcy case. Some of these debts are not discharged because the person owed the money is considered particularly worthy of repayment no matter what. Examples include domestic support obligations, some taxes, and student loans.

■ Debts not listed on the debtor's bankruptcy schedules do not get discharged for due process reasons. Creditors not listed will not receive notice of the case or the discharge of their claims, and cannot have their claims discharged without notice.

■ Other categories of debt do not get discharged because of bad acts by the debtor *prior* to filing the case, acts which led to the debt. Examples include debts incurred through actual fraud and presumptive fraud (for credit card debts incurred for luxuries during the 90 days prior to the filing and cash advances incurred during the 80 days prior to the filing), and debts resulting from intentional torts committed by the debtor.

■ Sometimes, in addition to these individual debts not getting discharges, a debtor can have his or her entire discharge denied (no debts get discharged). This typically happens because the debtor committed a bad act *during* the bankruptcy, such as hiding assets, lying in a creditors' meeting, or knowingly falsifying some of the bankruptcy disclosure documents. The entire discharge also can be denied for transferring assets with intent to hinder, delay, or defraud the creditors, during the year *prior* to the bankruptcy case.

■ The whole discharge, also called the **global discharge**, also will be denied if the debtor already obtained a bankruptcy discharge during the past eight years.

CONNECTIONS

Income and Property Taxes

Remember that only the taxes listed in Section 507(a)(8) are nondischargeable. This means that there are time limits on the dischargeability of some taxes, such as income taxes and property taxes. See Chapter 7 of this book for more details.

The Automatic Stay

Sometimes a person might file bankruptcy to get the benefit of the automatic stay rather than a discharge. If the automatic stay is the purpose, bankruptcy can be used as a strategic move more frequently than once every eight years. Some companies, particularly in very cyclical industries like oil and gas, have been know to file bankruptcy for this reason, just to make it through a downturn in the business cycle or a seasonal shift in gas prices caused by an unusually warm winter.

To File or Not to File

Chapters 3 through 10 describe the benefits and the nuts and bolts of bankruptcy. Without reading this chapter, one could easily get the impression that in most bankruptcies, the debtor walks away without a care in the world, with most or all debts discharged. This chapter explains the instances in which this is not the case because the discharge is either limited or denied. The fact that domestic support obligations, certain taxes, student loans, and debts incurred through fraud are not dischargeable, and that the debtor can lose the entire discharge for wrong-doing or filing within the past eight years, shows the rewards and punishments in the system. It is particularly important to keep these rules in mind when an attorney takes a step back to decide whether a client will benefit from a bankruptcy case or not.

Fraudulent Transfers

Under the avoiding powers described in Chapter 9, fraudulent transfers can be unwound by the trustee. However, transfers made with intent to hinder, delay, or defraud creditors can also lead to a successful objection to the debtor's entire discharge. If an attorney knows her client has intentionally made a fraudulent transfer, it may be best not to declare bankruptcy at all, and perhaps negotiate directly with creditors.

Keeping Secured Property in a CHAPTER 7 Case

12

As we discussed earlier, CHAPTER 7 rarely cures problems flowing from drastically past-due payments to secured creditors. CHAPTER 13 offers

much better options for dealing with past-due secured debt on property that the debtor would like to keep.

In a CHAPTER 7 case, however, the debtor does have at least two and in some cases three options for keeping property that is subject to a security interest: (1) redemption — basically paying the value of the property in cash to the secured party and thus extinguishing the security interest; (2) reaffirmation — essentially agreeing to honor the original loan agreement and pay off the whole loan as promised, including interest and penalties that are due, despite the bankruptcy;[1] and (3) simply keeping the payments current without agreeing to the original loan provisions — called "ride through," "keep and pay," or "the fourth option."[2] The first two options are specifically allowed in the Code and the third is court-created. Some jurisdictions allow only the first two options. Moreover, the Bankruptcy Reform Act specifically eliminates "ride through" for *personal property collateral*, as explained in this chapter. These options limit the effect of the debtor's discharge through the debtor's own choice.

---

[1]Reaffirmation allows the debtor and the creditor to work out new terms if they choose, but most creditors simply ask the debtor to sign the prior loan agreement again.

[2]It is actually called the *fourth*, not the *third*, option, because another option for dealing with secured debt is to give back the collateral. Since that is the third option (one we would not highlight in a discussion of how to keep the collateral), keeping the payments current and *not* signing a reaffirmation agreement is called the *fourth option*.

A. REDEMPTION

B. REAFFIRMATION: WHEN IS IT NECESSARY OR ADVISABLE?
1. General Principles of Reaffirmation
2. The Formal Requirements of Reaffirmation
3. "Ride Through" or "Keep and Pay"

A. Redemption

The first option we'll discuss is redemption. The name of this remedy has religious connotations and sounds so cleansing, but actually, all **redemption** means is that if the debtor has cash, the debtor can buy the secured property out from under the security interest for the lesser of the loan amount or the value of the property. This option is available to the debtor for any property used for personal, family, or household purposes. The debtor must pay the redemption price in cash up front, however, this is a virtual impossibility for most cash-starved debtors.

The big benefit, if the debtor can come up with the cash, is being able to buy the property at a discount because it has depreciated. Needless to say, redemption is most helpful when the value of the property is far less than the loan amount. Redemption allows the debtor to buy depreciated property at a deep discount as compared to what he or she would otherwise pay over time to keep the property. If the property has not depreciated and the loan amount is lower than the value of the property, redemption makes no economic sense. If the redeemed property is worth less than the claim amount, the rest of the secured party's claim becomes an unsecured claim, which is entitled to an unsecured distribution if there is one.

Sidebar

LOANS TO BANKRUPTS

There are now loan companies that specialize in making redemption loans to bankruptcy debtors, often at 25%-30% interest. Even at those rates, if the collateral value is low enough, this could be cheaper than reaffirming or retaining the collateral.

B. Reaffirmation: When Is It Necessary or Advisable?

Reaffirmation is another option for keeping collateral that is subject to a security interest. Just so you know, unsecured debts can be reaffirmed as well, although this is seldom a good idea.

(1) General Principles of Reaffirmation

Reaffirmation is a process by which the debtor agrees to pay a loan or debt, rather than having it discharged in his or her bankruptcy case. In essence, it is a voluntary waiver of the discharge of a particular debt. At its most basic, a **reaffirmation**

agreement is an agreement between the debtor and the creditor that a debt that otherwise would be discharged will be repaid. The agreement can contain new terms of repayment but most simply restate the original loan terms and ask the debtor to agree to pay as originally agreed, with all interest, fees, due dates, and so on.

(2) The Formal Requirements of Reaffirmation

Section 524(d) contains the rules for reaffirmation, which require that reaffirmation occur prior to the discharge in the case, that a written reaffirmation agreement be filed with the court, that the debtor's attorney certify that the reaffirmation will not impose an undue hardship on the debtor, that the agreement state clearly that reaffirmation is not required and is voluntary on the part of the debtor, and also that the debtor be given 60 days to revoke the reaffirmation agreement. These rules are stringent because in the past some creditors have abused the reaffirmation process by trying to cajole the debtor into reaffirming, and by trying to achieve reaffirmation without the court's knowledge or blessing.

The requirement that a debtor who is represented by counsel have counsel certify that the reaffirmation does not impose an undue hardship on the debtor is designed to make lawyers think twice before seeking reaffirmation on behalf of a client. Any reaffirmation will impair the fresh start and it is a big deal to sign a certification making this statement. This is particularly true if the debt being reaffirmed is unsecured. In cases in which an attorney does not represent the debtor, the court itself sets a hearing to decide whether to approve the agreement. The agreement will be approved *only if* the court finds that the agreement will not be an undue hardship for the debtor and also finds it to be in the debtor's best interest to sign the agreement.

Section 524(k), (l), and (m) now contain a tremendous number of conditions for reaffirmation. The creditor seeking to have his or her debts reaffirmed must now give long "truth-in-lending" type disclosures to the debtor before procuring the reaffirmation agreement. However, like most fine print, these are not likely to be read and thus will not likely curb abuses.

Sidebar

ABUSE BREEDS SKEPTICISM AMONG JUDGES

Why do judges dislike reaffirmation? Isn't it the debtor's choice? Well, creditors have abused the reaffirmation process, creating the perception that many consumers have reaffirmed their debts without wanting to or without understanding the ramifications. Reaffirmation also chips away at the benefits of a full bankruptcy discharge and a fresh start.

In an infamous case involving Sears, it was discovered that Sears was deliberately not filing reaffirmation agreements with the court because it feared that the court would not approve the agreements. *In re Latanowitch*, 207 B.R. 326 (Bankr. D. Mass. 1997). In a two-year period, in the District of Massachusetts alone, Sears knowingly failed to file reaffirmation agreements that it had solicited from unrepresented debtors in over 2,700 cases. This case and its progeny cost Sears over $400 million in settlements, which demonstrates the importance of following the reaffirmation rules and, more generally, being direct and honest with courts.

(3) "Ride Through" or "Keep and Pay"

Many creditors send reaffirmation agreements to debtors, or if the debtors are represented, to their counsel. A surprisingly large number of reaffirmation agreements are executed. Why? According to Professors Charles Tabb and Ralph Brubaker, there are four main reasons: (1) to allow the debtor to keep collateral that the creditor could otherwise repossess without the agreement;

(2) to settle litigation; (3) to protect a co-obligor on the debt (such as a guarantor); or (4) for personal reasons, such as to preserve a personal relationship with a creditor.[3] An additional reason is that, in some jurisdictions, the Bankruptcy Court requires the debtor to sign the agreement in order to keep the secured party's collateral.

However, in other jurisdictions, a reaffirmation agreement is not required. The debtor can simply keep the property and continue to make the payments without signing the agreement. This is a better option (where it is permitted) because if the debtor wishes to stop making the payments and return the goods to the creditor after the bankruptcy, he or she can do so at any time without being liable for the deficiency. The **deficiency** (meaning the part of the debt that was undersecured and not covered by the proceeds of the sale of the collateral) will be discharged by the prior bankruptcy.

Keeping the property while continuing to make payments, without signing a reaffirmation agreement, is the **ride through** or **keep and pay** option. In jurisdictions that allow this, judges think very poorly of attorneys that allow their debtor clients to reaffirm debts. It is almost always against the debtor's best interest. Even if the debtor lives in a jurisdiction that does not recognize **ride through** or **keep and pay** as an option, the creditor can agree to allow the debtor to simply continue paying on the loan as promised, without a reaffirmation agreement. Of course, the creditor would almost always prefer to get a formal reaffirmation agreement.

At first glance, the 2005 amendments appear to eliminate "ride through" or "keep and pay." See 11 U.S.C. §521(a)(6). But scholars and judges disagree about whether the language of the new bill achieves this goal. Some judges have interpreted the new law to make no change in this area, because Section 521(a)(2)(A) still allows the debtor three distinct and separate options: retain the collateral, redeem it, or reaffirm the debt. Other parts of the Code, as well as the official bankruptcy forms, suggest that "ride through" or "keep and pay" has been eliminated in some instances, but the form does not trump the statute.

Sidebar

TRYING TO ELIMINATE "RIDE THROUGH" OR "KEEP AND PAY"

Congress wanted to eliminate "ride through" or "keep and pay" because it was seen as unfair to allow the debtor to keep collateral while it depreciates, without deciding whether to pay the debt off or not. It leaves the risk of depreciation with the secured party, while the debtor enjoys the collateral.

Even if courts ultimately decide to eliminate these options, they are still available for real estate collateral, because the new Code language purporting to limit the fourth option applies only to personal property. 11 U.S.C. §521(a)(6).

SUMMARY

- In a CHAPTER 7 case, there are three basic ways to keep secured property. The first, "ride through" or "keep and pay;" is only helpful if the debtor is not behind on the payments. While the law technically requires the debtor to formally agree to repay the whole debt to keep most collateral (to formally reaffirm the debt), if

---

[3]Tabb and Brubaker, Bankruptcy Law Principles, Policies, and Practices 575 (Lexis Nexis 2006).

the debtor just keeps the payments current, some creditors may be happy with this and not require a formal reaffirmation agreement.

■ In the second option, if the creditor will not just take payments (as it would have without the debtor's bankruptcy filing) the debtor can reaffirm the debt, which means agreeing to pay back the whole debt post-bankruptcy, including any deficiency if the debtor returns the collateral.

■ The third option is to redeem the collateral, which helps if the debtor can get his or her hands on some cash and if the item is worth far less than the debt. The debtor can redeem—essentially buy back—the collateral for the lesser of the loan amount or the value of the collateral.

■ Redemption must be accomplished through a lump sum payment very close in time to the filing of the case. This amount cannot be paid over time.

CONNECTIONS

Objections to Dischargeability
As you think through the voluntary limits to a complete discharge, remember the involuntary limits, such as objections to dischargeability, described in the previous chapter.

Objections to Discharge
In addition to voluntary limits to a complete discharge and specific non-dischargeable debts, keep in mind the danger of a global denial of discharge pursuant to a creditor's successful objection to discharge. If this is a potential issue for your client, it is worth exploring the alternatives to bankruptcy.

Virtual Bankruptcy
If you anticipate nondischargeable debts or a global denial of discharge, virtual bankruptcy may be your client's best bet. Likewise, if your bankruptcy jurisdiction does not allow "ride through" or "keep and pay," it may be advisable to avoid bankruptcy altogether and do a "ride through" or "keep and pay" without even declaring bankruptcy, particularly if your client is judgment proof in other respects.

Negotiation
If there are potential voluntary or involuntary limits to complete discharge, direct negotiation with creditors may be a preferable alternative to bankruptcy, or at least worth considering before rushing into bankruptcy.

Secured Creditors
Redemption, reaffirmation, and retention are voluntary limits to total discharge that the debtor agrees to through personal choice, in order to keep certain

property that is subject to a security interest. Therefore it's important to be very clear from the beginning about the distinction between secured and unsecured creditors, as discussed in Chapter 1, and to be aware of which creditors have security interests in the debtor's property and how desperate the debtor is to hold onto that property. Remembering the distinction between secured and unsecured creditors was frequently important in Chapters 3 through 10 of this book, describing the benefits and the nuts and bolts of bankruptcy; it's also crucial for making the best strategic decision in respect to the limits to a complete discharge that are raised in Chapters 11 and 12.

Anatomy of a CHAPTER 13 Case

13

O V E R V I E W

This chapter contains a discussion of the rules for CHAPTER 13 cases. The general rules are discussed early, with the details left for the second half of the chapter. Bankruptcies have one of two themes: either *sell out quickly* or *pay out over time*. CHAPTER 7 cases are sell out cases, even though in most cases nothing actually gets sold because the debtor's assets are all exempt. The CHAPTER 7 model is based on the debtor selling all nonexempt assets (if there are any) and walking away.

In contrast, under CHAPTER 13 the debtor's assets are typically not sold. Rather, the debtor files a CHAPTER 13 case intending to use future income to pay back some debts over time and then discharge the rest.

If CHAPTER 7 is debtor's heaven — forgive past debt and start a new life — then CHAPTER 13 is debtor's purgatory. The debtor agrees to pay back some of his or her debts over time. The debtor proposes a plan of repayment called a CHAPTER 13 plan, which will be approved by the court as long as it complies with a set of rules governed, unsurprisingly, by CHAPTER 13 of the Bankruptcy Code.

A. **INTRODUCTION TO** CHAPTER 13

B. CHAPTER 13 **ELIGIBILITY**

C. **SECURED CREDITOR TREATMENT UNDER** CHAPTER 13

    1. Treatment of Personal Property Loans and Other Secured Loans That Are Not Home Mortgages: Is the Stripdown Rule Alive or Dead?

A. Introduction to CHAPTER 13

CHAPTER 13 is for individuals only, not corporations, LLCs, or partnerships. To qualify for CHAPTER 13, a debtor must have regular income, but this income can come from sources other than employment, such as public benefits and even payments from other people. In other words, the income need not come from regular *employment*, despite the fact that CHAPTER 13 is sometimes called "wage-earner" bankruptcy.

The duration of CHAPTER 13 plans is between three and five years. Although many debtors are better off in CHAPTER 7, there can be good reasons for choosing CHAPTER 13 over CHAPTER 7. The most common reason is to save a house from foreclosure. This works because CHAPTER 13 allows the debtor to restructure secured debt that has become way past due, and thus keep the house, the car, or other secured property. Recall that CHAPTER 7 accomplishes very little in this situation. Thus CHAPTER 13 may be the only way to save a house from foreclosure.

You'll recall that post-petition wages do not become part of the bankruptcy estate in a CHAPTER 7 case. The CHAPTER 7 estate is comprised of the assets in which the debtor has an interest at the time of the filing, and any income, rents, or proceeds flowing from those assets. In a CHAPTER 13 case, post-petition income, as well as other assets, become part of the estate. This income will be used to pay the debtor's obligations contained in the CHAPTER 13 plan. However, if the debtor has no extra income over and above everyday living expenses, the debtor cannot get a CHAPTER 13 plan approved.

All *secured debts* must be paid in full under a CHAPTER 13 plan but, in many cases, the debts are only defined as *secured debts* up to the value of the collateral. So the value of the collateral, with interest, is the amount that must be paid over the life of the plan. Home mortgages are treated differently and they generally must be paid in full, regardless of the value of the collateral. This treatment is extended, under the 2005 amendments, to car loans taken out within 910 days (about two and a half years) of the filing and all other purchase-money loans taken out within a year of the filing.

In addition, CHAPTER 13 requires that Section 507 priority debts be paid in full, but *without* interest. If the debtor has insufficient disposable income to cover these priority claims, there can be no CHAPTER 13 case. Also, the CHAPTER 13 trustee receives up to a 10% commission on every dollar that is paid through the case, and the debtor must pay for this expense in the plan as well.

F   A   Q

Q: How much do general unsecured creditors get paid under CHAPTER 13?

A: The amount depends on several things. First, the debtor must contribute all of his or her **disposable income** to the plan. If the debtor has enough disposable income to pay the secured and priority debts, as well as the CHAPTER 13 trustee's fees, and there is still money left over, this must be paid to the unsecured creditors under the plan. This is the **disposable income test**.

Additionally, in a CHAPTER 13 case, the debtor is not required to give up his or her nonexempt assets. Remember, the theme is *pay out*, not *sell out*. Calculating the exemptions is still very important in a CHAPTER 13 case because the debtor must pay the total value of all the nonexempt assets to creditors under the plan. In essence, the debtor is buying back the equity in the nonexempt assets, by paying their value to the creditors who would realize that value upon sale if the case were a CHAPTER 7 case. This means that if the debtor owns $10,000 in unencumbered, nonexempt assets, he or she must pay at least $10,000 to unsecured creditors under the plan. This is the **best interest of creditors test**, or for short, *the best interest test*. The plan must be in the best interest of the creditors, in that the creditors will get at least as much in CHAPTER 13 as they would have gotten in CHAPTER 7. There are two additional requirements. The plan must be filed in good faith and it must be feasible.

The bankruptcy judge is unlikely to approve a plan if there is a valid objection by the CHAPTER 13 trustee. If confirmation is approved, and the plan goes through, the debtor must then make every payment. At the end of the payment plan, the debtor is discharged from any unsecured debts that were not paid under the plan. Usually some debts do get discharged at this time, as it is unusual for a debtor to pay general unsecured creditors in full.

On October 17, 2005, the **means test** described in Chapter 10 went into effect. The practical result is that some people will now choose CHAPTER 13 over no bankruptcy, because they are ineligible for CHAPTER 7 based upon the means test. If a debtor is ineligible for CHAPTER 7 under the means test, the debtor *must* do a five-year payment plan, whereas in the past, all CHAPTER 13 debtors had a right to choose a plan of any length of time between three and five years.

Along with these changes came a much narrower discharge in CHAPTER 13 than was previously provided. Before these Code changes, the CHAPTER 13 discharge was more broad and lenient than a CHAPTER 7 discharge, to offer an incentive to debtors who were willing to use CHAPTER 13. Under the new law, the discharge one receives in a CHAPTER 13 case is very similar to the one received in a CHAPTER 7.

Another big change is that the debtor must pay the face value (not the stripped down value) of more secured loans on personal property. This is because *stripdown* is now available only for older loans, as is described in more detail later in this chapter.

The chart below summarizes the main differences between CHAPTER 13 and CHAPTER 7.

Comparison of CHAPTERS 7 and 13		
	CHAPTER 7	**CHAPTER 13**
Theme	sell out	pay out, reorganization, 3 to 5-year payment plan
Secured Claims	• redeem • reaffirm • surrender • keep and pay/ride through	pay "cramdown" amount (debtor's replacement cost) over time with present value interest rate (*Till* case)
Eligibility	§707(b) means test	§109(e) regular income debt limits: $336,900 unsecured, $1,010,60 secured
Priority Debts	discharged, unless some are nondischargeable under §523(a) or discharge is globally denied under §727(a)	paid in full (except assigned domestic relations claims under §1322(a)(4)) and some taxes
What Claims Get Discharged	all but §523(a) claims	all but §523(a) claims. Property settlements from marital settlement agreements are discharged.
General Unsecured Treatment	discharged, unless nondischargeable under §523(a) or discharge denied under §727(a)	discharged after debtor puts in disposable income • includes all disposable income for duration of the plan, but calculated under means test definition of current monthly income

		• debtor must pay at least the value of nonexempt property to unsecured creditors (creditors should do at least as well under Chapter 13 as under Chapter 7)
		• Example: Debtor owns a house with $20,000 of equity left over *after* exemptions. Debtor must pay the $20,000 to unsecured creditors over the life of the plan, under the best interest test.
Length of Stay	90 days	3 to 5 years
Time of Discharge	90 days (unless discharge denied under §727(a))	3 to 5 years — no discharge until the end of the plan
		• Note: If debtor limps along for 2 years and 11 months, and then stops paying, debtor gets no discharge after all that effort.
		• However, if debtor meets Code's minimum requirements, debtor can get a discharge anyway. See Section I of this chapter.

B. Chapter 13 Eligibility

Section 109(e) states that Chapter 13 is available to individuals with regular income that owe noncontingent, liquidated, unsecured debts of $336,900 or less, and secured debts of $1,010,650 or less. Stockbrokers are ineligible for Chapter 13, as are commodity brokers, but everyone else who meets these qualifications can file a Chapter 13 case.

The regular income requirement is quite flexible. The money does not need to be earned monthly, or even earned by the debtor. One recent case allowed the debtor's father to pay his plan. Public assistance benefits, as well as trust fund income, royalties, and similar earnings, also qualify as regular income.

C. Secured Creditor Treatment Under Chapter 13

One of the most common reasons for a debtor to use Chapter 13, as opposed to Chapter 7, is to keep property subject to a security interest. You'll recall that in a Chapter 7 case, the only way to keep property subject to a security interest is to keep the payments to the secured creditor current, reaffirm, or pay the value of the collateral in immediate cash to the secured party. This last option is called redemption under Section 722 of the Code, as we discussed in detail in Chapter 12. Some courts also recognize the ride through or keep and pay option, at least with regard to real property.

For many debtors, these options are not helpful. Few have the money to redeem the collateral by paying its cash value to the secured party. Moreover, many are already substantially behind on their payments, and thus simply cannot stay current. CHAPTER 13 provides welcome relief to those who are behind on their mortgage or car payments and would like to keep the property. Personal property such as cars and many unattached mobile homes are treated differently than home mortgages, so they will be discussed separately below.

As always, whether the secured property is personal or real estate, a home or something else, secured debt is always treated more favorably than unsecured debt, in recognition that security interests are property interests and are entitled to greater protection. This holds true under CHAPTER 13, which contains very explicit requirements for the treatment of secured debt. Given these rules, and the fact that all secured debt must always be paid in full (at least up to the value of the collateral), with interest or something very much like interest, many CHAPTER 13 plans are structured around meeting these secured debt requirements.

Because it is possible to propose a plan that makes no distribution to unsecured creditors, and because many debtors have no priority debts, some CHAPTER 13 plans do nothing more than pay secured creditors.

(1) Treatment of Personal Property Loans and Other Secured Loans That Are Not Home Mortgages: Is The Stripdown Rule Alive or Dead?

As you will shortly see, the debtor can sometimes reduce the amount that he or she pays on some personal property loans, through a concept known as **stripdown**, or **stripping down** the loan to the value of the collateral under Section 506. This can be done with all personal property loans and loans on rental real estate, *except* for auto loans incurred within 910 days of the filing (about two and a half years), and all PMSI loans taken out within a year of the filing. Outside these exceptions, the debtor can just pay the value of the secured property, along with interest, over the life of the plan.

Stripdown is conceptually similar to a CHAPTER 7 redemption that can be paid over time. Like a CHAPTER 7 redemption, the debtor can sometimes pay less than the full amount of the debt. CHAPTER 13 has the added benefit of allowing that reduced amount to be paid in installments, rather than up front.

(2) Bifurcation and "Stripdown" or "Cramdown"

Because many personal property items depreciate rapidly after they are purchased, they are often worth far less than the amount still owed on them. Because the debtor can sometimes reduce the debt to the value of the collateral, CHAPTER 13 can be very beneficial. The authority for this is Section 506(a), which defines a secured debt as secured "to the extent of the value of such creditor's interest . . . in such property."

The process of reducing the loan to the value of the collateral is called, in bankruptcy parlance, the stripdown or **cramdown**.[1] This literally just means reducing the claim to the value of the collateral under Section 506(a). The words "stripdown" or "cramdown" may not be official vocabulary words, but they describe a concept with

---

[1]Note that stripdown or cramdown is used here as a noun.

which every bankruptcy attorney (and every bankruptcy professor) is familiar, namely the process of reducing a secured claim to the value of the collateral underlying it.

Before the 2005 amendments, all personal property could be stripped down in a Chapter 13 case. This was one of the major benefits of Chapter 13. Even now, *all* Chapter 11 business loans can be stripped down to the value of the collateral.[2] Now, after 2005, there are broad exceptions to the stripdown rule in Chapter 13, but to us, this does not eliminate the need to first learn the stripdown rule and procedure before learning the exceptions. That's why in this section, we help you master the stripdown rule first. Then we tell you about the exceptions, for car loans that are at least 910 days old, PMSIs one year old or less, and home mortgages.

Again, one of the biggest benefits of both Chapter 13 and Chapter 11 is the ability to "**strip down**"[3] the secured debt to just the value of the collateral. Traditionally, one could strip down all undersecured loans on personal property or investment real estate. One could not and still cannot strip down home mortgages.

> ### Sidebar
>
> **STRIPDOWN AND CRAMDOWN TERMINOLOGY**
>
> Many attorneys use the word cramdown, not stripdown. Most law professors, however, prefer to call this concept stripdown. Using the word stripdown for this concept saves the word cramdown for another bankruptcy concept you'll learn about in the Chapter 11 materials of this book. Here we try to stick with stripdown for the same reason, but we also want you to know that the word cramdown is used by attorneys in practice. The U.S. Supreme Court also most commonly uses the word cramdown, not stripdown, for this concept.

Now let's learn stripdown through some concrete examples. You've often heard that once you drive a new car off the dealer's lot, it depreciates by some huge percentage, maybe even as much as 50%. In other words, a person pays $20,000 for a new car, but once it's off the lot, the car is only worth $10,000. Perhaps the depreciation is not that drastic, but, to be sure, the new car depreciates faster than the loan gets paid off. So for example, assume that you buy a car for $20,000 on credit, and three years later, the car is worth $7,000. With many cars, this is highly realistic. Also assume that because you have paid a lot of interest at a high rate, the amount of the car loan is still $13,000 after three years of payments. You have now fallen on tough times and need to file for Chapter 13.

As in a Chapter 7 case, the secured party who gave you the car loan (assuming it was incurred more than 910 days before any bankruptcy filing) now has a claim that is bifurcated, or split into two parts. One part of the claim, the $7,000, is a secured claim (you'll recall from Chapter 8 of this book that a secured claim is only as large as the value of the collateral supporting the claim), and the other part, the $6,000, becomes an unsecured claim. This unsecured part will be treated just like any other unsecured claim in the case. It does not matter that the $6,000 was once part of a secured claim. This procedure has allowed you to strip down your secured claim to $7,000, or the current value of your property.

Chapter 13 now considers the $7,000 owed a secured debt and requires it to be paid in full. But what is meant by "paid in full"? Just the stripped down amount. Payment of that amount will constitute payment in full of the secured claim. The

---

[2]This assumes the debtor in Chapter 11 has all business debt. If there is a home mortgage in an individual Chapter 11 case, that cannot be stripped down.

[3]Now "strip down" is used as a verb and is two words rather than one.

Sidebar

STRIPPING DOWN AUTO LOANS

The 2005 amendments preclude a debtor from stripping down certain auto loans taken out within the 910 days prior to the bankruptcy case. But which ones? The provision precludes stripdown only if the auto was "acquired for the personal use of the debtor." But what does that mean? Other provisions of the Code that distinguish between personal and business use almost always use the phrase "personal, family, or household use" to indicate "personal use only" — it's a legal term of art. And so there is uncertainty about what "personal use" means here. Of course, a car used solely for business purposes can still be crammed down. *In re Lowder*, 2006 WL 1794737 (Bankr. D. Kan. 2006). After that, the clarity ends.

Some courts have adopted a "totality of the circumstances" test. At least one court has held that if the debtor uses the car to get to work (and who doesn't, really?), the car was not acquired solely for the "personal use of the debtor" and can still be crammed down. See *In re Hill*, 352 B.R. 69 (Bankr. W.D. La. 2006). Other courts disagree, finding that "personal" simply means "non-business" and that if the debtor could take the bus or walk, but instead chooses to drive his or her car to work, that is a personal choice and a personal use. See *In re Solis*, 356 B.R. 398 (Bankr. S.D. Tex. 2006).

What if someone other than the debtor uses the car? If it is the debtor's adult child, who does not even live with the debtor, the car was not acquired for the personal use of the debtor and can be crammed down. *In re Jackson*, 338 B.R. 923 (Bankr. M.D. Ga. 2006).[6] If the car is used by the debtor's non-debtor spouse, some courts have said that it can be crammed down as well.

secured part of the debt is "stripped down" from $13,000 to $7,000. Of course, the creditor has an additional claim (a bifurcated unsecured claim) for the other $6,000, but the debtor's plan does not have to provide that all of this will be paid. In some cases the plan may provide that only a small portion of it, or even none of it, will be paid. So long as the plan provides for payment of the secured part (the $7,000), the debtor can keep the car. This $7,000 can be paid off over the life of a three- to five-year plan with so much paid each week or month.[4] As a result, the debtor may be able to keep the car, and indeed pay less for it than the original purchase price under CHAPTER 13, whereas it is unlikely that the debtor could have come up with the $7,000 to redeem it under CHAPTER 7.

The main thing to remember here is that paying the reduced or stripped down[5] amount fulfills the CHAPTER 13 requirement that all secured claims be paid in full, because the size of the secured claim is defined as the value of the collateral in Section 506(a). This is true any time the collateral has depreciated below the amount of the loan. The concept of bifurcation, or splitting the secured claim into two parts, is critical to understanding secured creditor treatment both in CHAPTER 13 and CHAPTER 11.

(3) Valuation

In the new car example above, we assumed quite a few facts, including the current value of the car. Valuation is probably the most common factual dispute decided by bankruptcy courts. Valuation arises in the context of exemptions, redemption, stripdown, relief from the automatic stay, lien avoidance, the best interest of creditors test, CHAPTER 11 confirmation, and many other areas.

Valuation is often accomplished in large business cases, as well as in some consumer cases, through an appraisal of the property in question. Appraisals may vary greatly depending on the purpose of the valuation, as well as the assumptions made by the appraiser. Judges often favor the value given by the most credible appraiser, when faced with more than one valuation. If both parties' appraisers are equally

---

[4]This example assumes the debtor passed the means test. If not, the debtor will need to do a five-year plan.
[5]Now "stripped down" is being used as an adjective. It's a very flexible phrase!
[6]The court found, however, that because the debtor's plan in this case favored the daughter over the auto lender, it was not proposed in good faith.

credible, the court will often just split the difference. Normally, only business assets and real estate are appraised. Smaller items of personal property are rarely appraised due to the cost of an appraisal. When it comes to vehicles and mobile homes, most creditors use Kelley's Blue Book, while most debtors prefer NADA, or another similar resource. Why? Kelley's tends to give higher values, which naturally favor creditors.

Creditors do not *always* want high values for their collateral. You might recall from Chapter 4 that a creditor can get the stay lifted and get its collateral back if there is no equity in the collateral, or if there is no substantial equity cushion.

Valuations made under Section 506 are made based upon the purpose of the valuation. At least in theory, the collateral can be valued differently at different times during the case, depending upon the purpose of the valuation.

In *Associates Commercial Corp. v. Rash*, 520 U.S. 953 (1997), the U.S. Supreme Court decided whether the proper measure of value for stripdown purposes is the *wholesale* or the *retail* value, as both are offered by these "blue book" type resources. After a long-standing split among the federal circuit courts about which of these two values was preferable, the Supreme Court followed neither approach, instead choosing the **replacement value**, presumably a number somewhere in between **wholesale** and **retail**. *Rash* indicates that the proper value of a debtor's used personal property, for stripdown purposes, is the price at which the debtor could purchase a comparable used item.

Regardless of how value is determined, it is the single most important determination with respect to whether a debtor will be able to afford to pay the stripped down value of a big-ticket item under his or her plan. Thus, as to any security interest that can be stripped down, the most critical question in the equation is the value of the collateral. *Associates Commercial Corp. v. Rash*, 520 U.S. 953 (1997).[7]

(4) The Present Value Interest Rate

The other variable in determining the cost of paying off property that has been stripped down is the **present value** rate that the debtor will be required to pay. Section 1325(a)(5)(B)(ii) provides that the debtor must pay the full value, as of the effective date of the plan, of the allowed secured claim. This has been interpreted to mean that the creditor is entitled to the value of that claim as if it were being paid all at once upon confirmation. Because the Code allows the payment over time, the debtor must compensate the creditor for the time value of money. A dollar paid a year from now is worth less than a dollar paid today. Thus the debtor must pay the creditor for what the creditor loses in interest, or the income the creditor could have earned by loaning that money to someone else, if the creditor had been paid its money up front.

Practically speaking, we provide the secured party with the present value of its claim, and compensate it by assigning an interest rate to the debt. We somewhat cavalierly refer to this as the **present value interest rate** or simply the **interest rate**,

---

[7]The 2005 amendments to the Bankruptcy Code adopt a test similar but not identical to *Rash*, by stating in Section 506(a)(2) that:

> (2) If the debtor is an individual in a case under Chapter 7 or 13, such value with respect to personal property securing an allowed claim shall be determined based on the replacement value of such property as of the date of the filing of the petition without deduction for costs of sale or marketing. With respect to property acquired for personal, family, or household purposes, replacement value shall mean the price a retail merchant would charge for property of that kind considering the age and condition of the property at the time value is determined.

but it is important to understand that it is not really interest. Rather, it is a payment to the secured party to provide it with the present value of its allowed secured claim.

Having said that, all courts discuss this concept in terms of "interest." In 2004, the Supreme Court held that the rate to be applied in a stripdown is the prime interest rate, *plus* an added one to three percentage points for a host of risk variables. See *Till v. SCS Credit Corp.*, 541 U.S. 465 (2004). This issue is discussed with more precision in Chapter 15 in the context of Chapter 11 plans.

Sidebar

PRESENT VALUE TERMINOLOGY

The debtor can reduce the rate on a loan on personal property even if the loan's value cannot be stripped down. The ability to reduce the interest rate on a loan, as the Court held in *Till*, applies even to loans for which the value cannot be stripped down. This means one can reduce the interest rate even on car loans taken out within two and a half years of the filing date or other loans taken out within a year of the filing date. This causes some attorneys to say things like "you can still strip down the rate, just not the value." More accurately, creditors still receive only the present value interest rate, not the contract rate. This compensates the secured creditor for the present value of the money that is owed, because the money will be paid over time. The principal due remains the same.

(5) Treatment of the Home Mortgage in Chapter 13

The rules described above for stripping down secured loans do not apply to home mortgages. The home mortgage industry convinced Congress that if people were allowed to strip down their home mortgages, the home lending market might collapse. As a result, Congress passed Section 1322(c), which states that a person may not modify or otherwise affect a secured loan upon which the lender's only collateral is a home. We sometimes refer to this as Section 1322's **anti-modification** clause.

Now, many personal property loans also must be paid in full, as we discussed above. This is because the new law significantly curtails the debtor's right to strip down personal property loans, in addition to the old rule on home mortgages.

In any event, as a result of effective lobbying efforts by home mortgage lenders, home mortgages are paid under Chapter 13 (and also Chapter 11) in a totally different way than the stripdown approach. As you'll soon see, a home mortgage payment that is in default will always require a larger payment in Chapter 13 than the debtor was paying before filing for Chapter 13 relief. As a result, feasibility (the debtor's ability to pay the plan) is often an issue. Many debtors cannot do what is required to cure the home mortgage, and thus cannot confirm or complete a plan.

Due to the anti-modification clause noted above, the debtor must continue to make the regular monthly payment to the lender and also pay off all the arrears over the life of the plan. The math is often easier to calculate with home mortgage lenders than with other secured creditors because there is no stripdown and thus no bifurcation. The debtor must, however, pay the present value of the arrears, so one must add present value interest to the arrears before dividing the arrears by the number of months of the plan and adding it to the regular monthly payment.

(6) Recognizing when Stripdown Applies

You have now learned several complex rules for treating secured claims in a Chapter 13 case, each in a vacuum depending upon the type of secured property that is at issue. You have learned that personal property loans can sometimes be stripped down but loans on real estate that is used as a principal residence cannot. Now we will describe an approach to determining which loans can be stripped down and which cannot.

A Conceptual Approach to Stripdown

Ask yourself three questions for each secured debt:

1. Is the loan *undersecured*? (If not, no need to strip down.)

2. Is this the *type* of loan that can be stripped down (i.e., a personal property PMSI loan, but not a home mortgage)?

3. Does the *timing* of the loan permit stripdown (i.e., is it a PMSI incurred within one year of the filing? Is it an auto loan incurred within 910 days of the filing)?

In summary, if the loan is *oversecured*, stripdown will accomplish nothing for your client because the goal of stripdown is to lower the loan amount to the value of the collateral. If the collateral is worth more than the debt, there is nothing to strip down. As to the *type* of loan, personal property loans are candidates for stripdown but home mortgages are not. Finally, consider the *timing*. Recent loans (car loans taken out less than two and a half years prior to the filing) and all other personal property loans taken out less than one year prior to the filing, that are PMSIs and that are for goods for the debtor's personal use, cannot be stripped down.

D. The Treatment of Priority Claims in Chapter 13

Section 1322(a)(2) provides that in order for a Chapter 13 plan to be confirmable, all claims entitled to priority under Section 507(a) must be paid in full under the plan. Thus, just as you saw that all secured claims (as they are defined in Section 506(a), up to the value of the collateral) must be paid in full under a Chapter 13 plan, the same is true of claims that have priority under Section 507(a). While priority claims also must be paid in full under a Chapter 13 plan, unlike secured claims, the holders of these priority claims are not entitled to present value interest on their claims. Thus, to determine how much the debtor must pay each month to satisfy the claim in full, the debtor's attorney need only divide the allowed priority claims by the number of months in the plan. No interest!

So what are the priority claims in a Chapter 13 plan likely to be? Well, while it is true that some Chapter 13 debtors run businesses and thus owe priority employee claims (like wages) and perhaps claims to suppliers and deposit holders, many Chapter 13 debtors do not run businesses. The most common priority claims for the average Chapter 13 debtor are likely to be past due taxes, and perhaps some past due child support. The debtor's attorney also is typically paid through the Chapter 13 plan and his or her fees are also priority claims. A debtor who has large tax liabilities can save a great deal on interest by filing a Chapter 13 case. As soon as the case is filed, both the interest and any penalties that would normally accrue outside bankruptcy cease. These benefits for dealing with past due taxes may be the primary reason to file Chapter 13.

We said above that one must divide the *allowed* priority claims by the number of months to calculate this part of the plan payment. But how does one determine how much of the claim is *allowed*? Because many types of taxes get priority treatment only if they are recent, the issue of allowance comes up most often in that context. Not all taxes will need to be paid in full in every case. Some taxes lose their priority status because they are too old. Others fall into categories that simply get less priority than others. Thus you should never assume that all taxes are entitled to priority.

Another allowance issue comes up in the context of domestic support obligations under a marital settlement agreement. All past due domestic support obligations must of course be paid in full under a CHAPTER 13 plan, but what about past due property settlements? While property settlement agreements flowing from a marital settlement agreement do not get *discharged* in a CHAPTER 7, these claims do not get any special *priority* in either chapter, so they do not have to be paid in full under a CHAPTER 13 plan.

Sidebar

A BROAD DEFINITION OF DOMESTIC SUPPORT OBLIGATIONS

The new definition of "domestic support obligations," which is one of the debts the debtor must pay in full in a CHAPTER 13 case under Section 1322(a), now applies to more claims. The definition includes support obligations arising before or after the case is filed, and also to a much broader group of obligees, including "a spouse, former spouse, or child of the debtor or such child's parent, legal guardian, or responsible relative." This language clearly covers unmarried parents of children as well as many others not previously covered. Quite significantly, the phrase also applies to domestic support obligations owed to governmental units. See §101(14A). These are acquired by assignment, and could be large enough to make a CHAPTER 13 plan infeasible.

E. The CHAPTER 13 Disposable Income Test

The disposable income test has been in the Code since 1984 and at least nominally requires that the debtor contribute to the plan all of his or her disposable income (meaning all amounts not necessary for the maintenance or support of the debtor, the debtor's dependents, or the debtor's business) during the plan period. The 2005 amendments now measure disposable income by using the means test (Section 707(b)) and the form it is calculated on, the Official Form B22A, for above-median income debtors.

(1) The Pre-2005 Disposable Income Test

At the time the pre-2005 disposable income test became part of the Bankruptcy Code, the "good faith" requirement was already in the Code but there was no explicit requirement that the debtor use his or her income to pay as much as possible to creditors under the CHAPTER 13 plan. The disposable income test was added to the Code to ensure that all CHAPTER 13 debtors made as substantial an effort to pay creditors as possible.

Prior to 1984, some judges imputed into the good-faith test a requirement that a debtor use *all* of his or her available income (after reasonable expenses) to pay creditors. The 1984 amendments made the requirements of CHAPTER 13 crystal clear: Use your disposable income to pay your creditors or your plan will not be confirmed.

How was disposable income calculated? By taking a debtor's **projected disposable income** and deducting the debtor's actual expenses, specifically those "reasonably necessary for the maintenance and support of the debtor and the debtor's dependents, including the debtor's business expenses." 11 U.S.C. §1325(b) (past version).

Built into this test was the explicit ability for courts and trustees to challenge expenses as too extravagant, where the debtor tried to claim expenses that went beyond what was necessary for the maintenance and support of the debtor and the debtor's dependents. This old test *still* applies to below-median income debtors under Chapter 13.

(2) The New Disposable Income Test

The new disposable income test has taken away some of the judicial discretion contained in the prior test. Congress has essentially imputed the means test into the disposable income test. Since the means test represents a fictional picture of the debtor's financial condition, based upon allowances rather than real expenses, and income from the past rather than the present, it may not accurately measure a debtor's genuine ability to pay creditors. To put it mildly, the imputation of the means test into the disposable income test has left a wake of confusion.

Recall that the purpose of the means test is to determine whether there is "abuse" under Section 707(b). But now courts are directed to apply the means test in order to determine the debtor's available income under the disposable income test. As you learned in Chapter 10, the income used in the means test is not the debtor's actual income but an average of the debtor's past income for the six months prior to the debtor's bankruptcy petition. This number, since it is all about the debtor's past, not about the future, can be easily manipulated by the timing of the petition. The resulting number could be more, but could also be far less, than the real income a debtor is earning while in Chapter 13. This income calculation also does not change as the debtor's circumstances change, making it a poor fit for determining what the debtor can afford to pay creditors. Some debtors may be able to pay creditors much more than the formula suggests, while others may be able to pay less. When you try to deduct the allowed expense, more confusion arises.

The new law splits debtors into two groups, those with current monthly income below the median income in their state, and those with income above it. 11 U.S.C. §1325(b)(2) and (3).

(a) Measuring Income

For *all* debtors, income is calculated according to the definition of current monthly income (11 U.S.C. §101(10A)), which looks *backward* rather than *forward*. Of course, what happened in the six months prior to the bankruptcy case may bear no relationship to the debtor's income after the filing. Thus, if the point of the disposable income test is to see if the debtor can afford to pay more to creditors in the plan, the test no longer effectively does that, at least in the way it measures income.

For instance, post-petition tax refunds are not necessarily part of a debtor's *projected* disposable income under this test. Because income now looks backward, debtors may not be required to contribute post-petition tax refunds to the plan. However, the debtor must do his or her best to accurately estimate his or her actual tax liability going forward and to deduct that amount from current monthly income on line 30, under Section 707(b)(2)(A)(ii)(I). Over-withholding for the purposes of reducing payments to creditors could cause the debtor to fail the good faith test. *In re Lawson*, 2007 WL 184733 (Bankr. D. Utah 2007).

F	A	Q

Q: Is there any leeway for a debtor whose income goes way down *after* filing a CHAPTER 13 case?

A: Yes, the debtor can apply for the special circumstances exception discussed below, but this requires more money for legal fees. This should allow the debtor to get out of doing a CHAPTER 13 case, however, if the debtor can afford to pursue it, and if the court does not feel the debtor has reduced his or her income on purpose.

(b) Measuring Expenses

For above-median debtors, the means test in Section 707(b)(2)(A) causes the same conceptual problems. The expenses allowed by the form are not the debtor's real expenses and thus could be too high or too low to measure the debtor's capacity to pay more. Moreover, the disposable income test by definition measures projected expenses. Does it make sense to compare future projections to past income? Accountants should be nervous.

(c) Below-Median Debtors and the Means Test

If the debtor is below the median income for his state and family size, however, the court is to use the old Schedule J (Official Form B7) (part of the disclosures the debtor fills out) to measure the debtor's expenses. This means the court will (as it always has) use the below-median debtor's actual expenses, albeit against the debtor's unreal income, to calculate the minimum amount due as disposable income.

For debtors with current monthly income below the median income for a comparable family in their state, the disposable income calculation works similarly to how it worked in the past (see 11 U.S.C. §1325(b)(2)(A) and (B)), except that all the appropriate and necessary expenses are deducted from the artificial "current monthly income" that we just talked about.

Studying the nuances of the old disposable income test (the one that now applies to only below-median income debtors) is one of the most interesting endeavors in bankruptcy law.

This topic raises at least two important policy questions. First, what should a person who has not paid his or her debts be allowed to spend money on; in other words, which expenses are really necessary within the meaning of the statutory language? Second, when a below-median income person is permitted to choose between walking away from his or her debts and paying some of them off over time, how attractive should we make CHAPTER 13 in order to induce people to choose the repayment plan option? How stringent should we be in answering the first question, given that we would like to create an incentive for people to pay off at least some debts?

You have heard that bankruptcy courts are courts of equity that have a great deal of discretion. In the extremely fact-sensitive area of the disposable income test for below-median income debtors, debtors' expenses are scrutinized heavily and judicial discretion is at an all-time high. One judge might find a $150 haircut outrageous, while another might find it a necessity. An animal lover might find pets to be a necessity while another judge might find the debtor's food and vet bills inappropriate for a bankruptcy debtor.

For items that are obviously necessary, the issue becomes *how much* is reasonable to spend on food, medicine, car insurance, and so on. One CHAPTER 13 trustee told me that she considered $600 per month per se reasonable for food for a family of four. However, some judges question the utility of per se budgets, claiming that there is no way to say that $700 or even $800 per month might not be reasonable in some situations, because the average family simply does not exist. Does the household include teenagers? Do the debtors have enough cash flow to take advantage of buying in bulk? Do they live in a remote area where food is expensive? Does the "food" category include toothpaste and toilet paper? Makeup for a teenage girl? What other expenses are reasonable? Is a $50 cable TV bill reasonable?

Many court opinions on the subject of the disposable income test or the **best efforts test** (as this test is also sometimes called) seem to allow the debtor to maintain the status quo. In other words, people who have always had high expenses will be allowed to continue to have high expenses, while really poor people will be allowed only the most basic expenses. For example, private school tuition has been found by some courts to be a reasonable and necessary expense as long as the cost is not excessive (whatever that means), and as long as the child has been attending the school for a considerable amount of time. *In re Nicola*, 244 B.R. 795 (Bankr. N.D. Ill. 2000); *In re Burgos*, 248 B.R. 446 (Bankr. M.D. Fla. 2000). Other courts flatly disagree, finding private school to be a luxury and not a necessity. *In re Nelson*, 204 B.R. 497 (E.D. Tex. 1996). One court recently held that the debtor could not continue to pay high veterinary bills for his elderly horses and dogs. See *In the Matter of Wyant*, 217 B.R. 585 (Bankr. D. Neb. 1988).

(d) Above-Median Income Debtors and the Means Test

CHAPTER 13 debtors with a current monthly income *above* the median income have their expenses deducted "in accordance with" the statutory formula for measuring abuse in CHAPTER 7 cases in Section 707(b)(2)(A) and (B) (the means test).

Above-median debtors are allowed to deduct all the expenses allowed on Form B22A, including apparently all secured debt regardless of its size and necessity to the debtor's quality of life. By the same token, some real expenses don't fit on the form, leaving great room for unfairness, manipulation, and even abuse!

Thus, for above-median income CHAPTER 13 debtors, the court's traditional expense-policing function of an objection to confirmation has been neutralized by the new law. Now Congress has substituted a mathematical formula that fixes expense deductions that may routinely be either insufficient to sustain life or (in many cases) in excess of any amount that would survive the reasonable and necessary test of the prior Code. Because current monthly income is not real income and because the expenses that can be deducted for above-median debtors are not real expenses, these numbers may bear no relationship to what a debtor could actually pay creditors.

Many scholars think that the disposable income test for these high-end debtors will no longer serve any meaningful function and that creditors could actually be hurt rather than helped by this test. This may turn out to be a case of unanticipated consequences flowing from legislation that the credit industry lobbied for intensely.

(e) How Are Above-Median Debtors' Expenses Really Measured?

Probably the biggest question left by the new disposable income test is whether Form B22A (which does not reflect the debtor's actual expenses and thus does not really measure the debtor's disposable income) governs the debtor's expense calculations under the disposable income test. The Code explicitly so provides, but some courts simply cannot live with this conclusion, and have instead decided that Form B22A simply creates a presumption of what the expenses are, which can be rebutted by using the debtor's actual expenses disclosed on Schedules I and J, *In re Grady*, 343 B.R. 747 (Bankr. N.D. Ga. 2006), or an anticipated change in financial condition in the future, *In re Casey*, 2006 WL 3071401 (Bankr. E.D. Wash. 2006). Other courts say that although the Code test seems to look backward, the court should consider the debtor's financial condition at the time of confirmation, not the time of the filing. See *In re Crittendon*, 2006 WL 2547102 (Bankr. M.D.N.C. 2006). Or perhaps the court can reduce the debtor's expenses for secured debts that are not necessary — imagine a debtor with three houses and five cars, all financed with secured debt. See *In re Edmunds*, 350 B.R. 636 (Bankr. D.S.C. 2006). Other, strict constructionist courts hold that Form B22A is dispositive, regardless of whether this is sensible, because that is what the statute says. *In re Farrer Johnson*, 353 B.R. 224 (Bankr. N.D. Ill. 2006); *In re Alexander*, 344 B.R. 742 (Bankr. E.D.N.C. 2006); *In re Barr*, 341 B.R. 181 (Bankr. M.D.N.C. 2006).

(f) Secured Debt

Another area of disagreement among courts is how to apply the disposable income test if the debtor has "contractually due" secured debt as of the bankruptcy filing that he or she does not intend to continue to repay. Some courts have held that under the clear wording of the statute, the debtor can deduct the payments from the income (thereby decreasing the amount of disposable income left over) even though the debtor will not actually make these payments, as long as the property has not been surrendered at the time of the filing of any Section 707(b) motion to dismiss. *In re Nockerts*, 2006 WL 3689465 (Bankr. E.D. Wis. 2006). Yet another issue is whether debtors can deduct the standard IRS ownership costs for vehicles on which they no longer owe any debt. Following Form B22A, at least one court says yes. See *In re Sawdy*, 2007 WL 582535 (Bankr. E.D. Wis. 2007). The court reasoned that we shouldn't punish debtors for paying off their debts, and we shouldn't treat debtors who have paid off their car debts differently from those who owe a very small amount and are allowed to take the full IRS allowance anyway.

(g) Applicable Commitment Period

The concept of an applicable commitment period (the time over which a debtor must pay a plan) makes no sense for above-median income debtors with negative monthly disposable income under line 58 of Form B22A. The debtors are "above median income" debtors, but because they have negative disposable income under Form B22A, they do not need to pay their plan for five full years. Thus, it appears to make no sense to require the plan to go on paying 0% to the unsecured creditors, when other creditors could be paid more quickly. See *In re Lawson*, 14 F.3d 595 (4th Cir. 1993).

F. The Good-Faith Test in Chapter 13

In addition to the disposable income test above, there is another equally powerful and complicated Chapter 13 test. It is called the **"good faith" test**. Section 1325(a)(3) provides that the plan must be proposed "in good faith and not by any means forbidden by law."

As noted above, the disposable income test was added to the Code in 1984. Prior to this time, the Code simply required that plans be filed in good faith. Before that, many courts had interpreted the good-faith requirement to mean that the debtor had contributed all of the disposable income that he or she had. But once the disposable income test was added to the Code in 1984, the good-faith test was left undefined. As a result, the good-faith test now means different things to different people. Some of those interpretations are discussed below.

(1) Overlap with the Disposable Income Test and Other Tests

When the debtor prepares his or her budget, some money falls to the bottom line as disposable income, or funds available to pay creditors. The debtor can then propose the plan. It is implicit in the Code's good-faith requirement, as well as the disposable income test, that the debtor will estimate all expenses in good faith and not inflate the expenses. Under some interpretations of the good-faith test, the debtor also should engage in some belt-tightening in the budget. If not, the plan may not meet the good-faith test. As the good-faith test allows the court to look at the debtor's overall behavior in a case in terms of expenses, disclosures, and testimony, the test allows for an objection to the plan that is hard to define. Lack of good faith is a test of overall fairness, and some of the facts and factors below may be tipoffs that good faith is at issue.

(2) Good-Faith Factor-Based Tests

Given the lack of guidance in the Code, some courts have adopted factor-based tests to determine whether a debtor has filed a plan in good faith. Both the Eighth and the Tenth Circuits have adopted the following factor-based test, which requires one to balance all the factors:

- the amount of the plan payments and of the debtor's surplus;
- the debtor's employment history, ability to earn, and likelihood of future increases in income;
- the duration of the plan;
- the accuracy of the plan's statement of debts and expenses, the percentage repayment of unsecured debts, and whether any inaccuracies are an attempt to mislead the court;

- the extent of preferential treatment in the plan between classes of creditors;
- the extent to which secured creditor claims are modified (this is presumably a respectable use of CHAPTER 13);
- the type of debt sought to be discharged and whether any such debt is non-dischargeable in a CHAPTER 7 case;
- the existence of special circumstances such as inordinate medical expenses;
- the frequency with which the debtor has filed for bankruptcy;
- the motivation and sincerity of the debtor in seeking CHAPTER 13 relief; and
- the burden that the plan's administration would place on the CHAPTER 13 trustee.

Somewhat amusingly, after enumerating this 11-part test, the Eighth Circuit court that drafted the test stated that "[t]his list is not exclusive and weight given to each factor will necessarily vary with the facts and circumstances of each case."[8] We repeat just one version of the test here, to give you a flavor of what a lack of good faith might mean. Again, judicial discretion is extensive.

Note that prior to 2005, the Code required that CHAPTER 13 *plans* be filed in good faith, but did not require that CHAPTER 13 *cases* themselves be filed in good faith. Now the Code requires both. See Section 1325(a)(3)(7).

What are some examples of plans that failed for want of good faith? Cases filed to delay foreclosures, with no intention to actually follow through with the CHAPTER 13 case, are often found to lack good faith. In one case, a debtor filed a CHAPTER 13 case and plan with no income from any sources, just to forestall a foreclosure. *In re Kollar*, 2006 WL 3759461 (Bankr. S.D. Fla. 2006).

Another common reason to deny confirmation of a CHAPTER 13 for lack of good faith is that the debtor wants to pay a small distribution to a creditor whose debt would not have been discharged at all in a CHAPTER 7 case. In one recent case, the debt resulted in a $300,000 judgment for assault on which the debtor proposed to pay a 1.5% distribution. *In re Nuttall*, 2007 WL 128896 (Bankr. D.N.J. 2007).

In another case, two married joint debtors agreed to the entry of judgment against them in the amount of $150,000 and agreed that such debts would not be dischargeable in any subsequent bankruptcy. One debtor went to jail for conspiracy and mail fraud and when he was released, the debtors filed for CHAPTER 13. The court found that because the debtors were solvent and also promised to pay most other debts, but not these two judgments, the plan was filed in bad faith. *In re Farber*, 335 B.R. 362 (Bankr. S.D. Fla. 2006).

Other cases in which good faith was lacking include cases in which debtors filed for bankruptcy for the sole purpose of rejecting a real estate lease or modifying a divorce decree.

---

[8]See *United States v. Estus (In re Estus)*, 695 F.2d 311, 314-16 (8th Cir. 1982), cited in *In re Flygare*, 709 F.2d 1344 (10th Cir. 1983). Other circuits have adopted other similarly complex tests. (See, e.g., *Kitchens v. Georgia Railroad Bank & Trust Co. (In re Kitchens)*, 702 F.2d 885 (11th Cir. 1983); *Deans v. O'Donnell (In re Deans)*, 692 F.2d 968 (4th Cir. 1982); *Barnes v. Whelan (In re Barnes)*, 689 F.2d 193 (D.C. Cir. 1982); *Goeb v. Heid (In re Goeb)*, 675 F.2d 1386 (9th Cir. 1982); *Ravenot v. Rimgale (In re Rimgale)*, 669 F.2d 426 (7th Cir. 1982)).

(3) Multiple Filings

The good-faith test is often raised, and used, as the basis for objection to a debtor's CHAPTER 13 plan when the debtor has filed more than one bankruptcy case. For example, a debtor will sometimes file a CHAPTER 13 plan in order to stop a home foreclosure, and then, before filing a plan, have the case dismissed. As the lender gets close to foreclosing again, the debtor may file yet another case, and may or may not comply with CHAPTER 13 in the process. Such cases, filed for delay purposes only, would violate the good-faith requirements of CHAPTER 13. This is quintessential lack of good faith. Although one or two previous filings could raise a flag and possibly an objection, it typically takes several filings to ensure success on a bad-faith claim based solely on serial filing. Don't forget that the new automatic stay provisions contained in Section 362(c) also discourage multiple filings.

One controversial topic is the question of whether it is bad faith to file a CHAPTER 7 case followed by a CHAPTER 13. We call this a "Chapter 20," meaning a 7 plus a 13. Why would anyone do this? If this is permitted, filing a CHAPTER 7 would first allow a debtor to discharge all of the nonpriority unsecured debts, so that he or she could concentrate in the CHAPTER 13 plan on just paying the priority and the secured debts. Assuming that it is acceptable to propose a plan that provides for no distribution to unsecured creditors (something we refer to as a **zero percent plan**), there seems to be nothing particularly wrong with a Chapter 20. As it turns out, zero percent plans are just as controversial as Chapter 20s.

Though the Code itself does not preclude one from filing a CHAPTER 7, followed by a CHAPTER 13, some courts find doing so to be per se bad faith. See *In the Matter of Strauss*, 184 B.R. 349 (Bankr. D. Neb. 1995).

(4) Zero Percent Plans

The preceding text asks whether it is acceptable to propose a plan that pays no distribution to unsecured creditors at all. Courts disagree about this. Some say a zero percent plan is per se bad faith. Others say this is one factor to consider in analyzing whether a plan has been filed in good faith. Still other courts believe the zero percent plan does not raise good-faith issues in and of itself, on the grounds that if the disposable income test is met there is no issue of good faith.

In the past, plan confirmation was regularly denied by some courts for a lack of good faith when the debtor carried unusually high secured debts (mortgages, car loans) resulting from living the high life. Obviously, uncommonly high secured debts also affect the disposable income test, by making less money available for a CHAPTER 13 plan.

G. The Best Interest of Creditors Test

The two tests we have just considered bear on the unsecured creditor distribution, namely the *disposable income test* and the *good-faith test*. We have focused on how much the debtor must give up in order to have the plan approved, or, put another way, how much belt-tightening the debtor must engage in.

The test we are going to learn about now relates to a totally different test, which should at least in theory be more objective. Now we will ask the question, "How much would the creditors get if this person just filed a Chapter 7 instead?" Why do we care about this? Because if the creditors would get more in a Chapter 7, the person should just file a Chapter 7 — why bother making payments for years, if the net result is *less* money for the creditors?

The money from a Chapter 7 liquidation would be a sure thing and the creditors are entitled to at least that much. The philosophy is that we should not allow a debtor to file a Chapter 13 case if the creditors cannot get at least as much in the Chapter 13 plan as they would get from the sale and distribution of the debtor's nonexempt assets, which is what they would receive in a Chapter 7.

F   A   Q

Q: But what if a person is not allowed to file Chapter 7 because he or she does not pass the means test?

A: It doesn't matter. The purpose of this test is to ensure that the creditors get at least as much as they would get in a Chapter 7, under a debtor's proposed Chapter 13 plan. The debtor is not trying to do a Chapter 7 case. We are just asking hypothetically what creditors would get in a Chapter 7 because the debtor must pay at least that much to unsecured creditors under a Chapter 7.

Slightly restating the test, in a Chapter 13 case, the creditors must get at least what they would get in a liquidation. If not, the Chapter 13 case is improper. It does not present creditors with the best-case bankruptcy scenario, and the Chapter 13 case would not be in their best interest. Rather, a Chapter 7 case would be in their best interest, thus the name *best interest of creditors* test.

But how do we know what creditors would get in a Chapter 7? By figuring out the debtor's exemptions. Whatever nonexempt property a debtor has would have been distributed to unsecured creditors in a Chapter 7. Thus a Chapter 13 must at least pay unsecured creditors the value of those nonexempt assets.

Sidebar

UNINTENTIONALLY UNDERMINED?

Under the 2005 amendments, the exemptions increased and the exclusions to the estate (such as pensions and qualified retirement plans) also expanded. This means that there may be fewer nonexempt assets in many Chapter 7 cases in the future and that as a result, it may be easier for Chapter 13 debtors to meet the best interest test in the future. In other words, this test is likely to be less useful as a screening tool than it was before the new law.

H. Chapter 13 Plan Feasibility

Section 1325(a)(6) requires the court to find that "the debtor will be able to make all payments under the plan and to comply with the plan." Although it sounds quite daunting (that the debtor be able to make *all* payments), the test is quite lenient. This test, known as the **feasibility** requirement, simply requires that the plan proposed be realistic and that the debtor have a reasonable chance of completing it.

(1) Do the Proposed Payments Meet the Plan Obligations?

One aspect of feasibility *is* stringent, namely that the payments proposed under the plan must actually add up to enough money to pay the total amount proposed in the plan. With the interest requirements and the trustee's fee, this can sometimes be tricky to calculate, but there are internet sites that can help. Or you can just make the payments a little bit bigger than the amount you calculate as necessary, to give the debtor a cushion in case of a slight error.

(2) Can the Debtor Make the Payments?

The other aspect of feasibility relates to the debtor's likelihood of being able to make the payments required under the plan, based primarily on his or her income. This requirement relates to eligibility. You might recall that debtors need regular income to qualify for CHAPTER 13. The feasibility test is far easier to meet than one might imagine, because courts tend to give debtors a fair chance to rehabilitate their financial lives. There is a similar test in CHAPTER 11, which is somewhat harder to meet.

I. Modification of a CHAPTER 13 Plan or Dismissal of a CHAPTER 13 Case

Once the plan is proposed, is the debtor stuck with it? Not exactly. Prior to actual confirmation, the debtor can modify the plan freely. 11 U.S.C. §1323. After confirmation, the court can order a modification at the request of the debtor, the trustee, or any other party-in-interest to increase or decrease the payments or the payment period, or to increase or decrease the distributions to be paid under the plan. 11 U.S.C. §1329. Obviously, the modified plan must still comply with the Code.

F	A	Q

Q: In CHAPTER 13, whose approval is required for confirmation of the plan?

A: The court decides whether to confirm the plan, based upon the objections filed and the requirements of the Code. The CHAPTER 13 trustee will object if the plan does not meet the Code, so practically speaking, the CHAPTER 13 trustee decides whether to oppose the plan or not. Why would he or she oppose it? Because the numbers do not add up or because creditors are not receiving as much as they should be, based upon the various tests. After hearing any objections, the court makes the ultimate decision.

What would justify modification of a CHAPTER 13 plan? If the debtor is requesting it, perhaps there has been a drop in income or an increase in expenses, either of which could justify modification.

Or perhaps the trustee or a creditor requests a modification because the debtor is making more money now and is no longer in compliance with the disposable income test. The trustee requires that the debtor provide tax returns for each year of the plan, so increased income will not go unnoticed.

If the debtor has missed a number of payments under the plan, the trustee or a creditor may ask that the case simply be dismissed. The court may dismiss a Chapter 13 case or convert it to a Chapter 7, for cause, including a failure to make payments, unreasonable delay in proposing a plan or otherwise proceeding with the case, or for denial of confirmation, among other reasons. See 11 U.S.C. §1307.

As you might imagine, after the debtor has failed to pay the plan, the trustee or a creditor may move to convert or dismiss at the same time that a debtor is requesting modification. Moreover, if the debtor is really hit with hard times, and has met the Code's most minimal requirements, the debtor may be freed from all further payments due to unexpected hardship under Section 1328(b). However, if the secured creditor payments due under the plan have not been paid in full, the debtor could lose the collateral securing those payments.

For the remainder of this book, we will dive into Chapter 11, the type of bankruptcy used to restructure businesses.

SUMMARY

- Chapter 13 is the chapter under which individuals file a bankruptcy that involves a repayment plan.

- While one can choose to file a Chapter 13 case rather than a Chapter 7 simply because one prefers to pay back some creditors rather than just discharging all of one's debts, most people who use Chapter 13 do so to avoid the repossession or foreclosure of property held as collateral, like a house or a car.

- Another common reason debtors use Chapter 13 is to pay off priority claims, such as taxes, over time.

- A big benefit of Chapter 13 has always been to pay debts subject to a security interest over time, at a reduced price.

- For some collateral the debtor can strip down the amount to the value of the collateral, even if the amount owed is far more than that. An example would be a $4,000 auto upon which $10,000 is owed. This is almost like a Chapter 7 redemption, which can be paid over time. The debtor can also pay the market interest rate rather than the contract rate, which can make a big difference in the payment if rates are dropping.

- Stripdown has never been available for homes. Instead, one must pay the regular payment and add to that the amount necessary to make up the past due amount over the life of the plan.

- Stripdown is now limited for automobile loans taken out within 910 days of the bankruptcy filing and for all purchase money secured loans taken out within a year of the filing. One can no longer strip down the amount, though one can reduce the interest rate on the loan if rates have dropped.

- A repayment plan lasts for three to five years. If a person fails the means test and is thus ineligible for Chapter 7, and then files a Chapter 13 case, that person must do a five-year plan. For all others, it is up to the debtor whether to do a three-year or a five-year plan.

- If one has priority tax claims to pay off in a Chapter 13 plan, those claims stop accruing interest once the case is filed.

- A debtor must pay unsecured creditors at least as much in a Chapter 13 plan as they would get in a Chapter 7 liquidation. This means the Chapter 13 choice must be in the best interest of creditors. This test, in which creditors receive as much in a Chapter 7 as in a Chapter 13, is called the best interest test.

- The debtor is to contribute all of his or her disposable income during the plan period to the payment of creditors under the plan. When the debtor has income below the median, under the first step of the means test, the disposable income is determined by subtracting the expenses necessary to support the family and run any business from the debtor's income. For debtors with income above the median, the means test determines the debtor's disposable income. For above-median income debtors, this test will not reflect the reality of the debtor's financial condition because the numbers used in the means test are hypothetical.

CONNECTIONS

Money for Retirement Is Excluded from a Chapter 13 Plan

Contributions to qualified retirement plans, regardless of amount or necessity, never come into the bankruptcy estate under Section 541(b)(7), and thus cannot be part of disposable income under Section 1325(b)(2). See Chapter 5, Section D for more detail and other exclusions that never come into the debtor's estate.

Alternatives to Declaring Bankruptcy

This chapter goes through the ins and outs of individual pay out plans under Chapter 13. Remember that Chapter 2 of this book addresses the alternative to declaring bankruptcy at all. After doing the calculations of whether a Chapter 13 plan is feasible and assessing the debtor's assets and liabilities, it's always worth-while to think about the advantages and disadvantages of simply staying in vir-tual bankruptcy, and the extent to which the debtor is judgment proof. Sometimes doing nothing really is the most advantageous, most affordable option for a low-income debtor.

Exemptions

In thinking about the alternatives to bankruptcy, in addition to looking at the debtor's assets and liabilities, it's essential to calculate how much of the debtor's property is exempt. Chapter 6 covers exemption law in detail, while Chapter 2, Section B focuses on exemptions in the context of the state law collection process.

The Overall Context for Chapter 13

Now that you know the details of a Chapter 13 case, it's a good time to review the Table of Contents for Chapters 4 through 9. That will give you a good overview, because those chapters cover the rules that apply to all bankruptcies. As you look over the automatic stay, the debtor's estate, exemptions, claims, the treatment of secured claims, and the avoiding powers, make sure you understand each concept. Here's a hint: Try to explain it to someone in plain English, without the legal jargon. If you can explain it to your grandma or a brother or sister or friend, that's a good sign that you understand that concept well enough to translate it in your own mind into regular words.

Chapter 11

Although the rest of this book focuses on Chapter 11 bankruptcies — business reorganizations — many of the requirements for Chapter 13 plans and Chapter 11 plans are similar. For example, both types of plans must be filed in good faith, must meet the best interest test, and must be feasible. Secured creditor treatment is also similar. So most of the concepts in this chapter are applied in the second half of this book to the business context.

The Means Test

We know that the means test can appear daunting. But if you found it confusing the first time around, this chapter provides a chance to revisit it for purposes of the disposable income test and, hopefully, understand it better. The key is to look back at Chapter 10, and work through the six steps listed in Chapter 10, Section C(3). Although the overall test seems complicated, each step by itself is straightforward. Practice by working through an example, and we're confident you can get it!

2

Business Reorganizations Under CHAPTER **11**

Overview of CHAPTER 11 and Its Alternatives

14

We now enter the foray of business reorganizations under CHAPTER 11, but for context, it is helpful to keep in mind that financially troubled businesses have alternatives to bankruptcy. For this reason, we introduce CHAPTER 11 by comparing CHAPTER 11 to its out-of-court alternatives. We cover the basic rules of CHAPTER 11, and discuss the most common alternative to CHAPTER 11, the out-of-court workout.

OVERVIEW

In beginning our discussion of CHAPTER 11 and its options, we leave the domain of personal bankruptcy and move into the business side of bankruptcy.[1] Many of the same principles apply (e.g., principles relating to the estate, the automatic stay, the treatment of secured and priority creditors, the feasibility test, and the best interest of creditors test), but there are also many new rules and concepts. If learning what makes a business tick interests you, this is the most interesting area of bankruptcy law.

A. THE OUT-OF-COURT WORKOUT PROCESS COMPARED TO CHAPTER 11

1. Default Triggers Negotiation
2. Negotiating in the Shadow of the Law
3. Advantages of Workout Plans
4. Disadvantages of Workout Plans: Unanimity Among Creditors

---

[1] CHAPTER 11 can also be used by individuals, but, because it is expensive, individuals rarely use it to restructure debt unless they are over the CHAPTER 13 debt limits.

The **debtor-in-possession** (a Chapter 11 debtor is called a debtor-in-possession because the debtor entity retains control of property — including, typically, the business itself) is faced with choices about which parts of the business to continue and which parts to discontinue, which contracts to honor and which to abandon, as well as restructuring options that may not be available outside bankruptcy. Because these choices must be made relatively quickly, Chapter 11 is an exciting practice area.

Before we even talk about Chapter 11, you should know that businesses have another option for sorting out financial problems: They can try to do an **out-of-court workout**, which involves restructuring the businesses' debts without involving a court, simply by negotiating with creditors. An out-of-court workout can be far superior to Chapter 11 if

- there are not too many creditors;
- no creditor is too aggressive;
- the debtor's business and debt structures are not too complex; and
- the debtor has had good relations with the creditors in the past.

An out-of-court workout saves the extremely expensive cost and time of a Chapter 11 case, costs that put the company further into debt. Therefore, the company may be more likely to survive an out-of-court workout. Further, Chapter 11 increases creditor antagonism toward the debtor.

While some companies may benefit from an out-of-court workout, some are simply too far gone to have any chance of working out their affairs without a bankruptcy court's help.

Sidebar

SICK COMPANIES EVERYWHERE NEED TREATMENT

In India, corporate bankruptcy law is known as the "sick companies' law." Continuing that metaphor, Chapter 11 is the intensive care unit, whereas the out-of-court workout is a holistic, homeopathic remedy. A workout is less drastic but Chapter 11, like modern medicine, is useful in a real emergency.

A. The Out-of-Court Workout Process Compared to Chapter 11

(1) Default Triggers Negotiation

When a business defaults on a secured loan, the creditor gets the right to take back assets. These business assets, whether equipment, the real estate where the business is located, or inventory and accounts, are the very assets needed to run the business. In these circumstances, the business must negotiate with the creditor, or risk losing the whole business. This need to negotiate is how an out-of-court workout typically begins.

(2) Negotiating in the Shadow of the Law

Sometimes the threat of a CHAPTER 11 case in the background can cause creditors to go along with an out-of-court workout. The parties negotiate in the **shadow of the law**. Unsecured creditors frequently fare poorly in a CHAPTER 11 case because once all the fees and other costs are paid, there's no money left for unsecured creditors, and if the business liquidates its assets, there might be no assets left to pay unsecured creditors. Against this backdrop, unsecured creditors are likely to prefer an out-of-court workout plan.

Many creditors are suppliers of the company that is in debt. Sometimes a creditor is entirely dependent on the debtor company, because it is the creditor's main client. Such creditors are often willing to forgo payments temporarily or waive them entirely because it is in their interest to keep the debtor alive as a customer. Often, this is the only way to get paid for even part of their unsecured claim, or to generate future business to prevent going bankrupt themselves.

On the other hand, unsecured creditors may belong to a trade association to which the debtor owes dues, and be actual competitors of the debtor. In that case, the creditor has no interest in keeping the failing company alive.

> ### S i d e b a r
>
> **WORKOUT PLANS CAN BE HUGE**
>
> In 1979, Chrysler Corp. (along with its subsidiary Chrysler Credit Corp.) completed the largest out-of-court workout in history, restructuring over $4.75 billion in debts with over 400 secured creditors. That was an incredible accomplishment, given the need for nearly complete unanimity.

(3) Advantages of Workout Plans

If the debtor is able to put the pieces in place, a workout plan costs much less. Attorneys' fees in CHAPTER 11 cases can be tens if not hundreds of thousands of dollars, and can eat up a large portion of the business's value. CHAPTER 11 also can take a long time, during which some of the debtor's reputation and goodwill is lost. While most CHAPTER 11 plans are confirmed within two years of the filing, it can sometimes take much longer to get a plan confirmed! Because of the time value of money and the value of receiving certain payment today rather than uncertain payment in the future, unsecured creditors might well prefer an out-of-court plan in which they receive earlier payments, even if they are not paid in full. Moreover, the CHAPTER 11 process is a huge burden on management, requiring endless hours dealing with legal issues rather than running the business. Out-of-court workouts, on the other hand, can be quite quick and create much less negative publicity. Overall, out-of-court workouts are much simpler.

Since the debtor and the creditors can figure out the treatment they would get in a CHAPTER 11, the results of many out-of-court workouts look just like the results of a CHAPTER 11 case, but without the high costs of going to court.

F   A   Q

Q: Since the out-of-court workout is not enforced by the bankruptcy court, how is it enforced?

A: Like any other private contract, it's governed by contract law. All of the parties sign a complex contract governing how the debtor will pay the debts, and how the creditors will forbear from collecting the debts.

(4) Disadvantages of Workout Plans: Unanimity Among Creditors

One disadvantage of an out-of-court workout is that every creditor needs to agree to the workout plan. So as soon as one creditor steps out of line and starts aggressively pursuing its state court collection rights (remember, it's a **race of the diligent**, each creditor for himself) all creditors will want out of the deal. Because out-of-court workouts are collective in nature, they require fairly amicable relations. CHAPTER 11, by contrast, contains rules that allow a court to force the CHAPTER 11 plan on dissenting creditors, and therefore the debtor need not obtain unanimous consent from all the creditors. 11 U.S.C. §1129(b).

Out-of-Court Workouts Require Consensus			
Vote Tally: Out-of-Court Workout		Vote Tally: Chapter 11 Plan	
Yes	90	Yes	90
No	2	+No	2
= NO GO		= APPROVED (a cramdown plan)	

(5) Advantages of CHAPTER 11

There are some situations in which CHAPTER 11 is so beneficial that it would be much better for the debtor just to file bankruptcy than to attempt an out-of-court workout. For example, as discussed in Chapter 9, if a creditor has obtained a lien during the 90 days prior to the filing, the debtor can avoid that lien. 11 U.S.C. §547. Or the debtor may have provided a security interest to a creditor, thus favoring that creditor over other creditors, and other creditors may file an involuntary petition to reverse the transfer. 11 U.S.C. §§303, 547. Another advantage of filing a CHAPTER 11 is the protection of the automatic stay. 11 U.S.C. §362. As explained in Chapter 4, the automatic stay prohibits the immediate seizure of assets, and prohibits any action to collect a debt or to obtain possession of property of the debtor's estate. 11 U.S.C. §362. The debtor may need the protection of the automatic stay during the time it takes to negotiate a plan with creditors. CHAPTER 11 allows the debtor to operate its business free of collection activity, subject to the need to provide secured creditors with adequate protection of their property interests.

How many businesses survive Chapter 11? Chapter 11 statistics vary but they are not as high as one might hope. Depending on the study, success rates range from 10% to 25%. It depends on how you measure success. Some cases are filed merely to sell assets as a going concern, with no intention to survive. We are aware of no data on the success of out-of-court workouts — this would be a good subject for empirical research.

In addition, the debtor may find it advantageous to reject certain leases and contracts, which essentially means to breach or not perform its obligations. Section 365 of the Bankruptcy Code not only permits but also encourages debtors to reject contracts and leases in order to revitalize the business, leaving the non-debtor party with a general unsecured claim for damages. 11 U.S.C. §365.

Finally, Chapter 11 can help a company to restock inventory. Here's how it works: While the debtor is putting together the Chapter 11 plan, payments on general unsecured claims are frozen, thereby freeing up cash to buy new product.

Believe it or not, secured creditors also may prefer Chapter 11, because the debtor-in-possession is required to file disclosures that give a blow-by-blow account of its business activities. See Bankruptcy Rule 1007 (requiring the filing of bankruptcy schedules and statements). This allows creditors to monitor the debtor's business activity.

Further, in most Chapter 11 plans the debtor does not pay general unsecured claims in full. Accordingly, unsecured debt is reduced, leaving more money available to operate and to pay secured claims. Fully secured creditors are often more than happy to squeeze out unsecured creditors.

(6) Disadvantages of Chapter 11

Chapter 11 is disadvantageous to creditors because creditors can be forced to live with a plan they do not like. 11 U.S.C. §1129(b). Moreover, secured creditors in Chapter 11 can be forced to accept less than they're owed — payments equal to the value of their collateral (the "stripped down" value). 11 U.S.C. §1129(b)(2)(A)(i).

Sidebar

SELLING ASSETS AS A GOING CONCERN

Section 363(b) allows assets to be sold free and clear of all liens, claims, and encumbrances, which allows the buyer to purchase the assets without fear of encumbrances, liens, or successor liability claims. The policy reason is that assets sold free of all claims can be sold at a higher price, thus raising more money for the debtor's creditors.

B. Introduction to the Basic Chapter 11 Rules and Major Parties-in-Interest

If you represent a Chapter 11 debtor, the first thing you must determine is whether there is a realistic plan to get the company out of its financial difficulties. An exit plan is the most critical aspect of a Chapter 11 case because Chapter 11 is incredibly expensive. It would be a senseless waste of time to file a Chapter 11 case for a client if there was no chance it would turn the business around. And if the case goes on for too long, lawyers' fees can eat up any potential profits and make reorganization impossible.

Here's an example of a typical company's monthly bills while it's in CHAPTER 11:

- phone, electric, internet, gas
- debt service
- rent
- cleaning service
- debtor's counsel's fees
- debtor's accountant's fees
- creditors' committees counsel fees
- CHAPTER 11 administrative fee

As with CHAPTERS 7 and 13, only certain **pre-petition claims** can be paid at a discount in CHAPTER 11. The debtor will be responsible for paying *all* of its post-petition obligations. In addition, secured debt may need to be **serviced** (paid) during the CHAPTER 11 case.

To assess whether a client can succeed in CHAPTER 11, the debtor must prepare budgets and financial projections, explaining how the case will help its business return to profitability.

The debtor does not need creditor consent to file a CHAPTER 11 case. 11 U.S.C. §109. Conversely, creditors occasionally force a debtor into CHAPTER 11. In the rare event of an involuntary case, a creditor normally files an involuntary CHAPTER 7 case, and the debtor later converts it to a CHAPTER 11 case. 11 U.S.C. §303.

(1) Major Players in a CHAPTER 11 Case

(a) The Debtor-in-Possession

In most CHAPTER 11 cases, the debtor's management, not a trustee, runs the case. See 11 U.S.C. §§1104, 1107. In CHAPTER 11 the focus is on how the debtor's operations can support future payments to creditors. The debtor-in-possession continues to run the business, and has virtually all of the rights and powers of a trustee under the Bankruptcy Code, including the right to operate the business, the right to enter into transactions in the ordinary course of business without court approval, and the right to avoid preferential transfers and fraudulent conveyances. See 11 U.S.C. §§1106, 1107.

The appointment of a trustee is a rare and drastic move in CHAPTER 11. Section 1104 provides that a trustee may only be appointed for "cause," such as fraud, dishonesty, incompetence, or gross mismanagement. 11 U.S.C. §1104 (a)(1).

Remember that a debtor-in-possession, like any trustee in bankruptcy, is a fiduciary for all creditors. 11 U.S.C. §1107. This means that a trustee in bankruptcy has an obligation to create the largest possible distribution for creditors and to fulfill the duties of loyalty and care to creditors. Indeed, the debtor's management (the officers and directors of the corporation) now have dual fiduciary duties, to creditors in addition to shareholders. Indeed, once the debtor is within the zone of insolvency,[2] the primary fiduciary duty shifts away from the shareholders, in favor of the creditors.

---

[2]Most scholars and courts agree that at some point *prior to insolvency*, justice requires that directors be more sensitive to risking creditors' funds. See *Credit Lyonnais Bank Nederland, N.V. v. Pathe Communications Corp.*, 1991 WL 277613, n.55 (Del. Ch. 1991); *In re Ben Franklin Retail Stores, Inc.*, 225 B.R. 655-56 (Bankr. N.D. Ill. 1998).

Once a case is filed, the debtor-in-possession has an obligation to run the company and to comply with the rules of CHAPTER 11. The debtor's goal is to make a profit and continue its business into the future or, if it so chooses, to sell its assets, depending on what approach maximizes the value of its assets for creditors.

(b) The United States Trustee's Office

The United States Trustee's Office was created as part of the Bankruptcy Reform Act of 1978, when Congress greatly expanded the jurisdictional powers of bankruptcy judges. The U.S. Trustee's program started as a pilot project in 18 districts to ease the transition during that time. In 1986 the program was expanded nationwide, except in Alabama and North Carolina.

The U.S. Trustee is different from a case trustee. The U.S. Trustee is a government officer, functionally equivalent to a United States Attorney for bankruptcy cases. 28 U.S.C. §581.

The U.S. Trustee's Office was created with the purpose of further removing judges from the administration of CHAPTER 11 cases, thereby allowing judges to focus on disputes within those cases. The duties of the U.S. Trustee's Office include appointing committees, including unsecured creditor committees and equity committees (who represent the interests of owners — shareholders in a corporation); appointing a CHAPTER 11 trustee in the rare event that the court orders one and creditors do not elect their own choice for trustee; monitoring cases to ensure that debtors file their monthly operating reports and pay their administrative fees; protecting unsecured creditor interests in cases in which there is no unsecured creditors' committee; and appearing before to court to be heard on any relevant issue in a case. 11 U.S.C. §307.

In addition to paying the fees of its own lawyers and the lawyers for the creditors' committees, the debtor also indirectly pays the U.S. Trustee's lawyers' fees as well. The attorneys in the U.S. Trustee's Office are government employees, part of the Department of Justice. But debtors in CHAPTER 11 do pay administrative fees every month they remain in bankruptcy and these fees help fund the U.S. Trustee program.

The U.S. Trustee's Office plays a much larger role in CHAPTER 11 cases than in CHAPTER 7 and CHAPTER 13 cases, particularly in reviewing and approving fees for the debtor's counsel, counsel for the creditor's committee, and other professionals who are paid from the debtor's assets. Remember, these fees can be substantial, in some cases running to millions of dollars.

(c) Creditors' Committees

The claims of individual unsecured creditors are often quite small, and thus may not be worth fighting for. The Bankruptcy Code deals with this problem by allowing general unsecured creditors to organize into committees, who are permitted to hire counsel that is paid from the debtor's assets. 11 U.S.C. §§1102, 330. By forming an unsecured creditors' committee, the general unsecured creditors gain a powerful, unified voice that the judge can hear through the din of the secured creditors. Thus unsecured creditors' committees often counterbalance powerful secured creditors.

The most important activities of the creditors' committee include

- negotiating the CHAPTER 11 plan;
- reviewing the debtor's budgets and other financial information;

■ hiring accountants and other professionals to review the debtor's financial data;

■ reviewing the debtor's cash collateral order and post-petition financing order; and

■ reviewing the debtor's motions to sell assets, and assume and assign leases.

See 11 U.S.C. §1103. The creditors' committee is often the most important party in the case after the debtor-in-possession and the primary secured creditor. Normally, the 20 largest unsecured creditors receive notice of the meeting to form a creditors' committee, and the U.S. Trustee's Office forms a committee from that group, with at least three and no more than nine members. Ideally, the committee will have five or seven members, because a smaller committee is easier to manage and an odd number of members prevents tie votes.

Like the debtor-in-possession, committee members owe fiduciary duties, including the duty of loyalty and the duty of care, to the entire general unsecured creditor class, meaning all of the general unsecured creditors in the case. *In re SPM Mfg. Corp.*, 984 F.2d 1305 (1st Cir. 1993). Fiduciary duties run not only to creditors that have the same interests as a particular committee member, but to all general unsecured creditors. If an unsecured creditor has a particular interest unique to his or her own position, it may be best for that creditor to refrain from membership in the creditors' committee and to obtain its own counsel. Other creditors that should be excluded from the creditors' committee include those that are competitors of the debtor and those that are involved in litigation with the debtor.

As mentioned above, the creditors' committee may retain counsel in the case, as well as other professionals (such as accountants) with court approval. These professionals will be paid from the debtor's estate, just as the debtor's own professionals will be paid. As you can see, committee participation levels the playing field and allows the general unsecured creditors (who would not otherwise have a strong voice individually) to be represented and play an active and meaningful role in the case.

In larger cases, other committees may be appointed as well. For example, in a publicly traded company, the U.S. Trustee's Office often appoints a committee of equity holders to represent the shareholders. 11 U.S.C. §1102. In larger cases, there may also be a bondholders' committee and more than one general unsecured creditors' committee, particularly if some unsecured creditors have interests that are different from other unsecured creditors.

Sidebar

NO FREE LUNCH

Notice that the professional services, which look like they are free for unsecured creditors, are not really free. Instead, the professionals will be paid out of the estate as first priority administrative expenses, leaving less money to repay general unsecured claims. As usual, there is no free lunch!

However, the best way for the unsecured creditors to protect their interests is by hiring their own accountant to review and verify the debtor's financial information. This is almost always money well spent.

(d) Secured Creditors

It is common to have multiple secured creditors with overlapping liens of different priority on the same or different assets. Why is there more than one lien on the same asset? First, a company grants voluntary liens in order to borrow money. This is just like a first mortgage on your home, followed by a home equity loan or second mortgage. Second, anyone who is owed money can file an involuntary lien. This is just like a plumber who is owed money, and can then file an involuntary "mechanics' lien" on your house. If there is only one secured creditor that holds a lien on all of the debtor's assets, we call that creditor the **primary secured lender**.

All secured creditors, regardless of their priority, are entitled to adequate protection of their security interests throughout the bankruptcy process. Adequate protection can mean monthly payments on the secured debt, or it might simply mean maintaining the collateral in its present condition and insuring it against damage. Adequate protection is designed to protect the value of the creditor's collateral from diminution during the case. 11 U.S.C. §363(c)(2).

Also, every secured creditor has a right to be adequately protected before any of their **cash collateral** (collateral that becomes cash at some point, such as inventory and accounts receivable, as discussed in detail in Chapter 16) is used by the debtor during the Chapter 11 case.

Overall, secured creditors have a very strong bargaining position in Chapter 11, just as they do in other types of bankruptcy as well as outside bankruptcy. Under a Chapter 11 plan, the debtor must either surrender the secured party's collateral, pay the allowed secured claim in full with **present value interest** over the life of the plan, or provide the creditor with what is called the "indubitable equivalent" of its secured claim. 11 U.S.C. §1129(B)(2)(A). In addition, if the secured creditor is **oversecured**, it will be entitled to post-petition interest and attorneys' fees to the extent of the value of its collateral under Section 506(b).

As discussed in the context of Chapter 13 cases, in cases where the secured party's collateral is worth less than its debt, the secured party's claim will be **bifurcated**. Some of the claim (the **deficiency claim**) will end up in the general unsecured creditor class under the plan, while the rest (the part supported by the value of the collateral) will be treated and paid as a secured claim. This is at times a great benefit to the debtor, as it allows the debtor to **strip down** the secured party's claim to the value of the collateral, and thus more easily fund a plan.

The debtor hopes that each class will vote in favor of its ultimate Chapter 11 plan, or that at the very least *one class* will vote in favor of its plan. Without one accepting class, the debtor cannot confirm a plan. If the secured party's deficiency claim is large and dominates the unsecured creditor class, and if the debtor and the secured party are adverse, the large deficiency claim could make it very difficult for the debtor to gain a favorable vote from its unsecured class.

Voting is calculated by both number of creditors and by amount, so this could cause the whole class to vote no. Consequently, stripping down a secured creditor's claim can make it difficult for the debtor to obtain the unsecured creditor votes that it may need to confirm a Chapter 11 plan.

(e) Unsecured Creditors

Unsecured creditors have a powerful tool in obtaining favorable treatment in the plan: the absolute priority rule. If an unsecured creditor class does not accept the plan and the class is not paid in full with interest, the debtor's equity holders (think stockholders) cannot keep their equity interests (think stock). Instead, the owners must either sell these interests and give creditors the proceeds or distribute the equity interests to the creditors. This is a great incentive for owners to work with unsecured creditors to provide a distribution that creditors can live with.

C. Overview of Thoughts on CHAPTER 11

We hope that thinking through CHAPTER 11 legal issues helps your understanding of bankruptcy law overall and perhaps intrigues you to learn more about business law and the many policy issues and societal ramifications it involves.

All thinking and strategizing about the case begins and ends with the CHAPTER 11 plan process. The end game for all CHAPTER 11 cases is the plan. Thus the last big thing that a debtor must do in any successful CHAPTER 11 case, after filing first day orders, keeping the business afloat, restructuring, determining the claims against it, and rejecting or assuming and assigning contracts and leases, is draft and circulate a voting plan. Unlike an out-of-court workout, creditors in a CHAPTER 11 case are entitled to very specific treatment under the Bankruptcy Code.

The backdrop for any plan negotiations, be they with an unsecured creditors' committee or a secured creditor, is a party's assessment of what the debtor can get from a court if the creditor objects. In other words, if the debtor would be able to force a certain treatment on a secured creditor, the secured creditor is likely to agree to that treatment. Similarly, if unsecured creditors could be forced to accept a certain distribution, the creditor is likely to vote in favor of a plan that provides that treatment, without the expense and delay of litigation. This is why it's worth remembering that parties always negotiate in the shadow of the law.

The other important backdrop to CHAPTER 11 plan negotiations is that the creditor must determine what it would get if the plan were to fail and the debtor were to liquidate. General unsecured creditors often receive little in liquidation and are typically motivated to support a plan that proposes more than liquidation payments, even if the proposed amount is far less than they are owed.

The chart below offers a chronological overview of the CHAPTER 11 process.

CHAPTER 11 Chronology of Key Concepts		
Section Number	**Concept Name**	**Usefulness**
327 330	Hire attorneys, accountants	For debtors, creditors' committees, and equity holder committees
1108	Debtor-in-possession	Debtor continues to run business if no trustee is appointed
363(c)(2)	Use of cash collateral	Debtor needs agreement or court approval
364	Post-petition financing	Needed when there is not enough cash

362(a)	Automatic stay	Stops collection efforts
362(d)	Lift the stay	Creditor can have stay lifted
361	Adequate protection	Debtor can avoid having stay lifted by providing adequate protection
363(c)(1)	Debtor uses and sells assets in ordinary course of business	Court permission is not needed
365	Debtor assumes, assumes and assigns, or rejects executory contracts and unexpired leases	Provides flexibility useful to reorganization
363(b)	Debtor sells assets free and clear of liens and claims	Increases asset value
1122	Debtor classifies claims in contemplation of getting a plan confirmed	No gerrymandering, only classify for legitimate legal or business purposes
1125	Debtor drafts and circulates a disclosure statement	Provides enough information so creditors can decide whether to vote for the plan
1129	Debtor formulates a plan that meets • the good-faith test • the feasibility test • the best interest test • the fair and equitable test • the absolute priority rule	Exit Plan: At least some of this strategizing should have occurred *before* the case was filed
1126(c)	Creditors vote on the plan	Accepting class = 2/3 in amount and 1/2 in number in each class
1129	Debtor proceeds to confirmation either consensually or through cramdown	Plan must be crammed down if any one class votes no
1141 1142	Confirmation order is binding on all parties in interest for the rest of time	Only exceptions are creditors with no notice because there is no due process

SUMMARY

■ An out-of-court workout is more likely to be successful if there aren't too many creditors, no single creditor is too aggressive, and the debtor has good relationships with creditors. Out-of-court workout plans can be much faster, can save money on attorneys' fees, and can allow management to focus on running the company rather than focusing on the legal issues regarding the bankruptcy.

■ Chapter 11 can be advantageous because the automatic stay halts collection efforts and thereby temporarily improves cash flow that can be used to restock inventory or pre-pay for services. The Code allows the debtor to reject certain leases and contracts and allows debtors to sell assets free and clear of liens, claims, and encumbrances, which increases the value of the assets.

■ The debtor-in-possession, i.e., the debtor company's management, rather than a trustee, usually continues to run the business, even though those are the guys who ran the company into the ground to begin with. Why? The management team has knowledge about the company and the industry. Management also becomes a fiduciary for the creditors.

■ The U.S. Trustee's Office approves fees for attorneys and other professionals, such as accountants, which can run into millions of dollars.

■ The creditors' committee represents all the claims of unsecured creditors, many of which may be small.

■ In general, secured creditors have a lot of power in a Chapter 11 case, because the debtor must usually either surrender the secured creditor's collateral or pay the allowed secured claim in full, over the life of the plan, with present value interest.

CONNECTIONS

Fiduciary Duty

Once a case is filed, the debtor-in-possession has an obligation to run the company and to comply with the rules of Chapter 11. The debtor's goal is to make a profit and continue its business into the future or, if it so chooses, to sell its assets, depending on what approach maximizes the value of its assets for creditors.

Shifting Loyalties

Managers' loyalties are supposed to shift in favor of creditors when a company approaches insolvency. But we suspect that, in the real world, managers do not know that their loyalties are supposed to shift. We'd also be surprised if they could really change their behavior overnight, as loyalties are from the heart.

The Creditors' Legal Fees

The debtor pays the secured creditor's post-petition, pre-confirmation legal fees, in addition to its own, *if* the creditor and the debtor have a contract that provides for payment of legal fees (nearly all commercial loan agreements have this provision), and *if* the secured creditor is oversecured, meaning its collateral is worth more than the amount of its debt. See Chapter 15, Section B, and Chapter 8 for a discussion of oversecured and undersecured creditors, and the consequences that follow from those conditions.

Making Peace with Creditors

Remember that an overriding goal of Chapter 11 is to negotiate and confirm a consensual plan, meaning a plan that all classes of claims have accepted. This is done by making peace with the secured creditor classes as well as the unsecured creditor class or classes.

Keeping Perspective

In the next five chapters, we take an in-depth look at the complex issues that arise in Chapter 11. If you start to get bogged down in the details and lose sight of the forest for the trees, feel free to come back to the overview in this chapter to remind yourself of the big picture. In addition, if you're a visual learner, there's the handy chart at the end of this chapter that summarizes all the major Chapter 11 issues, and lists the Bankruptcy Code section that goes with each. You can use the chart to look up key provisions in the Bankruptcy Code, which is another valuable way to use these materials.

The Execution Process

Remember that the execution process prescribed by state collection law, described in Chapter 2, still applies in the business context. If the debtor doesn't file bankruptcy, and cannot get the creditors to sign off on a workout plan, the creditors' recourse is to state collection law—obtaining a judgment and executing on the debtor's property to take it and sell it in order to satisfy the debts they're owed.

The CHAPTER 11 Plan Process: Creditor Treatment, Plan Confirmation, and Post-Confirmation Issues

15

This chapter describes how the CHAPTER 11 plan must treat different types of claims and interests — secured claims, priority claims, general unsecured claims, and equity holder interests (i.e., ownership of the company). We discuss how the confirmation process works, how creditors with different legal rights are put into different classes, how they vote on the plan, and which post-confirmation issues come up most frequently.

OVERVIEW

Once the debtor gets the disclosure statement approved and puts together a plan that complies with the basic creditor treatment rules, it presents the plan to all the classes of creditors. The creditors vote to accept or reject the plan. If not all the creditor classes consent to the plan, there are additional rules to determine whether the debtor can force ("cram down") the plan on creditors that do not consent. Finally, post-confirmation issues include interpreting the legal effect of the confirmation order, and enforcing the plan and the confirmation order.

The CHAPTER 11 plan is the debtor's ticket out of bankruptcy and back into the world of business as usual. Even though the debtor-in-possession and its attorneys must do a lot of things before circulating the plan and seeking creditor votes to approve it, we think the next four chapters will make more sense if you first understand the plan requirements. If you understand the goal, the process of how to get there will make more sense.

A. BASIC CHAPTER 11 REQUIREMENTS

  1. Feasibility

B. SECURED CREDITOR TREATMENT

  1. The Treatment of Oversecured and Undersecured Claims After the Filing but Prior to Confirmation of a CHAPTER 11 Plan
  2. Secured Creditor Treatment Under the CHAPTER 11 Plan

C. PRIORITY TREATMENT UNDER CHAPTER 11

D. THE BEST INTEREST TEST: TREATMENT OF GENERAL UNSECURED CLAIMS

E. THE CONFIRMATION PROCESS

  1. Confirmation
  2. Consensual Plans Versus Cramdown Plans

F. SOLICITING VOTES FOR THE PLAN

  1. The Disclosure Statement
  2. Plan Voting
  3. Classification
  4. Impairment

G. FORCING THE PLAN ON DISSENTING CREDITORS: THE CRAMDOWN PLAN

  1. Cramdown of a Secured Class
  2. The Specific and General Requirements of the Fair and Equitable Test
  3. The Present Value Interest Rate
  4. Obtaining Positive Votes from at Least One Accepting Class: If You Are Stripping Down, This Is Harder Than It Looks
  5. The Absolute Priority Rule When Cramming Down the Plan on Unsecured Creditors
  6. The New Value Exception

H. POST-CONFIRMATION ISSUES: THE EFFECT OF CONFIRMATION

  1. The Confirmation Order Is *Res Judicata* as to All Issues Dealt with in the Plan and Also Discharges All Claims Except as Otherwise Provided for in the Plan
  2. Enforcing the Plan

A. Basic CHAPTER 11 Requirements

The CHAPTER 11 requirements are very similar to the CHAPTER 13 requirements (discussed in Chapter 13 of this book), as the following chart shows.

Comparison of CHAPTER 13 and CHAPTER 11 Plan Requirements

Test or Treatment	CHAPTER 13	CHAPTER 11
Good-Faith Test	Plan must be proposed in good faith	Plan must be proposed in good faith
Feasibility Test	Debtor must have sufficient income to fund plan	Debtor's projections must be based in reality, cannot be "pie in the sky"
Best Interest Test	Creditors must get at least as much under the plan as they would get in a CHAPTER 7 liquidation	Creditors must get at least as much under the plan as they would get in a CHAPTER 7 liquidation
Treatment of Priority Claims	Pay in full over life of plan	Pay most in full by the effective date; taxes can be paid over 5 years from the date of the petition
Secured Creditor Treatment	Must pay present value of allowed secured claim over the life of the plan (3 to 5 years)	Must pay present value of allowed secured claim over the life of the collateral (varies) unless creditor agrees to other treatment
Unsecured Creditor Treatment	Must pay debtor's disposable income over the life of the plan	Get whatever money is negotiated; voting replaces requirement to pay all disposable income plus, unless unsecured creditors either agree or are paid in full, equity owners cannot keep their ownership

In any CHAPTER 11 plan, the debtor must prove that the debtor proposed the plan in **good faith** and not by any means forbidden by law, a test similar to the CHAPTER 13 good-faith test. 11 U.S.C. §1129(a)(1). The debtor must also meet the **feasibility test**, which means that the debtor must prove, based on cash flow projections and its overall financial picture, that the plan is not likely to be followed by a liquidation or need for further reorganization of the debtor. 11 U.S.C. §1129(a)(11). In other words, the feasibility test requires the court to find that the debtor can probably afford to pay the plan. Further, the plan must treat secured creditors and priority claims as they are entitled to be treated under the overall priority scheme. Next, the plan must treat the general unsecured creditors as they are entitled to be treated under the ever present **best interest test** — they are entitled to receive at least as much under the CHAPTER 11 plan as they would receive under a CHAPTER 7 liquidation. 11 U.S.C. §1129(a)(7). Finally, all transfers of property

S i d e b a r

AIRLINES IN CHAPTER 11

How common is CHAPTER 11? That depends upon the industry. As of 2006, over half of all seats on U.S. airlines were on airlines that are in CHAPTER 11. If you are worried that airlines' cost-cutting measures could affect safety, try to put it out of your mind — it is almost impossible to avoid traveling on airlines that are or have been in CHAPTER 11.

under the plan must comply with non-bankruptcy law. For example, debtors must comply with state laws that govern the transfer of assets from a nonprofit corporation to a for-profit corporation.

(1) Feasibility

The feasibility test essentially requires that the plan be more than just a pipe dream. Section 1129(a)(11) specifies that "confirmation of the plan is not likely to be followed by the liquidation, or the need for further financial reorganization, of the debtor or any successor to the debtor under the plan, unless such liquidation or reorganization is proposed in the plan." The big question that arises here is *how certain* must it be that the debtor can actually make the payments proposed in the plan.

Because the feasibility test deals largely with the very factual and contingent issue of the debtor's future business prospects, few courts require absolute proof that a debtor will succeed. The question, though, is whether the debtor is likely to succeed at least long enough to make the plan payments. Other than that, the feasibility test is applied by the courts on a case-by-case basis within the very broad discretion of the bankruptcy court.

F   A   Q

Q: How can the debtor prove feasibility?

A: The debtor can present business projections and projected cash flow statements determining how much money the debtor can generate on a net basis during the plan period. The debtor also lists all other sources of payments for the plan, including asset sales, equity contributions, potential lawsuits (in which it is the plaintiff), and future contracts that will come to fruition during the repayment period.

In addressing feasibility concerns, the debtor may be required to explain to the court (through management or an expert witness) what caused the debtor's financial problems in the first place, and what will be or has been done to correct these problems. In other words, the debtor must prove that its cash flow statements and other financial projections are realistic and credible, and show how it will raise the funds necessary to make the plan payments. In some cases, this involves presenting information regarding financial conditions and trends in its industry, if that information will help prove the projections.

Feasibility issues can be hotly contested. Naturally, if the debtor is relying on future litigation proceeds or future contracts to fund its plan, creditors and the court should ask how likely it is that the revenue from litigation or future contracts is really going to come to fruition. Section 1129(a)(11) does not require the bankruptcy

Sidebar

FEASIBILITY: FROM THE COURT'S MOUTH

Here's a sample of language that courts have used to determine whether a plan is feasible: Is the plan a visionary scheme that promises more than the debtor can possibly attain? Is it really pie in the sky, regardless of the sincere and honest intention of the plan proponent? Are the debtor's financial statements mere speculation? Even worse, does it look as though the debtor will continue to operate at a loss throughout the life of the plan?

court to find that the plan will definitely be paid or is guaranteed to succeed, only a reasonable assurance of commercial viability. *Kane v. Johns-Manville Corp.*, 843 F.2d 636, 649 (2d Cir. 1998); *In re New Orleans Ltd.*, 116 F.3d 790 (5th Cir. 1997). But the court *does* need to determine the adequacy of the capital structure, the earning power of the business, the economics surrounding the business, the ability of management, the probability of the continuation of the same management, and any other matters that could determine the prospect of a sufficiently successful operation. *In Re Georgetown Ltd.*, 209 B.R. 763 (Bankr. M.D. Ga. 1997).

B. Secured Creditor Treatment

Now we'll look in greater detail at the plan's **treatment** of secured claims, priority claims, and general unsecured claims, that is, the overall priority scheme. Note that "treatment" means payment. So when we talk of the "treatment of secured claims," we are talking about the debtor's payments to secured creditors.

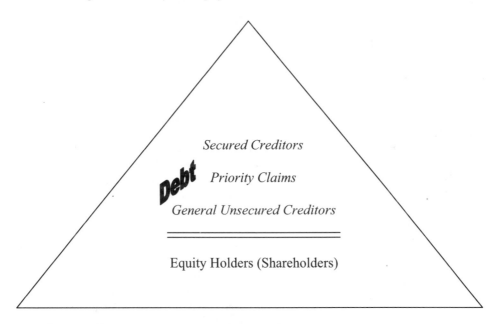

Secured Creditors

Debt *Priority Claims*

General Unsecured Creditors

Equity Holders (Shareholders)

FIGURE 15.1 **THE OVERALL PRIORITY SCHEME**

The above diagram shows that debt (creditor claims) is higher in priority than equity in the business (meaning the ownership interests of the owners of the business). *Debt* is above the double line and *equity* is below the double line.

Secured creditors can take themselves out of the whole priority structure by pulling their collateral out of the case. They do this by filing a motion to lift the stay.

The debtor's most complex task in a CHAPTER 11 case is to figure out how it will pay secured creditors. Keep in mind that, under Section 506(a), if a claim is oversecured, it must be paid in full, with interest, costs, and reasonable fees incurred during the CHAPTER 11 case and before confirmation of the plan, as specified in the security agreement. Conversely, if a claim is undersecured, it is bifurcated. Thus an undersecured creditor is secured *only* to the extent of the value of its collateral, and any remaining debt over and above the value of this collateral will be placed in the general unsecured creditor class. The undersecured portion of the debt is called a **deficiency claim**, and like all unsecured claims, interest, costs, and fees freeze upon filing for bankruptcy. The reason is that bankruptcy treats similarly situated creditors equally (unlike the race of the diligent under state collection laws).

General unsecured creditors get a pro-rata payment. Therefore, we need to pick a point in time at which all those debts freeze, so we can calculate each creditor's pro-rata share. Instead of allowing interest to build up while the debtor is in bankruptcy and then recalculating each creditor's proportionate share when the plan is confirmed, the Bankruptcy Code resolves this needless complexity by simply freezing interest on the date of filing. This makes it straightforward: Each unsecured creditor gets its proportional fair share based on the amount it was owed on the day the debtor filed for bankruptcy.

(1) The Treatment of Oversecured and Undersecured Claims After the Filing but Prior to Confirmation of a CHAPTER 11 Plan

The most important rule with respect to secured creditor treatment, explained above, is that the secured claim is only as valuable as the value of the collateral. 11 U.S.C. §506(a). Whether a secured creditor is oversecured or undersecured will drastically affect the secured creditor's treatment while the bankruptcy case is pending and before the plan is confirmed. As a practical matter, it takes time for a debtor-in-possession to confirm a CHAPTER 11 plan. While the confirmation process is at work, the secured party that is oversecured is entitled to accrue interest and attorneys' fees at the contract rates. 11 U.S.C. §506(b). Undersecured creditors, like all unsecured creditors, are not entitled to accrue interest or fees during the post-petition period. 11 U.S.C. §506(b). In addition, the interest and attorneys' fees provided for in the original loan document are paid to oversecured creditors, but only until the claim becomes as large as the value of the collateral. 11 U.S.C. §506(b). At that time, continuing interest and fees come to a halt. All interest and fees that are unsupported by collateral simply go "poof" and disappear.

(2) Secured Creditor Treatment Under the CHAPTER 11 Plan

Once a plan has been confirmed, the treatment (or payment) of secured claims is described in the plan itself. At that time, the interest and fees being paid under the original loan documents cease, and the pre-petition loan terms no longer apply. The rules totally change. Although the secured creditor treatment is negotiated between the debtor and the secured creditors, these creditors cannot be forced to take less than the terms specified in Section 1129(b)(2)(A). In essence, Section 1129(b)(2)(A) provides that secured creditors are entitled to keep whatever lien or secured interest they have on their collateral, and also the **present value** (including present value interest to account for the time value of money) of their secured claims (measured by the lesser of the loan amount or the value of the collateral), over the life of the plan. While this rule is only required, technically, in a cramdown (forced plan), practically speaking secured creditors regularly insist upon this treatment and withhold their consent if they don't get it. Consequently, this is the default treatment that is most common, even though a secured party could agree to accept less favorable treatment.

As in so many areas, Chapter 11 is similar to Chapter 13 when it comes to the concept of present value.

C. Priority Treatment Under Chapter 11

Chapter 11 plans must pay Section 507 priority claims in full. 11 U.S.C. §1129(a)(9). So what *are* the most common priority claims in a Chapter 11? See 11 U.S.C. §507(a). Section 507(a)(2) provides that all administrative expenses listed in Section 503(b) (including debtor's and creditors' committee's fees for attorneys and accountants) get second priority. Section 507(a)(3) provides third priority for wages owed, up to $10,000 per person, that were earned within 90 days before the filing date. These 507(a)(3) wages arise when a debtor is unable to obtain an order of the court allowing it to pay pre-petition wages pursuant to its first day motions (discussed in Chapter 16), or if the debtor doesn't time the filing to coincide with the end of a pay period so that wages get paid prior to filing. The fourth priority, Section 507(a)(4), describes unsecured claims for contributions to employee benefit plans earned within 180 days before the filing of the petition, up to $10,000 per person. A corporate debtor is likely to have claims in this fourth category. Category six, Section 507(a)(6), makes claims for customer deposits up to $2,425 entitled to priority. Finally, taxes, Section 507(a)(8), are always crucial for any business. Some taxes only get priority for a short period of time, and others are always entitled to priority.

Priority Claims Common for Businesses	
Section Number	**Type**
507(a)(2), 503(b)	Administrative expenses
507(a)(4)	Wages, salaries, and commissions, up to $10,000 per person
507(a)(5)	Contributions to employee benefit plans, up to $10,000 per person
507(a)(7)	Deposits, up to $2,425
507(a)(8)	Various taxes (read the statute carefully)

The timing of the payment of priority claims, pursuant to Sections 507(a) and 503(b), is different in a CHAPTER 11 than in a CHAPTER 13. Compare 11 U.S.C. §§1129(a)(9) and 1322(a)(2). Section 1129(a)(9) states that, unless a holder of a particular claim has agreed to different treatment, the plan must pay Section 507(a)(1), 507(a)(2), 507(a)(3), 507(a)(4), 507(a)(5), 507(a)(6), and 507(a)(7) claims on the effective date of the plan. Debtors often designate the effective date as the date 30 days following confirmation, to give them time to prepare to pay claims under the plan, and to allow the appeal period to run. However, virtually any effective date can be chosen.

Thus attorneys' fees (and all professional fees) are paid earlier in a CHAPTER 11 than in a CHAPTER 13. In a CHAPTER 11, they are paid on the effective date of the plan, unless the holder agrees to different treatment. In a CHAPTER 13, the debtor has the entire plan period to pay these claims — up to five years! 11 U.S.C. §1322(a)(2).

In addition to the professional fees that Section 507(a) cross references from Section 503(b), other creditors in the administrative category include businesses that have provided goods and services to the debtor post-petition. Most of these creditors will be paid prior to the plan, in the ordinary course of business before the plan is confirmed, and thus few typically remain unpaid at the time the plan becomes effective. Those that are still unpaid, however, will hold first priority claims. 11 U.S.C. §§503(a), (b).

Tax claims, unlike all the other priority claims (which must be paid in full on the date the plan takes effect) can be paid in "regular installment payments in cash . . . over a period ending not later than 5 years after the date of order for relief." 11 U.S.C. §1129(a)(9)(C). Accordingly, the debtor may pay tax claims over time, but must pay them off completely within five years of the filing date. Most debtors take advantage of this very beneficial tax provision, because it stops the interest from building up even though the debtor is making payments over five years.

Because of the different treatment (payment) of pre-petition and post-petition taxes, and the difference between taxes and non-tax 507(a) priority claims, it is generally advisable for the debtor to separately classify the tax claims. Even though tax claims are separately classified under most plans, they are deemed not to be impaired (because even pre-petition taxes are paid in full, albeit without interest), and therefore the holders of these claims do not vote on the plan.

D. The Best Interest Test: Treatment of General Unsecured Claims

The best interest test establishes the minimum treatment for general unsecured creditors. 11 U.S.C. §1129(a)(7). You might recall that under CHAPTER 13, the debtor must prove that he or she is paying as much to creditors under the CHAPTER 13 plan as creditors would receive in CHAPTER 7 liquidation. 11 U.S.C. §1324(a)(4).

CHAPTER 11 contains essentially the same best interest test as CHAPTER 13. Section 1129(a)(7) provides that, with respect to each impaired class of claims or interests, each holder of a claim has to either accept the plan (this is somewhat unlikely in larger cases because it refers to each and every creditor, not a creditor class) or each holder of the claim must receive an amount that is not less than what the holder would receive if the debtor were liquidated under CHAPTER 7. 11 U.S.C. §1129(a)(7).

F   A   Q

Q: What is a reorganizing debtor hoping that a liquidation analysis (or best interest analysis) will show? Does the debtor want the distributions to look high or low?

A: The debtor wants the hypothetical liquidation calculation to be low. The debtor passes the best interest test by offering to pay creditors more than they would have gotten in a hypothetical liquidation.

In CHAPTER 11, the debtor (assuming it is a corporation and not an individual) will have no exemptions. Thus, to calculate whether the plan passes the best interest test, the debtor must perform a liquidation analysis by doing a hypothetical liquidation of all its assets, and subtracting all the secured claims it owes from the sales price of its assets. Also, remember that whether the plan is consensual or not, the Code requires the debtor to pay *all priority claims in full*, usually on the effective date of its plan. Once all the claims that must be paid are subtracted from the hypothetical liquidation of the assets, the result yields the amount the general unsecured creditors would receive if the debtor liquidated rather than reorganized.

Here's a simple way to think of the best interest test: Compare the amount of the plan payments to the amount that would be realized in the liquidation. The plan payments must be at least as much as the liquidation amount, but, in addition, because the plan payments are paid over time, we must compensate the creditor for the time value of money.

> **Sidebar**
>
> **THE TIME VALUE OF MONEY**
>
> The philosophy behind the best interest test is that a debtor should not be permitted to pay creditors over time for free. Ten dollars today is worth more than ten dollars in five years. After all, if a creditor receives ten dollars today, that ten dollars can be invested and earn interest for the next five years. The way creditors are compensated for this lost time value of money is with present value interest. Thus the creditor is entitled to receive the amount that it would have received if the debtor's assets were liquidated today.

E. The Confirmation Process

CHAPTER 11 is designed as a consensual, negotiated process. Ideally, creditors negotiate with the debtor to achieve an acceptable treatment (payment) plan from the debtor, who will then propose a plan that pleases as many creditors as possible. However, the Code also recognizes that we don't live in an ideal world: Sometimes creditors won't agree to a plan. Nonetheless, it may still make sense for the court to approve the plan, so long as the plan meets the tests discussed above to protect the creditors on the whole, including the dissenters.

To start the confirmation process, the debtor places the creditors into classes of claims. See 11 U.S.C. §1122. Next, the debtor and its attorneys attempt to negotiate with the creditors regarding the treatment (payment) they will receive under the plan. After these two steps, the debtor and its attorney draft and circulate a plan, and work to get the votes needed to approve the plan.

The debtor is hoping all classes will vote to accept the plan (be an **accepting class**). If they do, the plan is a **consensual plan**.

In order for a class to be an accepting class, the debtor needs favorable votes from **two-thirds in amount** (the holders of two-thirds of the dollar amount of the total debt in the class) and **one-half in number** (one-half of the actual number of creditors in the class). 11 U.S.C. §1126(d). If any class votes no, the debtor can try to force the plan on the creditors (a cramdown plan). Whether the plan is a consensual plan or a cramdown plan, at least one impaired class must vote yes. 11 U.S.C. §1129(a)(10).

(1) Confirmation

Confirmation is the process by which a debtor-in-possession gets a Chapter 11 plan approved by the court. See 11 U.S.C. §1129. The rules for consensual plans include the basic rules discussed above, the good faith test, the feasibility test, secured creditor treatment, priority treatment, and general unsecured treatment under the best interest test. See 11 U.S.C. §1129(a). If the plan is not consensual, i.e., if at least one class of creditors has voted against the plan, the debtor must comply with the rules for cramdown plans, in addition to the rules for consensual plans. See 11 U.S.C. §1129(b).

(2) Consensual Plans Versus Cramdown Plans

If at least one class votes no, the plan is non-consensual and debtor will need to **cram down**[1] the plan. 11 U.S.C. §1129(b). This is a new way to use the term **cramdown**[2] and in this context, it means "to force the plan on a class of creditors." Rather than cramming down the value of an asset,[3] you might think of this as cramming the plan down the creditor's throats, over their objections.

Why does it matter if the plan is consensual, given that the debtor can do a plan anyway, over the creditors' objections? Is it even worth the effort to try to get every class on board? Yes, indeed, for several reasons. First, the court will be much more hesitant to approve a plan that is not consensual.

The decision about whether to let the debtor reorganize and continue to operate, rather than forcing the debtor to liquidate, is typically considered a choice for creditors, not the debtor's management or owners. This is because the claims of creditors are higher in priority than the claims of equity shareholders (the owners of the company) or management (which has no recognized interest in the case). If creditors want the company liquidated, should it just be liquidated?

If all creditors prefer that the company be liquidated, courts pay attention to that. But sometimes different types of creditors disagree, and that is where cramdown plans come in. It is also where the special rules come in, which are designed to protect creditors when there is a cramdown plan.

---

[1]This is a verb.
[2]Here the word is a noun.
[3]Remember that many professors call this **stripping down** the value, not cramming it down. Both are used so listen carefully to your own teacher.

F. Soliciting Votes for the Plan

If the negotiations have been going well, a debtor's plan is normally approved consensually. The debtor starts by obtaining court approval of a disclosure statement, and then circulates the plan for voting. 11 U.S.C. §1125. If the votes are not all positive, the debtor will have to do a cramdown plan. 11 U.S.C. §1129(b). A debtor-in-possession must ensure that the plan voting and solicitation process comply with the Bankruptcy Code requirements, discussed next.

(1) The Disclosure Statement

A plan cannot be circulated for voting unless it is accompanied by a court-approved disclosure statement. Sections 1125(a) and (b) of the Code contain the requirements for obtaining approval of a disclosure statement, as do Bankruptcy Rules 3001(6), 3001(7), and 3001(8). Putting together a disclosure statement can be difficult because the debtor must provide creditors with information sufficient to decide whether or not to vote for the plan. While a large portion of the disclosures simply restate the provisions of the plan, the beginning part of the disclosure statement contains a history of the debtor's operations, as well as an explanation of what went wrong prior to the bankruptcy filing. The disclosure statement also contains a detailed description of all litigation matters to which the debtor is a party, as well as all of the methods through which the debtor will fund the plan. The description of these funding mechanisms is important because it explains how creditors will be paid under the plan.

The disclosure statement also explains in detail how the debtor will meet the best interest test. 11 U.S.C. §1129(a)(7). This is where the debtor reports the results of its liquidation analysis, explaining what claims there would be if the debtor were to liquidate, and the corresponding distribution to creditors. The disclosure statement also describes how the debtor will meet the feasibility test, which requires a description of its cash flow projections and other financial information to show that it can afford the proposed payments.

Once the debtor has drafted its CHAPTER 11 plan and the accompanying disclosure statement, the debtor circulates the disclosure statement to the major parties-in-interest in the case, notifies everyone in the case that the disclosure statement has been filed, and requests a hearing on the adequacy of the disclosure statement pursuant to Section 1125(b). The court holds an initial hearing, the "disclosure statement hearing," to determine if the disclosure statement contains adequate information. 11 U.S.C. §1125. Once the disclosure statement is approved, it is sent to all creditors, along with the plan and a ballot for voting. Once the votes have been counted, the court holds another, more substantive hearing, this time to decide whether to approve (confirm) the plan. See 11 U.S.C. §§1125, 1128, 1129.

Sidebar

THE DANGER OF TOO MUCH FINE PRINT!

If you have ever invested in stock and received a corporate disclosure statement, or looked at the fine print in your credit card agreement, you know that few people actually read these documents. Really, how could they, given their length and complexity? Thus too much information defeats the disclosure statement's purpose, burying the important parts in an avalanche of less relevant information. Despite this concern, when creditors object to a disclosure statement, the common remedy is to simply ask debtor's counsel to add more information regarding the issue. Thus, when approving a disclosure statement, courts sometimes balance the need for the information against the harm caused by too much information.

Some creditors, particularly if they are creditors with whom the debtor is in litigation or with whom the debtor otherwise has strained relations, may object to the disclosure statement on the basis that it contains information they believe to be biased or inaccurate. Some creditors also may object to the disclosure statement because it describes a plan they believe is not confirmable. Consequently, they may wish to tell the court that it would be a waste of estate money to circulate and solicit votes on an unconfirmable plan. As you can see, these are veiled objections to the plan itself, rather than the disclosure statement, and some courts do not like to hear them. Other courts appreciate the heads-up, as they want to know whether the plan has problems and whether the debtor should consider modifying the plan prior to soliciting votes.

If the court approves a disclosure statement, that means the court has found that the disclosure statement provides "information of a kind, and in sufficient detail, as far as is reasonably practicable in light of the nature and history of the debtor and the condition of the debtor's books and records, that would enable a hypothetical reasonable investor typical of holders of claims or interests of the relevant class to make an informed judgment about the plan." 11 U.S.C. §1125. That's a mouthful, but it just means the disclosure statement contains enough information for creditors to make an informed decision about whether to vote for the plan.

(2) Plan Voting

The debtor is not allowed to *solicit votes* on its plan until it has circulated the plan with an approved disclosure statement. 11 U.S.C. §1125(b). This does not mean, however, that the debtor cannot negotiate with creditors about plan treatment (payment). The debtor is free to hold meetings to talk about plan treatment, and to discuss the plan prior to circulation. The only thing that is forbidden outright is soliciting votes on the plan, yet many attorneys consider it inadvisable for the debtor to circulate an actual plan, prior to getting the disclosure statement approved. The whole point of requiring a disclosure statement is to make sure creditors have the information they need, *at the time* they are considering whether to vote for a plan. 11 U.S.C. §1125(a).

Once the court has entered an order approving the disclosure statement, the debtor distributes the plan and the disclosure statement to creditors for voting. 11 U.S.C. §1126. You will recall that when the debtor drafted the plan, it placed creditors into different classes. Now the classes get to vote, and Section 1126(c) provides that a *class* has accepted the plan if it is accepted by creditors that hold at least two-thirds in amount and more than one-half in number of the allowed claims in the class that have voted on the plan. The debtor needs two-thirds in amount and over one-half in number of the creditors who *actually vote* to approve the plan, not all the creditors in each class.

(3) Classification

Classification is often simple, as the debtor is required to put creditors with the same legal rights into the same class and treat every creditor within a class the same. 11 U.S.C. §1122. Section 1122(a) requires *merely* that the debtor classify only substantially similar creditors in the same class. It is silent about whether it is acceptable to place similarly situated creditors in separate classes. Courts interpreting the Code, however, disapprove of gerrymandered classification schemes created for the purpose of getting an affirmative vote on the plan. In practical terms, therefore, the debtor is generally required to put all creditors with the same legal rights into the same class.

Typically, classification issues arise in CHAPTER 11 where the debtor is trying to isolate hostile creditors into their own class, so that the rest of the similarly situated creditors (presumably friendly creditors) will be in a different class. By so doing, the debtor can get the "friendly," or at least non-hostile yet similarly situated, creditors to vote in favor of the plan and thereby satisfy the requirement that at least one class vote in favor of the plan. Although ideally the debtor would like every class to vote in favor of the plan, the debtor can also force the plan on dissenting classes (a cram-down plan), but *only if at least one impaired class votes in favor of the plan.*

Whether a classification scheme meets the requirements of Section 1122 depends, on one hand, upon whether the classification scheme is in the best interest of creditors and fosters the reorganization effort, or, on the other hand, whether it violates the absolute priority rule or some other rule or policy.

Classification matters because if one creditor dominates a whole class, which is typical when a secured creditor's deficiency claim is large, it cannot be overruled through the voting process. The debtor wants to push a huge claim like that out of the general unsecured creditor class, so it can get the other unsecured creditors to vote yes, and have at least one accepting class. This may or may not be possible, depending on the reason for the separate classification.

But if a creditor gets improperly classified, it can file an objection to the classification.

The most important thing about classification under Section 1122 is that creditors with similar legal interests must be placed in the same class. The converse is also true: If a creditor has legal rights that are unique to its own position, it should not be thrown into a class with other creditors that are not similarly situated. Because secured creditors normally have different collateral securing their claims (or different lien priority positions), and are subject to different pre-petition rights under their respective loan documents, each secured creditor is usually classified separately in a CHAPTER 11 plan.

(4) Impairment

We've said that the debtor needs *at least one* **accepting class** to confirm a plan, but that's really just half the story. The debtor needs at least one **impaired class** to accept the plan. Actually, only impaired classes of claims are entitled to vote on the plan. Under Section 1124(1), a class of claims is impaired unless the plan "leaves unaltered the legal, equitable, and contractual rights to which such claim or interest entitles the holder of such claim or interest." This means that a class is impaired if it is not paid in full on the effective date of the plan, or if its pre-bankruptcy rights are somehow otherwise affected by the plan. Because only impaired classes are entitled to vote on the plan, the debtor can only count impaired classes in determining whether one or more classes has voted in favor of the plan.

If you think about it, this makes good sense: Only creditors who are being hurt get to vote on a plan. If a creditor is completely unaffected by the bankruptcy, there's no need to vote on the plan.

F   A   Q

Q: Aren't most creditors impaired in a bankruptcy proceeding? Or are there certain classes of creditors that are generally unimpaired?

A: Administrative claims, which must be paid in full on the effective date, are never impaired. They are not allowed to be impaired by definition. Tax claims are not considered impaired if the debtor complies with the required plan treatment. Finally, each secured claim gets classified separately. Often some of these are paid pursuant to their contract rights with the debtor, meaning they also are unimpaired. It is not uncommon to have just one impaired class of unsecured creditors and one or two classes of impaired secured creditors. Obviously, the smaller the number of impaired classes, the harder it can be to find an accepting class.

G. Forcing the Plan on Dissenting Creditors: The Cramdown Plan

The rules and tests we've been discussing apply to all Chapter 11 plans — the good-faith test, the feasibility test, basic secured creditor treatment, priority claim treatment, the best interest test and general unsecured treatment, confirmation, classification, voting, and impairment. Here, we discuss the additional steps required to cram down the plan (force the plan) on nonconsenting classes of creditors. 11 U.S.C. §1129(a). We also discuss stripping down the value of secured creditor claims in this section.

What must the debtor prove to force the plan treatment (payment) on a class of unsecured creditors? Section 1129(b)(1) permits cramdown of a rejecting class, but only if at least one impaired class votes in favor of the plan, the plan does not discriminate unfairly between classes, and the plan treatment is "fair and equitable." The fair and equitable standard codifies a long line of cases addressing the fair and equitable treatment of creditors under the old Bankruptcy Act. Section 1129(b) of the current Bankruptcy Code contains the *minimum* requirements for a plan to be found fair and equitable, leaving equitable discretion in the hands of the court to impose additional requirements if justice so requires. The rights of secured creditors are contained in Section 1129(b)(2)(A) and the rights of unsecured creditors are contained in Section 1129(b)(2)(B).

F	A	Q

Q: What right does a creditor have if its treatment (payment) is not equitable?

A: A creditor can object to the plan and have its objection heard at the confirmation hearing. This is the remedy for any creditor who feels its treatment does not comply with the requirements of the Code.

(1) Cramdown of a Secured Class

Section 1129(b) requires that in order to cram down a secured creditor class, the class must receive "**fair and equitable**" treatment. Section 1129(b)(1) requires that a non-consensual plan be "fair and equitable" in general, and Section 1129(b)(2) states that to be fair and equitable, the debtor must pay the secured party at least the present value of its secured claim over the life of the collateral, and also allow the secured party to retain its liens during the payment period. The result is that, at a minimum, secured claims must receive payments equal to the full value of the collateral, plus present value interest (which is not really an interest payment but rather compensation to the creditor for the time value of money). Remember, the creditor is entitled to money *now*, but won't get the money until some time in the future, when each dollar will be worth less, because of inflation, than it is today.

(2) The Specific and General Requirements of the Fair and Equitable Test

You might recall that CHAPTER 13 provides for similar treatment of secured creditors, pursuant to Section 1325. There are, however, two significant differences between the treatment provided to secured creditors under Section 1325(b)(2)(A) and that provided under Section 1129(b)(2)(A). The first difference is the length of time over which the debtor may pay a secured creditor. The second difference is that Section 1129(b)(2)(A) contains an amorphous general fairness standard that is absent in Section 1325(b)(2)(A).

(a) Duration of Payments to the Secured Party

In a CHAPTER 11 case, there is no statutory time limit for a debtor to pay secured creditors. Instead, the secured creditor retains its security interest while waiting to be paid. 11 U.S.C. §1129(b)(2)(A)(i). Therefore the outer time limit for paying a secured creditor is determined by the lifespan of the collateral. Payments on secured claims cannot extend beyond the **useful life of the collateral**, because that would leave the secured party in the uncomfortable position of being owed money that is backed up by collateral worth nothing.

For example, assume a secured creditor loaned money to a business to buy office equipment, and retained a security interest in a copy machine, fax machine, and computer. The useful life of this type of office equipment is generally about four years, give or take. Assuming that the debtor has already had the office equipment for a year, the debtor must pay the secured creditor within three years, the period of time in which the copy machine, fax machine, and computer retain some value.

Now take an example on the other end of the spectrum, and assume that the secured party has a mortgage on an office building. Real estate typically doesn't depreciate. Thus the debtor could pay the secured party over a much longer period of time. When the courts apply a reasonableness standard, the cases suggest that such payments can extend for 15 or 20 years. Imagine that! A bankruptcy plan that spans 20 years!

The result is that different secured creditors in a case (creditors holding liens on different collateral) will be paid over different periods of time, depending on the useful life of their collateral.

(b) General Fairness and Section 1129(b)(1)

Now let's talk about the fair and equitable test in Section 1129(b)(1). One practical problem that arises in Chapter 11 cases is **negative amortization**. Negative amortization occurs when a secured creditor is paid the present value of its allowed claim over the life of the plan, but not in equal monthly installments. Instead the payments are very small in the beginning of the plan, so that initially, the payments do not even cover the interest on a monthly or quarterly basis. We call it negative amortization because the debt is not being paid down. In fact, because interest is accruing, the amount of debt is actually increasing during the early part of the plan. Even worse (from the creditor's perspective), many plans that propose negative amortization also involve a big payment, called a **balloon payment**, at the end of the plan. This places most of the risk of the reorganization on the secured party rather than the debtor. This type of plan can run aground on the "fair and equitable" test, depending on the financial circumstances. In addition, a negative amortization plan may fail the feasibility test because there are no assurances that the debtor will be able to make the balloon payment in the future.

(3) The Present Value Interest Rate

Section 1129(b)(2) also requires the debtor to pay the secured creditor the present value of its allowed secured claim, starting on the effective date of the plan.

The concept of **present value** is that a dollar today is worth more than the same dollar a year from now. Thus the debtor must compensate the creditor for the present value of the money if it won't be paid until later. This is accomplished by assigning an interest rate to the payments to compensate the creditor for the time value of money. This is *not* a real interest payment. It simply reimburses the creditor for accepting late payment.

In 2004, the United States Supreme Court held that the present value interest rate to be applied in a cramdown Chapter 11 case, or any Chapter 13 case, is the prime rate plus one to three percentage points. The extra percentage accounts for a host of risk variables. *Till v. SCS Credit Corp.*, 541 U.S. 465 (2004). As the Court explained,

> [b]ecause bankrupt debtors typically pose a greater risk of nonpayment than solvent commercial borrowers, the approach then requires a bankruptcy court to adjust the prime rate accordingly. The appropriate size of that risk adjustment depends, of course, on such factors as *the circumstances of the estate, the nature of the security, and the duration and feasibility of the reorganization plan.* The court must therefore hold a hearing at which the debtor and any creditors may present evidence about the appropriate risk adjustment.

Id. at 1961 (emphasis added).

The 1 to 3%, over and above prime rate, is sometimes called a **risk kicker**. The Supreme Court went on to explain that if a court were tempted to assign a risk kicker larger than 3%, the plan is likely too risky and may not be feasible. The Court also held that the creditor has the burden of proving the amount of the risk, and if nothing but the prime rate is established, the debtor can simply pay the prime rate.

(4) Obtaining Positive Votes from at Least One Accepting Class: If You Are Stripping Down, This Is Harder Than It Looks

Cram down plans often involve stripping down a secured party's claim. Reducing, or stripping down, the value of a secured creditor's claim has its costs, however. Remember that any time a creditor is undersecured by a large amount, and the debtor decides to strip down the lien, the creditor will have a large deficiency claim, and thus a large voice in the general unsecured creditor class as well. As a result, the creditor may be able to cause the unsecured creditor class to vote no and thus block confirmation of the plan. 11 U.S.C. §1126(c).

However, stripdown of the secured creditor's lien is *optional for the debtor*. In some cases, it may be easier and cheaper (and make little difference in terms of the plan payments) to simply pay a lender the full amount of its claim as a secured claim, rather than attempting to strip down the lien. In many cases, the debtor will have numerous secured creditors and may not want to wage a valuation battle with all of them. The debtor also may not want a disgruntled secured party's substantial deficiency claim to move into and vote with the unsecured creditor class. Such a creditor is likely to vote no (when your loan has been stripped down, you tend to be disgruntled), and this could make it hard to obtain an accepting class.

On the other hand, if the debtor decides to pay at least some secured creditors pursuant to the original terms, and maintains payments during the case, those creditors are unimpaired. Unimpaired creditors do not get to vote and cannot count as an accepting class. Thus the debtor must evaluate its options on a case-by-case basis.

F   A   Q

Q: But is it fair and equitable to the unsecured creditors if the debtor *does not* strip down some loans when he is able to?

A: The fair and equitable test for general unsecured creditors is set out below. It deals with the question of whether equity holders or owners are getting something that should be given to the general unsecured creditors. We appreciate the thinking behind this question, though. It seems that unsecured creditors should be able to object on some basis (perhaps good faith) if secured creditors are taking more than their share. This question also raises the issue of whether there is a general fairness test for unsecured creditors. Paying more than would be required to a secured creditor may also implicate the best interest test because unsecured creditors may do better in a CHAPTER 7 liquidation.

(5) The Absolute Priority Rule When Cramming Down the Plan on Unsecured Creditors

Unsecured creditors are protected by a very different cramdown rule. If unsecured creditors are not paid in full under the plan, any party "junior to them" (i.e., share-holders) cannot receive or retain anything. Thus, if a class of unsecured creditors rejects the plan, the plan cannot be forced on them (crammed down) unless all of the equity owners receive and retain *nothing* under the plan on account of their equity interests. See 11 U.S.C. §1129(6)(2)(B).

At first glance, that might seem okay, because in most CHAPTER 11 plans equity holders do not receive any payments under the plan anyway. But this misses the point of the **absolute priority rule**. The absolute priority rule forbids shareholders from *retaining* their equity interests. In other words, if unsecured creditors are either not paid in full under the plan or do not consent to the plan, the owners cannot keep their ownership of the company. Instead, the **equity** in the company must be sold or given to creditors. Equity here means ownership interests, profits, control over the business, and the possibility of future returns.

F   A   Q

Q: If shareholders don't get to keep their interest in the business, where does that ownership interest go?

A: To the unsecured creditor class. The general unsecured creditors become the owners of the company. They can keep their new interest in the company or sell it. The absolute priority rule makes sense because all creditors, including general unsecured creditors, are higher in priority than equity holders. As a result, cred-itors must be paid in full (or accept the plan) before equity owners get to retain ownership of the business.

Considering that the entire CHAPTER 11 model assumes that management and equity remain in place during a CHAPTER 11 case, the absolute priority rule is somewhat surprising. While the owners and the managers are two different groups of people in very large bankruptcy cases, in the smaller cases, owners typically manage the company. For these cases, the absolute priority rule seems harsh.

But in reality, this rule merely requires equity owners to get unsecured creditors to agree to the plan. Otherwise, they lose everything—all their ownership interests in the company. Remember that, generally speaking, the debtor's management is controlled by shareholders (also called equity holders) and equity holders are attempting to keep their interest in the reorganized debtor. That's why the absolute priority rule creates a powerful incentive for the owners to get all creditor classes, particularly general unsecured creditors, to vote in favor of the plan.

(6) The New Value Exception

While many courts have interpreted the absolute priority rule strictly, in the manner just described above, others have recognized an exception to the rule. This exception, which is not found anywhere in the Code, is known as the **new value exception**. Under this exception, equity holders must buy back their equity interests in the company by having their equity interests valued, and then contributing cash equal to the value of their interests. The cash is then used to help fund the debtor's CHAPTER 11 plan — to reorganize and become profitable again.

Dan Defaulter   1187
333 Free Parking Apt. 7
Bankruptcia, NN 77654

                                                          Date: Mid-Bankruptcy

Pay to the Order of *Unsecured Creditors*
In the Amount of *All my Equity*

For *Unable to Pay Unsecured Creditors in Full*   *Dan Defaulter*

:505087643:   11335577993:   1187

Thus the shareholders, or old equity holders, may represent a welcome source of capital. They can invest new money in the debtor, help the debtor reorganize, and thereby retain (or buy back) their equity interests, using the new value exception.

Although the new value exception sounds straightforward, it has been controversial. Some courts fear that equity holders might try to buy back the equity interests in the debtor at a bargain price, because the actual value of the company's equity has not been subjected to market conditions, such as an auction or advertisement for sale. However, the U.S. Supreme Court stated in dicta in *Bank of America National Trust and Savings Association v. 203 North LaSalle Street Partnership*, 526 U.S. 434 (1999), that while old equity holders *could not* have the exclusive right to buy the equity interests in a debtor, old equity holders can buy back equity interests if these equity interests are first exposed to market conditions.

Under this reading, if other parties are allowed to bid on the equity of the debtor, the new value exception can be used. The Court reasoned that old equity holders could not have an exclusive right to buy the equity in a CHAPTER 11 business because that exclusive right is itself a retention of some interest in the debtor. Further, the Court noted that the terms "absolute priority rule" and "new value exception" are judicially made law, and are to be reviewed against the backdrop of a larger concern, namely that a CHAPTER 11 debtor's plan could be too good a deal for the debtor's old owners, who then gain an unfair advantage in the reorganization process. Ultimately, the Court held that some form of market valuation must be available to test the adequacy of the old equity holders' proposed contribution. However, the Court did not decide whether market exposure requires an opportunity for competing bids or could simply be satisfied by a different valuation procedure. Instead, the Court concluded that "it is enough to say . . . that plans providing interest holders with an exclusive opportunity free from competition and without benefit of market valuation fall within the prohibitions of §1129(b)(2)(B)(ii)."

Prior cases interpreting the new value exception to the absolute priority rule had established various requirements for dealing with the problem of equity holders who contribute too little in exchange for keeping their ownership of the company. These tests are still being used, and are thus worth mentioning:

1. The debtor's equity holders' contribution must be in money (rather than services or "sweat equity," which the owners of a small company were hopefully planning to contribute anyway).
2. The contribution must be equal in value to the equity interest being retained under the plan (based on an analysis by accountants or investment bankers).
3. The contribution must be necessary to the debtor's reorganization.

H. Post-Confirmation Issues: The Effect of Confirmation

Sidebar

ABSOLUTE PRIORITY IN SINGLE ASSET REAL ESTATE CASES

Some scholars have noted that the absolute priority rule comes up most often in the context of single asset real estate cases. Single asset real estate cases don't really affect society. In many ways, these are unimportant as reorganization cases because there are no (or few) employees and the businesses generally have little effect on the economy. Thus there is no strong interest in keeping the business afloat to preserve jobs. Further, these may be thought of as simple disputes between two parties, the debtor/developer and the mortgage lender, which would probably be better handled in a setting other than CHAPTER 11.

Confirming a CHAPTER 11 plan is a tremendous accomplishment, the day the parties have been hoping for. But confirmation does not mark the end of the case. Creditors don't even *start* getting paid until confirmation has occurred. Post-confirmation, the debtor will attempt to perform the plan, and the debtor's lawyers will be called upon to interpret the plan and the order confirming it. See 11 U.S.C. §1142. The plan, the order confirming it, and the Bankruptcy Code govern the effect of the plan on the debtor, its creditors, and all other parties-in-interest. The post-confirmation period can be filled with complexity, but we'll just discuss a couple common issues here.

(1) The Confirmation Order Is *Res Judicata* as to All Issues Dealt with in the Plan and Also Discharges All Claims Except as Otherwise Provided for in the Plan

Section 1141 of the Bankruptcy Code does a number of radical things, including binding "the debtor, any entity issuing securities under the plan, any entity acquiring property under the plan, and any creditor, equity security holder, or general partner in the debtor, whether or not the claim or interest . . . is impaired under the plan and whether or not such creditor, equity security holder, or partner, has accepted the plan." 11 U.S.C. §1141(a). The plan is *really* binding! Thus, the confirmation order approving the plan is *res judicata* as to all of the matters addressed in the plan. The only exceptions are orders that violate due process or were accomplished through fraud. Although courts are often called upon to reverse a confirmation order or to interpret a prior order that is inconsistent with the confirmation order, the order is what it is — final and binding.

(2) Enforcing the Plan

The plan forms a new contract between the debtor and the creditors, which replaces all prior contractual obligations between the parties. Further, the bankruptcy court's jurisdiction over the case is severely limited after confirmation. This is a far cry from the broad jurisdiction that the bankruptcy court exercised *during* the case, in which it heard business disputes of the debtor and essentially all other matters the debtor needed resolved. Moreover, creditors may choose to sue the debtor on their contract rights in a different court, in which case non-bankruptcy courts will be interpreting the confirmation order.

SUMMARY

- The debtor meets the feasibility test by producing projected cash flow statements, as well as other sources of revenue, such as asset sales, equity contributions, and future contracts. The idea is to get a good estimate of how much net revenue the debtor will have during the repayment period.

- Secured creditor treatment under the Code means that the debtor pays the present value of allowed secured claims over the life of the collateral, unless the secured creditor agrees otherwise. This includes present value interest to account for the time value of money.

- Priority claims must be paid in full under CHAPTER 11, generally at the time the plan becomes effective, which the debtor frequently designates as 30 days following confirmation.

- Unlike other priority claims, taxes can be paid over time, without interest, but must be paid in full within five years. This is a very favorable provision that most businesses take advantage of, because it stops interest from accruing on back taxes.

- Unsecured creditor treatment is governed by the best interest test, which provides that unsecured creditors must get at least as much in a CHAPTER 11 plan as they would have gotten under a CHAPTER 7 liquidation. This is why a liquidation analysis is necessary.

- If the debtor-in-possession complies with the rules for consensual plans — the good-faith test, the feasibility test, secured creditor treatment, priority treatment, and general unsecured treatment under the best interest test — *and* all the classes of creditors vote in favor of the plan, the Court will approve the plan.

- If a class of creditors votes against the plan, the debtor-in-possession has to comply with extra rules to cram down the plan. To cram down a plan, at least one impaired class must vote for the plan, the plan must not discriminate unfairly among classes of creditors, and the plan must be "fair and equitable" (meaning secured claims are paid in full over the life of the collateral, with present value interest). Moreover, unsecured creditors are protected by the absolute priority rule (meaning ownership of the company must be sold or given to unsecured creditors if unsecured creditors reject the plan).

■ Practically speaking, the most important thing for a secured creditor is whether it is oversecured or undersecured, because oversecured creditors collect interest and attorneys' fees after the filing and before confirmation of the plan, which can be substantial. These are paid only up to the value of the collateral, at which point the secured creditor is no longer oversecured.

■ The disclosure statement contains the history of the company's operations, what went wrong, litigation matters, methods for funding the plan, provisions of the plan, and a liquidation analysis (which is used to show that the debtor passes the best interest test).

■ The confirmation order is final and binding, and forms a new contract that replaces all prior contractual obligations of the parties.

CONNECTIONS

Unsecured Creditors and Interest Payments

Unsecured creditors do not earn interest on their claims during a CHAPTER 11 case or in a CHAPTER 11 plan, even if they have a contract with the debtor providing for interest. The Code modifies the contract, in an effort to be fair to all creditors. Only fully secured creditors earn interest during a case. This may seem unfair, but remember that unsecured creditors would only get partial payments anyway, so they're not losing anything.

Post-Petition Taxes Versus Pre-Petition Taxes

Be careful! Post-petition taxes, as opposed to pre-petition 507(a)(8) priority taxes, do accrue interest and penalties if they are not paid on time. Some debtors fail after confirmation because they did not keep post-petition taxes current. When it comes to taxes, the Code only helps debtors in respect to pre-petition taxes.

Collateral Value — After Filing but Before Confirmation

If the value of the collateral changes after filing but before confirmation of the plan, the amount the secured creditor may collect is not supposed to change. The secured party's claim is supposedly valued as of the filing of the case. If the value goes up, the secured party is still only entitled to what it would get based upon the value at the time of the filing. If the collateral goes down, the creditor is still entitled to get what it would have been entitled to at the beginning of the case. In fact, the debtor is not allowed to diminish the collateral during the case. That's the whole point of the adequate protection doctrine.

However, in reality, debtors do sometimes diminish the value of a secured creditor's collateral. To complicate matters, there sometimes is no valuation done at the time of the filing, making it hard to prove the diminution in value.

Assumption or Rejection of Contracts and the Best Interest Test

One potential complication in the best interest test is that if a reorganizing debtor would assume some contracts (perform them), but a liquidating debtor would be forced to reject them, rejection creates large unsecured claims in favor of the other party to the contract. This can result in a much smaller unsecured distribution, and thus can make the liquidation distributions much lower than the plan distributions. Thus it's important to take into account the information in Chapter 19 when thinking through the best interest test.

The Value of a Consensual Plan

Classification issues aside, the debtor hopes that each and every class votes yes, because then it need not comply with the rules for cramdown plans, discussed below. This makes the confirmation process easier and much cheaper, because it won't be litigious.

Post-Confirmation Obligations

If an obligation, such as a tax debt, is discovered after the plan is confirmed, and the debt is supported by a lien or security interest, it is a property interest that remains unaffected by the confirmation order or the bankruptcy. This is true whether the creditor received notice of the bankruptcy or not. In other words, the debt survives the bankruptcy.

The Forest and the Trees — Keeping Perspective

This chapter builds on concepts described in the beginning chapters of this book, as well as the overview in the prior chapter, including the good-faith test, the feasibility test, and the treatment of priority claims, and cramdown requirements such as the best interest test, the fair and equitable test, treatment of secured creditors, and the absolute priority rule. The goal here is to get to the heart of a CHAPTER 11 plan and explore the details in depth. If after reading Chapter 14 or looking at the chart at the end of Chapter 14, you want to understand the details and policy reasons behind each provision, this is the chapter for you!

Starting a CHAPTER 11 Case

Whereas this chapter described the end game of CHAPTER 11 — the nitty-gritty of how to get a plan confirmed — the following chapters describe the preparations needed to get to the plan stage. Next up, Chapter 16 describes the procedural and technical steps that an attorney must take to start a case.

Cash Collateral, Post-Petition Financing, and Other First Day Orders

16

In the real world, what happens at the beginning of a case? At this early stage, the debtor and its counsel focus on staying in business, stabilizing operations, and restructuring the business to bring it back to profitability. This chapter describes how to get the case started.

O V E R V I E W

E. APPLICATIONS TO BE EMPLOYED AS COUNSEL, ACCOUNTANT, OR OTHER PROFESSIONAL

F. CASH MANAGEMENT ORDERS

Before a CHAPTER 11 case is filed, a lot of preparation is required. The petition and the schedules of assets and liabilities described in Chapter 10 must be completed. The debtor (or at least the debtor's counsel) must appear in court just hours after the actual bankruptcy petition is filed, with a handful of motions and other paperwork for the court to consider and approve. These are loosely called **first day orders** and vary somewhat in form from district to district.

First day orders typically include a motion to approve the appointment of debtor's counsel and accountants, under Section 330; a motion to use cash collateral under Section 363(c)(2) (because most debtors have pledged their cash proceeds to secured lenders); a motion for post-petition financing (new loans) under Section 364; a cash management order addressing how pre-petition bank accounts will be handled; a motion to pay trust fund taxes; a motion to pay critical vendors; and, if needed, a motion to pay pre-petition payroll.

These motions and proposed orders are presented to the court on very short notice, with a request for almost immediate approval. Secured creditors receive notice of these motions, as do the largest unsecured creditors. Unsecured creditors are often in no position to actually participate in these matters, however, because they have not yet formed a committee or appointed counsel. Nevertheless, the largest unsecured creditors typically receive notice of the hearings.

Before we go into each of these separate motions, let's review the difference between a **motion**, an **order**, and a **notice of hearing**, and the purpose of each. When the debtor makes a motion before the court, *it is asking the court for permission to do something.* If the court grants the motion, it enters an order approving the motion, often under specified conditions. Hence the motion requests the entry of an order approving the motion. The debtor (or whoever is making the motion) drafts the requested order and, depending on local practice, either attaches it to the motion or brings it to the hearing on the motion. Remember that the motion and the order serve very different purposes. One makes a request to the court and the other becomes the law of the case.

A. The Cash Collateral Motion and Order

The hard and fast rule is that debtors-in-possession *must* obtain court approval before using a creditor's cash collateral. 11 U.S.C. §363(c)(2). This rule is hard to understand and remember if you do not know what cash collateral is.

(1) What Is Cash Collateral?

Recall that collateral is property the debtor has pledged to a secured creditor as security for a secured loan. It turns out that almost every company's cash is cash collateral, because the cash comes from property that is used as collateral. For example, if a secured creditor has a lien on a company's inventory, its lien automatically continues when the inventory is sold for cash. Or if a debtor has pledged its accounts receivable as collateral for a loan, the accounts receivable become cash collateral when the debtor is paid cash for its services. Either way, the security interest transfers to the cash.

In fact, the most common business assets, and the ones that most debtors use to acquire a working capital loan (a loan that provides ongoing cash for operations, such as paying a lease, employees' salaries, and utilities), are the inventory and the accounts receivable. Other business assets that may be used as collateral include equipment, intangible assets like patents and trademarks, goodwill, customer lists, interests in lawsuits, and interests in leases and contracts.

There are numerous ways to finance a business, but the point of the following discussion is to make sure you understand the two or three main types of collateral. Equipment is easiest to visualize, and is defined as long-term assets that are used in business operations. For a butcher, equipment might include forklifts, cash registers, meat cutters, and freezers. Inventory is also easy to grasp. Inventory means short-term assets, made or held by the business for sale or short-term use in the business. These would include groceries in a grocery store, shoes in a shoe factory, and lumber in a lumber mill. See U.C.C. §9-102(a)(33), (48).

Accounts receivable are the most important type of assets to learn to identify because they are more difficult to spot if you are unfamiliar with them. Accounts receivable are money (accounts) that other people owe the debtor. U.C.C. §9-102(a)(2). Picture a corporate cleaning service. The company owns vacuums, steam cleaners, and two vans. These assets are **equipment**. It has soaps and cleaning supplies, which are used by the business on a short-term basis. These assets are **inventory**, even though they are only "sold" indirectly when the cleaning services are performed. Now, notice that the vast majority of the cleaning company's valuable assets are **accounts receivable**.[1]

The cleaning company cleans office buildings every night and then bills customers for payment within 30 to 60 days. Each time the debtor cleans an office building an account receivable (an amount owed to the debtor) is created. The cleaning company's customers pay these accounts receivable by sending checks to the company, which the company then deposits into its bank account. Voila! The resulting cash is cash collateral if the accounts receivable have been pledged for a loan. That is why accounts receivable are so important for service companies.

F   A   Q

Q: Why do we care which category an asset or piece of collateral falls into?

A: The secured party cares because it must correctly identify its collateral in its filing documents and keep track of its collateral. But here, we are concerned with how assets are characterized because there are special bankruptcy rules that govern the debtor's use of cash collateral, and cash collateral almost always comes from the sale of the debtor's inventory and accounts receivable. Thus, if you can recognize these two types of assets, and distinguish them from other types of

---

[1]Article 9 of the U.C.C. calls these **accounts**, which has a specific legal meaning. Business people, however, call these either **accounts receivable** or just **receivables**. Attorneys need to know all three terms, so they understand what their clients are talking about.

assets such as equipment, you will know when to be concerned about the use of cash collateral.

Let's try another example. Here the business is a paper factory that has pledged all its assets to a secured lender to secure a working capital loan. What are the paper factory's assets? First, picture the equipment—large industrial metal paper presses, forklifts, metal carts on wheels, furniture in the employee workrooms, computers—anything that is tangible, long-term property. It need not be used to make paper. How about the inventory? Well, there is the finished paper. There are also raw materials—the wood pulp, recycled paper, and glue that are used to make new paper. There is also **work-in-progress**, which is paper in the process of being made that is not currently in salable form either as raw material or finished product. Finally, the soap in the bathrooms is inventory because it is for short-term use in the business.

While the soap in the bathroom does not create cash collateral, some of the other assets do. The paper products may be sold directly to the public for cash, in which case the cash that the factory gets in exchange for the paper is cash collateral. Most of the paper, however, will probably be sold to other businesses, in which case the paper will be sold by the factory on credit. The company will ship to a customer and then bill the customer for the shipment, payment to be made by the customer within 30 to 60 days. At this point, the obligations of its customers are accounts receivable. Therefore, just as with the cleaning company example above, when payment is made by the paper factory's customers, the payments are cash collateral of the lender.

Although cash collateral can technically arise from the sale of the debtor's equipment when the equipment is sold by the business, this is not typically the subject of a cash collateral order.

(2) Special Rules for the Debtor's Use of Cash Collateral

So now you know what inventory and accounts receivable are, and that if these assets are pledged to a lender to secure a loan they become cash collateral. So what? Well, outside bankruptcy, the debtor is free to use the lender's cash collateral under whatever terms the parties have contractually agreed. In bankruptcy, however, the debtor is not free to use cash collateral without court approval.

Cash collateral is given special protections under the Bankruptcy Code because it is so hard to keep track of and easy to spend. That's why the Code requires the debtor to get court approval before using any cash collateral. A typical debtor must move quickly to obtain approval to use cash collateral because most debtors cannot go even one business day without using the cash generated from the sale of inventory or the collection of accounts receivable, and most debtors have pledged these assets to secure operating loans.

F   A   Q

Q: Once the debtor has asked the court for permission to use cash collateral, how long does it typically take to get approval?

A: Not long. The court will order the interim (temporary) use of cash collateral within 24 hours of the request and there will usually be a final hearing on the same issue in a couple of weeks.

The motion must be accompanied by a **notice of motion**, which tells creditors where and when to appear if they would like to participate in the hearing on the motion, and also sets the deadline for filing objections to the motion. The court schedules a hearing on the motion, during which the moving party argues that the motion should be *granted*, and other parties support or oppose the motion. Sometimes first day orders are entered without a traditional hearing, given the time constraints, with another hearing to follow at a later time.

To gain the right to use cash collateral during a CHAPTER 11, against the creditor's will, the court must find that the creditor's interest in the collateral will not be harmed or impaired by the debtor's use. In the parlance of Section 363, the creditor's interest must be adequately protected. 11 U.S.C. §363(a)(2).

Note that the debtor must provide adequate protection to the secured party in other situations as well, which are enumerated in Section 363. For example, in the context of relief from the automatic stay, if a court finds that all of the requirements of Section 362(d) are met, and that the secured party is thus entitled to have the automatic stay lifted, the court can still refuse to lift the stay and order the debtor to make adequate protection payments instead. 11 U.S.C. §361. The debtor also must provide adequate protection if it plans to grant new liens on collateral that has already been pledged to an existing creditor. 11 U.S.C. §364(d).

F   A   Q

Q: How common is cash collateral?

A: Very common — any business that has pledged its cash for a loan will need a cash collateral order. This means that any business that sells inventory will need a cash collateral order. Cash collateral is also generated from the liquidation of accounts receivable, which are frequently a large part of the asset base for a service business such as a cleaning service or a construction business.

Accounts receivable generated from the debtor's *post-petition* services are free of a secured party's lien, despite any **after-acquired property clause**,[2] so a business that generates most of its revenue from *post-petition* accounts receivable might be able to get by on the cash generated from the services without a cash collateral order. Of course, any business that has not granted a security interest in its inventory or accounts receivable doesn't need a cash collateral order.

(3) Three Ways to Provide Adequate Protection for the Use of Cash Collateral

Returning to our discussion of the debtor's use of cash collateral, Section 361 provides three nonexclusive ways for the debtor to provide adequate protection to a

---

[2]An after-acquired property clause is a provision in a security agreement granting the secured party a security interest in, say, inventory and accounts, whether the debtor owns them now, or acquires them in the future. These clauses are perfectly enforceable outside bankruptcy and fully enforceable inside bankruptcy, *except* for on post-petition accounts, which are freed of these liens in recognition that they are generated by the debtor's post-petition labor, rather than the creditor's collateral.

creditor to gain the right to use cash collateral. First, the debtor can make periodic cash payments to the creditor in order to protect the secured party from loss. 11 U.S.C. §361(1). Second, the debtor can provide the creditor with a lien on new collateral, in addition to the collateral the creditor is already holding, which is called a **replacement lien** or a **supplemental lien**. 11 U.S.C. §361(2). A third and more controversial way to provide adequate protection is through an **equity cushion**. Oversecured creditors have an equity cushion, which means that the value of their collateral is greater than the face value of the secured party's claim. 11 U.S.C. §506(b).

Why are equity cushions a controversial way to provide adequate protection? First of all, as you know from Chapter 8 of this book, oversecured creditors are allowed to accrue interest and attorneys' fees on their claims. At least in theory, if a creditor starts the case oversecured, the creditor should stay oversecured because the case is not supposed to impair a secured creditor's position over time. For this reason, equity cushions are not a favored means of providing adequate protection. However, the U.S. Supreme Court has explicitly held that it is *not necessary* to preserve an equity cushion, and consequently an equity cushion is a correct way to provide adequate protection. *U.S. Savings Assn. v. Timbers of Inwood Forest Associates, Ltd.*, 484 U.S. 365 (1988). As the Supreme Court reasoned, if there is plenty of collateral to cover the debt, there is no need to make adequate protection payments to protect the creditor against loss so long as the losses do not eat up the equity cushion. This makes good sense, particularly when the debtor needs to use the collateral to keep the business going and to continue paying employees and suppliers.

F A Q

Q: So if there *is* an equity cushion, and the court accepts this as a way to provide adequate protection for the use of cash collateral, can the debtor just freely use the cash collateral until the equity cushion is used up?

A: No, the cushion should not be shrinking unless it is really huge. If the cushion gets used up, the court should then order payments or replacement liens so as not to reduce the creditor's likelihood of being paid in full.

We briefly mentioned replacement or supplemental liens as one way of providing adequate protection. These are liens in property in which the creditor *does not currently hold an interest.* The debtor has to find new collateral to create a replacement lien. Further, the replacement liens secure obligations of the debtor to the creditor, but only to the extent of any diminution in the original collateral resulting from the debtor's use. The new lien merely replaces the diminution amount.

Let's say the secured party's claim is $5 million, secured by original collateral worth $5 million. The debtor grants replacement liens in *new collateral* to adequately protect the secured party in exchange for the use of cash collateral. If the original collateral does not decrease in value during the case, the *new collateral* is returned to the debtor (it wasn't needed after all), and the creditor ends up in the same position it was in originally—with a $5 million loan secured by $5 million worth of collateral. In contrast, if the collateral decreases in value by $100,000, at the end of the case, the other collateral is returned to the debtor, less $100,000 for the creditor, and so on.

Collateral is always used in that way. It secures a debt but must be returned once the debt is paid.

Regardless of how adequate protection is provided, a few things are clear: The debtor cannot operate its business in bankruptcy without cash; most of its cash will probably be cash collateral; and the debtor cannot use cash collateral over a secured party's objection without a court finding that the creditor with an interest in the cash collateral is adequately protected. If the debtor cannot find some property that it can use to provide adequate protection to the creditor, the case is over before it even starts.

(4) Cash Collateral Stipulations

Fortunately, in most Chapter 11 cases parties do not contest the debtor's motion to use cash collateral. Instead, the debtor and the secured creditor try to work out the terms of cash collateral use consensually, and then present the court with a negotiated order, often called a cash collateral stipulation.

Chapter 11, however, is a multiparty proceeding. Even if the debtor and the secured creditor agree on the terms of cash collateral use, other creditors may object on the grounds that the order gives the secured party too much, forcing the court to decide whether to grant or deny the motion.

A cash collateral order or stipulation contains many terms that protect the secured party as well as some that protect the debtor. Virtually every stipulation contains a budget prepared by the debtor's management outlining how much cash the debtor can spend during the time covered by the cash collateral stipulation. The budget is the most important thing to negotiate because it determines specifically how the debtor can use the creditor's cash collateral. The debtor can only spend money on the items outlined in the budget, up to the amounts permitted in the budget, typically with a 5% overall margin of error. Debtors often propose a larger budget than they actually need during negotiations, knowing that some items will be cut. Items over which there is often a fight include management's fees and salaries, professional fees, and sometimes advertising.

After the ever-important budget, the next most common issue to negotiate is payments to the lender, if any. Many secured parties want to receive ongoing payments during a Chapter 11 case. If these payments are called **adequate protection payments**, the court will likely approve them. The debtor must think long and hard about whether to offer payments (are payments really necessary, or is there other collateral or an equity cushion?), and, if so, how much? The creditors' committee (if there is one at this early stage) or individual unsecured creditors can object to the debtor's offered adequate protection payments but the court may allow the payments anyway. What is the risk to the debtor of promising payments? If the debtor cannot keep them up as the case goes forward, it is unlikely that the court will modify the agreement to reduce the payments against the secured party's will. This often marks the end of the case, as the creditor's swift motion to lift the stay will usually be granted.

In addition to the budget and the payments, the stipulation contains many other terms. First, reporting requirements often require the debtor to tell the secured party on a weekly or even daily basis what the inventory and accounts receivable are worth, the amount of cash on hand, daily sales, and the status of accounts receivable. The debtor is also normally required to prepare financial projections indicating how much business it expects to do over the cash collateral period. Usually the stipulation will require that the debtor meet or exceed its projections, so this is no time for pie-in-the-sky accounting. Remember the stipulation's purpose, namely, to allow the debtor to use the creditor's cash collateral without hurting the creditor.

Other things you might find in the stipulation are statements that the debtor is granting replacement liens to provide adequate protection (up to the amount of the diminution in the value of the collateral), definitions of what constitutes a default under the stipulation, and what happens upon default, which can include relief from the stay for the creditor. Some stipulations also contain an acknowledgment of the debtor that the secured party has a valid and perfected security interest in the collateral and that the debtor has no claims against the lender. As in most other situations both in and outside bankruptcy, the secured lender holds most of the bargaining power.

(5) The Creditors' Interests

Finally, the secured party should be vigilant to make sure that the debtor is maintaining the collateral and keeping it insured. The secured party wants the period in which the debtor is using cash collateral to be as short as possible, so that it ends before the collateral loses much value.

B. Post-Petition Financing Orders

Sometimes the cash generated by a business in CHAPTER 11 is insufficient to turn the business around. In other words, the debtor needs to borrow more money. Normally, a debtor needs unencumbered assets (assets with no liens attached) before it can raise significant cash, but there are some other good options for borrowing money post-petition.

F	A	Q

Q: Why in the world would anyone lend money to a company that is already in bankruptcy?

A: Because the Bankruptcy Code creates incentives for lenders to lend money to troubled companies, by providing high priority to money lent post-petition, and by providing special rights to those who procure new collateral post-petition. 11 U.S.C. §364. High priority means the new creditor gets paid ahead of most other creditors, or that the new creditor gets a first lien on something that is already encumbered by another lien. The bottom line? There are very strong assurances of repayment.

(1) Special Sources of Funding for Debtors in CHAPTER 11

Before we talk specifically about the special rights that creditors can acquire by lending money to the debtor post-petition, let's look at the different sources a debtor might have for new, post-petition capital. Some creditors will have supplied goods or services to the debtor on credit pre-petition. Most suppliers will have an outstanding unpaid invoice resulting from the bankruptcy case, which will be an account receivable for them, and an account payable for the debtor. Some suppliers may even be owed more money for sales over a long period of time. Yet many will be willing to continue to supply the debtor, because a supplier who supplies a CHAPTER 11 debtor with goods or services post-petition is entitled to a first position administrative priority claim for those goods and services. See 11 U.S.C. §§503(b), 507(a). The debtor also may be a very large customer of the supplier, thereby forcing the supplier to choose between continuing to supply the debtor or going out of business.

In addition to suppliers and service providers, the *business owners* may be willing to put in new cash post-petition in order to keep the business afloat. Current secured lenders also may be willing to put in additional cash, and perhaps other new lenders will be happy to do so. A final possible source for cash is investors who are willing to buy an equity interest at a bargain price.

(2) The Code's Incentives to Provide Post-Petition Financing: Priming

Some of the Bankruptcy Code's most innovative provisions deal with post-petition financing. Section 364 allows the court to grant some unsecured creditors super-priority status for post-petition loans, grant liens on new collateral for new secured loans, and even grant new security interests to new creditors for new lending on collateral that is already pledged to another creditor. 11 U.S.C. §364. Finally, if none of these efforts are enough to generate the cash the debtor needs, the court can **prime** existing secured creditor liens, meaning grant new liens on previously pledged collateral, that are senior in priority to existing liens on the same collateral.

Priming is radical and controversial because it reduces the position of a secured creditor by placing a new lien in front of it, simply because the debtor needs new cash to operate and is unable to come up with cash in any other way. See id. §364(d). A court will not grant a priming lien unless it believes the new influx of cash will almost certainly turn the company around. To convince a court of this, the debtor must present the court with a very thorough business plan, and financial projections that show how the new cash will allow the company to prosper. Further, to prime a loan the court must also find that the existing creditor (who is now "being primed") is adequately protected despite the priming. This is yet another use of the adequate protection concept. See 11 U.S.C. §361.

To illustrate, let's say that Betty's Day Spa borrowed $150,000 from First State Bank, secured by a building worth $200,000. Betty's is now in CHAPTER 11 and needs another $25,000 to revamp its business. Without the new cash, the business will likely close its doors in the next few days. There are no other liens on the building, and Betty's has no other unencumbered assets. Second Bank is happy to lend Betty's $25,000, but they insist on a first priority lien in the debtor's building. This would push First State Bank into the second position. Can the court approve the new loan? Only if it finds that First State Bank remains *adequately protected*, but the court will then have to face the fact that without cash, Betty's may simply close its doors. Notice the Hobson's choice here: Hurt First Bank, the secured creditor who did everything right, or allow the business to go under.

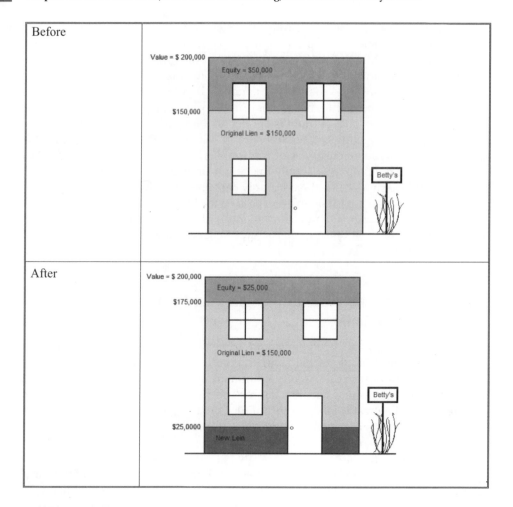

FIGURE 16.1   HOW PRIMING CHANGES THE EQUITY PICTURE

C. Payment of Pre-Petition Trust Fund Taxes

Although a debtor is generally not supposed to pay pre-petition claims post-petition except under a confirmed plan of reorganization, some exceptions to this rule have developed. Recall, for instance, that if a debtor fails to pay taxes that it withheld from its employees' paychecks, the debtor is considered a trustee of these funds, pursuant to Section 507(a)(8)(C) and therefore, the debtor is required to pay these pre-petition withholding tax claims in full. These claims are nondischargeable in bankruptcy and also carry personal responsibility for some managers. As a result of this rule, courts frequently allow a debtor-in-possession to pay **trust fund taxes** that just happen to be caught up in bankruptcy. These are pre-petition claims but would be entitled to priority in a CHAPTER 11 case, and thus will eventually be paid in full in most plans.

D. Payment of Pre-Petition Deposits, Warranties, Reclamation Claims, and Wages

In addition to critical vendors and taxes, the debtor may ask for permission to honor customer deposits and warranties. Of course, deposits are entitled to priority pursuant to Section 507(a)(5). Moreover, part of the debtor's goal is to keep the business running more or less in the same way that it ran prior to the bankruptcy, and destruction of customer goodwill would be counterproductive. Similarly, to preserve goodwill with suppliers the debtor may request permission to pay reclamation claims — claims by vendors for goods sold and delivered to the debtor during the 20 days prior to the filing.

In addition, the debtor should make sure that it has paid its pre-petition wage claims prior to filing the bankruptcy. If the case cannot be timed so that it is filed right after a payroll period, the debtor may make a first day motion requesting authorization to pay its pre-petition wage claims.

Obviously, the debtor's work force needs the money badly, but perhaps more important from management's perspective, workers may threaten to quit or start looking for other employment if they aren't paid. Certainly, missing a paycheck sends employees the wrong message, and, in any case, these claims are also entitled to priority under Section 507(a)(4). The debtor's goal is to not miss a beat, so leaving workers out in the cold is a serious misstep.

E. Applications to Be Employed as Counsel, Accountant, or Other Professional

As the debtor's lawyer rushes across the street with the packet of first day orders, she also carries her own application to be appointed as counsel for the debtor. Debtor's counsel also may apply for the appointment of other professionals, such as an accountant or an investment banker for the debtor. See 11 U.S.C. §327. It is critical that debtor's counsel *not be* one of the debtor's creditors at the time that the attorney applies to be general counsel to the CHAPTER 11 debtor, because Section 327(a) requires that debtor's general counsel be **disinterested**. Disinterested means that the attorney is not a creditor of the debtor, and also that the attorney does not represent any of the creditors or other parties-in-interest in the case. This requires debtor's counsel to do a thorough check for possible conflicts of interest prior to accepting the appointment.

Not becoming one of the debtor's creditors is a bit more complicated. As you may have guessed by now, there is a great deal of work for debtor's counsel before a case can even be filed. We have been discussing numerous first day orders that

> **Sidebar**
>
> **EVERGREEN ORDERS**
>
> In the debtor's counsel's application to be retained, counsel will request that it be permitted to submit interim fee applications for approval by the court. See 11 U.S.C. §330(a). These fee applications are required by the Bankruptcy Court so that the court can approve all fees for debtor's counsel prior to the debtor paying the fees. In some jurisdictions, the debtor is permitted to pay these fees on a regular basis and the court approves them retroactively. These types of compensation schemes, sometimes called evergreen orders, are quite controversial and are frowned upon in other parts of the country. As the name suggests, it is "ever green" for debtor's counsel, as the green keeps flowing and there is no need to obtain court approval prior to receiving payments in the case.

need to be filed with the court immediately upon the bankruptcy filing, many of which must be negotiated with other creditors. All of these first day orders require time and attention on the part of debtor's counsel. This time is not free. If the lawyer wants to be paid for his or her pre-petition time in the case (and who wouldn't?), she must get a pre-petition retainer and apply the retainer on a regular basis.

With respect to the need to ensure that the debtor's counsel does not become a creditor in the case, and is owed no outstanding fees at the time of the bankruptcy filing, some courts have rejected this strict doctrine under a theory called the **nunc pro tunc** doctrine. Literally, nunc pro tunc means "now for then," meaning that a thing is done at one time that ought to have been done at another time. But, practically speaking, nunc pro tunc simply means means "after the fact" or "retroactively." The nunc pro tunc doctrine provides that if debtor's counsel had good cause, such as an emergency, or no way of obtaining either payment or court approval to be retained as counsel prior to rendering services to the debtor, the court may, at its discretion, approve the fees on a retroactive basis. This means that the debtor's counsel could be paid for services rendered prior to the time that it applied to be debtor's counsel. Be aware that the nunc pro tunc doctrine is an exception to the general rule and is not accepted everywhere in the country. It would not be a sound idea to rely on the nunc pro tunc doctrine rather than following the correct procedure to get retained as counsel.

F. Cash Management Orders

Some debtors also request the entry of a **cash management order** as part of the first day orders. A cash management order is an order permitting a debtor-in-possession to keep pre-petition bank accounts open. The order also governs the flow of cash among debtor-in-possession bank accounts. For example, if a company has retail operations in many cities, it is common for the company to have local depository accounts, in which case the funds are swept daily into a central operating account. Because no checks are written from the depository accounts, there is no risk that, by keeping the accounts open, outstanding pre-petition checks will be honored post-petition. Why does this matter? Because the debtor is not permitted to *pay* or *allow* pre-petition claims post-petition, except with court approval.

Practically speaking, it would be burdensome to make the debtor close and reopen a large number of depository accounts and to reset the sweep system for those accounts. Accordingly, courts often allow pre-petition depository accounts to remain open pursuant to the *cash management order.*

COMMON FIRST DAY ORDERS

Cash Collateral Motion or Stipulation
Post-Petition Financing Motion
Motion to Pay Pre-Petition Wages
Application to Retain Debtor's Counsel
Application to Retain Debtor's Accountant
Cash Management Order

SUMMARY

■ Cash collateral is the money a company receives when it sells assets that are encumbered by a security interest. The security interest in the asset becomes a security interest in the cash. For instance, when a company sells inventory that is the collateral for a loan, the secured creditor gets a security interest in the proceeds of the sale. Similarly, when a secured creditor has a security interest in accounts receivable, and the accounts are paid, the secured creditor retains a security interest in the proceeds of the accounts.

■ The debtor must get court approval to use cash collateral. This is important because most companies cannot go even a day in business without using cash from the sale of inventory or the collection of accounts receivable.

■ The most common way to get court approval to use cash collateral is to give the creditor a lien on new collateral, such as the new inventory or new accounts receivable that replace the old. This provides adequate protection. Cash payments or, controversially, an equity cushion, can also be used to provide adequate protection to a secured creditor.

■ Usually, the debtor and secured creditor work out a plan to provide adequate protection and present it to the court in a cash collateral stipulation. This includes the debtor's budget, outlining the items the debtor is permitted to purchase with cash collateral.

■ The Code provides innovative incentives to lenders that are willing to lend money to a company that is trying to come out of bankruptcy. These include super-priority status for unsecured, post-petition loans; liens on new collateral for new secured loans; new security interests on collateral that is already encumbered; and, if all else fails, priming existing secured creditors by giving new lenders senior priority on the same collateral.

■ First day orders include the lawyer's and accountant's applications to be employed.

■ A cash management order permits the debtor to keep bank accounts open, and governs the flow of cash among bank accounts, which can be important for a company that has retail outlets with depository accounts in many cities. It would be a hassle to reopen bank accounts, and there's no risk that money will be lost because checks are not written on depository accounts.

CONNECTIONS

Cash Collateral Increases

What happens when the debtor's use causes the value of the collateral to increase rather than decrease? The secured creditor ends up with more collateral, but that does not mean it gets paid more. It still just gets paid the amount it is owed. Indeed, the court could allow the debtor to place an additional lien on the same collateral, if the debtor needs to raise money and the equity cushion is so large that there's no danger that the secured creditor won't be adequately protected.

Taxes Versus "Critical" Vendors

Motions to pay pre-petition withholding taxes are much more justifiable than critical vendor motions. Unlike unsecured supplier claims, these are priority claims, and are therefore required under Section 1129(a)(9) to be paid in full under the CHAPTER 11 plan. So it's not grossly unfair to pay them now. They are not receiving more than they would receive under the plan.[3]

Providing Post-Petition Services to the Debtor

Even if a supplier provides services to the debtor post-petition, that does not change the priority level of their pre-petition claims. Only the post-petition claims get administrative priority. The pre-petition claims remain general unsecured claims. Some debtors have tried to get around this, however, by filing what is called a critical vendor motion, a motion asking for special permission to pay some creditors their pre-petition claims, so they will continue working with the debtor. While these motions were popular in big cities for a number of years, they are rarely used today in most parts of the country.

Timing the Payroll

It is not only permissible but highly advisable to take the timing of payroll into account when filing a bankruptcy. This is not a preference. A debtor can file whenever it chooses and this is an appropriate strategy. In fact, even if the court enters an order allowing the debtor to pay pre-petition payroll in the case, this is not a preference. Wages fit within the ordinary course of business because they are paid regularly (not usually antecedent), and are an ordinary course expense for any business.

Avoiding Powers

The avoiding powers do not come into play to reverse ordinary course business expenses, such as payroll. But the avoiding powers do become an issue for other expenses paid on the eve of filing a CHAPTER 11. See Chapter 9 for the full explanation of avoiding powers.

Lifting the Automatic Stay

Once a case is instituted, it is time for the debtor to focus on the preservation of the estate's assets so the debtor can use them to reorganize. Creditors, on the other hand, may have other plans for their collateral. They may wish they could take the collateral back, sell it, take their losses, and move on to more profitable loans and ventures. The next chapter describes the standards for lifting the stay.

---

[3]This of course assumes that priority claims will be paid in full in the case, which may be untrue if the case fails.

Adequate Protection

Chapter 17 also explains the requirements adequately protecting secured creditors' interests in collateral. If the collateral for a loan is needed to run a business, the secured party must be made happy or must at least be adequately protected. This subject matter was also discussed in more general terms, as applied to all types of bankruptcy, in Chapter 4.

The Automatic Stay and Adequate Protection

17

In CHAPTER 11, like other types of bankruptcy, the automatic stay of Section 362 is one of the best benefits of filing a bankruptcy case. It is certainly the most immediate benefit. This chapter discusses the scope of the stay (11 U.S.C. §62(a)), its exceptions (11 U.S.C. §362(b)), as well as the grounds for relief from the stay (11 U.S.C. §362(d)), all in the context of CHAPTER 11. It also discusses the court's option of ordering adequate protection payments rather than granting relief from the automatic stay.

OVERVIEW

A. THE SCOPE OF THE AUTOMATIC STAY

B. EXCEPTIONS TO THE AUTOMATIC STAY

C. RELIEF FROM THE AUTOMATIC STAY

1. Relief Under Section 362(d)(1)
2. Relief Under Section 362(d)(2)
3. Relief from the Stay Under Section 362(d)(3): Single Asset Real Estate Cases

D. ADEQUATE PROTECTION

A. The Scope of the Automatic Stay

As we discussed in some detail in Chapter 4, the automatic stay stops collection activity against the debtor and the debtor's property. It also stops attempts to obtain possession or control of estate property, perfect a security interest, and continue lawsuits. Thus the automatic stay comes in handy in a number of ways. Attempts by lenders to repossess collateral or to lien property are stayed. Lawsuits in which the debtor is a defendant[1] are also stayed as to the debtor. For companies like Mattel or Firestone Tires, which have been hit in recent years with a barrage of lawsuits, stopping the lawsuits is a tremendous feat in and of itself. The stay is an injunction against suits and collection efforts, and allows the debtor to breathe a long sigh of relief.[2]

B. Exceptions to the Automatic Stay

Again, as discussed in Chapter 4, some actions against the debtor are not stayed, so the debtor's sigh of relief is not complete. See 11 U.S.C. §362(b). For example, the exercise of police powers taken by a governmental entity to protect the health and public welfare of citizens is not stayed by Section 362. 11 U.S.C. §362(b)(4). The classic example is where a county sues a company to enjoin it from polluting a stream. Another is where the government sues a company for fraudulent activity aimed at consumers. Such a suit is not stayed, because it constitutes an exercise of governmental police powers (for the health and welfare of citizens) rather than an action to collect revenue.

C. Relief from the Automatic Stay

The relief the debtor feels upon filing is limited not only by the exceptions to the automatic stay but also by creditors, circling like vultures, asking the court to lift the stay. The stay is a very powerful general injunction against collection, but individual creditors can move to have the stay lifted as to their own debt, so they can pursue their contractual or state law remedies notwithstanding the debtor's bankruptcy. 11 U.S.C. §362(d). Stay litigation is so ubiquitous that Section 362(d) is the most litigated subsection of the Code.

Sometimes the threat of having the stay lifted is no big deal. Let's assume that the debtor is a huge manufacturer of farm equipment, and that it pledged a $20,000 certificate of deposit (CD) to a lender who financed an overseas sales transaction. The debtor owes this lender about $22,000. This lender has moved to lift the stay ("relief from the stay") to liquidate the CD in partial satisfaction of its claim. Does the debtor care? Not particularly. The debtor is not using the CD to run the business. It's just money, and not much money at that.

But now assume that the same debtor has financed its operations through a $10 million line of credit that is collateralized by its entire inventory, accounts receivable,

---

[1]The stay will not stay suits in which the debtor is the plaintiff because these are not suits against the debtor.
[2]In her 2007 hit, "Umbrella," Rihanna sings, "now that it's raining more than ever, you can stand under my umbrella." The automatic stay is like a big umbrella, protecting the debtor from the rain of lawsuits and creditors' collection efforts.

and equipment, which have a total value of $9 million. Assume that the current loan balance is $9 million. If *this* lender moves to lift the stay, does the debtor care? If it wants to stay in business, it does! If this lender gets relief from the stay, it will take all the company's assets and sell them, and the case will be over. Here, the motion for relief from the stay is a threat to the debtor's entire existence, and, if granted, will mean bye-bye to all operations, employees, management, and payments to unsecured creditors.

| FIGURE 17.1 | SUCCESSFUL LIFT STAY MOTIONS OFTEN KILL THE BUSINESS |

(1) Relief Under Section 362(d)(1)

There are two primary ways for a secured creditor to get the stay lifted,[3] contained in Section 362(d)(1) and (2). Under Section 362(d)(1), the stay must be lifted if the court finds that there is "cause, including **lack of adequate protection** of an interest in property of the moving party." This test requires that the creditor's interest in its collateral be safe and steady. The creditor is not adequately protected under Section 362(d)(1) if its position might be worsened through the debtor's use of the collateral.

In practical terms, this often means that the debtor doesn't have an **equity cushion**, that the property is depreciating, or that these conditions combine to leave the creditor unprotected against loss if the debtor continues to possess and use the collateral. Naturally, if the creditor is already undersecured, there is probably lack

Sidebar

STAY LITIGATION — THE ADVANTAGE OF BEING UNDERSECURED

This is a rare instance when being undersecured has its advantages. Having less collateral than the amount of its loan will allow a creditor to get its collateral back quickly, and thus get out of the CHAPTER 11 case quickly. On the whole, it's probably not a good strategy for a creditor to be undersecured, but it is interesting to realize that at this stage the creditor argues that the collateral values are very low, while the debtor argues the collateral is worth a lot. When it comes time to confirm a plan, the parties will take opposite positions: The creditor gets paid the value of its collateral (the "stripped down" value), so it wants a high collateral value; the debtor, on the other hand, wants the collateral values to be low so it can "strip down" the value to a lower amount.

---

[3]There is also a third way, as the chart at the end of this section shows. The third way, dealing specifically with single asset real estate cases, is not as common. See 11 U.S.C. §362(d)(3).

of adequate protection, but that's also true if there is a small equity cushion that is not large enough to cover the diminution in the value of the collateral resulting from the debtor's use.

Alternatively, sometimes even an undersecured creditor is *not* entitled to relief from the stay where the debtor's use is not further diminishing the value of the collateral, but rather the value of the collateral remains constant or is appreciating. Note that Section 362(d)(1) is a one-part test.

If there is no equity in the collateral, will the stay be lifted? Be careful here. That is what most people assume but it is not accurate. The creditor must also prove that the collateral is diminishing in value. Remember, the point of the test in Section 362(d)(1) is that the creditor lacks adequate protection in respect to the interest it already has. If the creditor is not *losing* any collateral value, there is not a lack of adequate protection.

(2) Relief Under Section 362(d)(2)

Section 362(d)(2) contains a two-part test, under which the creditor must prove, first, that the debtor has **no equity in the property** (meaning the collateral); and, second, that the property is not **necessary to an effective reorganization** of the debtor. While (d)(1) only looks at the position of the *moving party* to determine whether there is equity in the property over and above the moving secured party's claim, the equity described in the first prong of (d)(2) refers to the **total equity** in the property, i.e., *all* secured claims against the property (not just the moving party's claim). In other words, the first prong of (d)(2) looks at the total of all secured claims, not just the amount of the moving party's claim. This distinction makes a big difference.

The second prong of (d)(2) examines whether the property is necessary for an *effective* reorganization. The court must first determine if the property is needed for the reorganization, and then determine whether an effective reorganization is even likely. This second part of the test is easiest for the creditor to win after several months have passed without significant rehabilitation progress. After a certain amount of time has passed, the court will likely grant relief from the stay where there is no equity, even if this property *would* be necessary for an effective reorganization of this debtor. That is because an *effective* reorganization is looking less and less likely.

But how can you tell if a business is *effectively* reorganizing? First, every month the debtor must file operating reports that show if the debtor is losing money. If it is, the debtor is not successfully reorganizing, especially if this happens for more than a month or two. Second, as time passes, if little or no progress is made toward formulating a plan of reorganization, the debtor's chances of successfully reorganizing decrease. So read the monthly operating reports and look for plan progress.

Going back to our earlier example, suppose a company pledged a $20,000 CD as collateral, and the secured creditor's claim (the principal due on the note) is $22,000.

This certificate of deposit is not the type of collateral that the debtor needs to run its business. In addition, the debtor has no interest in the collateral, as the creditor's claim ($22,000) is larger than the value of the collateral ($20,000). As a result, the creditor wins and the stay gets lifted in respect to this debt under (d)(2), even though it is the very beginning of the case.

This test is consistent with common sense. If the debtor does not need the collateral for its operations (unlike equipment or inventory), and if the debtor has no interest in the collateral anyway, why would we let the debtor keep it? There are no overriding reorganization goals that would justify keeping the collateral from the creditor under these facts, so it makes sense simply to give the collateral to the creditor.

In our second example, the equities are different. The debtor financed its operations with a $10 million line of credit, collateralized by all of its inventory, accounts, and equipment (worth $9 million), and the outstanding principal is $9 million also. The creditor likely lacks adequate protection, because the equipment and inventory are probably depreciating. In that case, the creditor wins under (d)(1). The court must either grant relief (lift the stay), or the company must find other unencumbered assets to use as collateral to provide adequate protection.

But if the collateral is not depreciating, the creditor would have to argue (d)(2) to try to get the stay lifted. Under (d)(2)'s two-prong test, the creditor must prove that there's no equity in the property, and that the property is not necessary to an effective reorganization. The creditor loses under (d)(2) because the collateral is clearly critical to the debtor's reorganization efforts (the equipment and inventory are necessary to keep the company in business), and because (d)(2) gives the debtor time (at least a couple months) to reorganize its affairs before the creditor is granted relief and effectively shuts down the business.

The text above focuses on the primary grounds for lifting the automatic stay under Section 362(d)(1) and (2). Again, under (d)(1) there is cause to lift the stay if there is a lack of adequate protection, while under (d)(2) there is cause to lift the stay if the debtor has no equity in the property and the property at issue is not necessary for an effective reorganization of the debtor.

(3) Relief from the Stay Under Section 362(d)(3): Single Asset Real Estate Cases

Section 362(d)(3) contains a unique test for lifting the stay in cases in which the debtor's sole asset is a piece of passive real estate (not a business, but an apartment or office building). In those cases, the stay can be lifted by the secured party if the debtor does not, within 90 days (or within 30 days from the determination that the debtor is a single asset real estate debtor), file a plan of reorganization that has a reasonable chance of being confirmed within a reasonable period of time, unless the debtor has started making monthly payments that at least cover the monthly interest due.

The new Code also allows the stay to be lifted if the court finds that the filing of the case was part of a scheme to delay, defraud, or hinder creditors, after the debtor transferred the property away or filed multiple bankruptcy cases affecting the property.

Grounds to Lift Stay	
Section 362(d)(1)	Cause, including lack of adequate protection
Section 362(d)(2)	No equity in the property and the property is not necessary to an effective reorganization
Section 362(d)(3)	In a single asset real estate case, within 90 days of filing (or within a later date set by the court or within 30 days of a court order finding that the case is a singe asset real estate case), the debtor has filed a feasible plan or has started annual monthly interest payments to the secured lender

D. Adequate Protection

Sometimes a creditor's interest is not adequately protected by an equity cushion, but the debtor can keep the stay in place by offering some other form of adequate protection. This issue ties into the cash collateral issue discussed earlier. Section 361 provides that a debtor may need to provide adequate protection in various instances, including when the debtor is using a creditor's cash collateral, when a debtor is obtaining post-petition financing from a third party and thus priming an existing creditor's lien, and also when the secured party has moved to lift the stay under Section 362(d)(1). See 11 U.S.C. §§361, 362(d).

If a court finds that cause exists to grant relief under Section 362(d)(1), it can either grant relief from the stay or order the debtor to provide additional protection (adequate protection) to protect the creditor's interest. How? The usual ways include ordering the debtor to make periodic cash payments to the creditor, or ordering the debtor to provide the creditor with additional or replacement liens. See 11 U.S.C. §361. For example, the debtor may be required to grant the creditor a lien on previously unencumbered assets to the extent of diminution in the creditor's interest in the original collateral to adequately protect the creditor's interests.

SUMMARY

- The automatic stay is a very powerful general injunction against collection. It stops all sorts of creditors' collection efforts — including attempts to take collateral and perfect security interests. It also stops almost all lawsuits against the debtor.

- The most important exception to the automatic stay for businesses is lawsuits involving the exercise of police powers by a governmental entity to protect the health and public welfare of citizens. These lawsuits are not stayed.

- Secured creditor requests to lift the stay are so common that Section 362(d) is the most litigated subsection of the Code.

- The one-part test in Section 362(d)(1) requires that the secured creditor's position is getting worse — it's not safe and steady. This typically means the value of the collateral is decreasing and the secured creditor has no equity cushion.

- The two-part test in Section 362(d)(2) looks at whether the *debtor* has any equity in the collateral (meaning the total of all secured claims, not just the moving party's secured claim), and whether the property is necessary to an effective reorganization.

- If the creditor could otherwise have the automatic stay lifted (because it is not adequately protected), the debtor can usually keep the stay in place by making periodic cash payments to the creditor or providing the debtor with replacement liens — these are alternative ways to provide adequate protection.

CONNECTIONS

Business Decisions — Navigating Through Chapter 11

If the debtor can make it through the first day motions and automatic stay litigation, holding secured parties at bay while retaining encumbered assets, the debtor can focus on operating the business. Chapters 18 and 19 discuss these decisions in detail, as well as basic business restructuring methods and methods for keeping the business afloat while the plan is being formulated.

Secured Creditors — Taking Back Their Collateral

It might seem that once a creditor has met the elements of Section 362(d)(1) or 362(d)(2), the creditor is entitled to take back the collateral. But that's not true. The court can either grant a motion to lift the stay (which allows the creditor to take back the collateral), or grant a form of adequate protection instead. It is up to the judge, not the moving secured party.

Filing Bankruptcy to Avoid Paying a Large Judgment

What would happen if a company filed bankruptcy simply because it did not want to pay a huge judgment from a lawsuit against it? This is a legitimate reason to file for bankruptcy. There is no requirement that a debtor be insolvent to file for bankruptcy. Texaco did this very thing to avoid paying a huge judgment to Pennzoil. See *In re Texaco*, 73 B.R. 960 (Bankr. S.D.N.Y. 1987). At the time, Texaco had over $36 billion in assets.

The Debtor's Estate

Remember that the automatic stay does not cover assets that never came into the debtor's estate to begin with. So make sure you're clear on the material in Chapter 5 and recognize that an attorney will need to determine whether an asset is really in the estate before bringing stay litigation to have the stay lifted. If the asset is owned by someone other than the debtor, the stay does not apply to the asset.

Keep It All in Perspective

Chapter 14 gave an overview of the options that a company in financial trouble has, including bankruptcy or an out-of-court workout plan. Chapter 15 explained the CHAPTER 11 plan process in depth, so that you could begin with the goal in mind. Then in Chapter 16 and this chapter, we began a chronological tour of the issues that come up in a typical CHAPTER 11 case, starting with first day orders and moving to the most litigated areas in bankruptcy, creditor requests for relief from the automatic stay under Section 362(d)(1) and (2), and adequate protection as it applies in that context. Next, in Chapters 18 and 19, we continue our chronological tour of a typical CHAPTER 11 case, as we explain the scope of the debtor-in-possession's authority, day-to-day operations, and restructuring options of a company in CHAPTER 11.

The Debtor-in-Possession's Scope of Authority and Basic Goals

18

In this chapter we explain the rights and goals of the debtor-in-possession, and pin down what the debtor-in-possession is authorized to do without court approval. We cover the grounds for appointment of a CHAPTER 11 trustee or examiner. We also explain the debtor-in-possession's basic goals, and the issues that management faces during day-to-day operations once a company is in CHAPTER 11.

OVERVIEW

A. **ACTIVITIES THAT THE DEBTOR-IN-POSSESSION CAN ENGAGE IN WITHOUT COURT APPROVAL WHILE IN** CHAPTER 11

B. **THE APPOINTMENT OF A TRUSTEE**

C. **THE APPOINTMENT OF AN EXAMINER**

D. **MAINTAINING THE DEBTOR'S OPERATIONS AND STRUCTURING A SUCCESSFUL** CHAPTER 11 **CASE: THE DEBTOR-IN-POSSESSION'S BASIC GOALS AND REQUIREMENTS**

A. Activities that the Debtor-in-Possession Can Engage in Without Court Approval While in CHAPTER 11

The debtor-in-possession has almost all the rights and duties that a trustee would have if there were a trustee appointed in the case under Section 1107(a). So the debtor-in-possession is the representative of the estate and a fiduciary to creditors. Specifically, the debtor-in-possession has the right to operate the business under Section 1108; the power to use, sell, or lease property of the estate pursuant to Section 363; the power to borrow money or obtain credit on behalf of the estate pursuant to Section 364; and the power to assume, assume and assign, or reject executory contracts and unexpired leases on behalf of the estate under Section 365. The debtor-in-possession also has the power to object to claims on behalf of the estate pursuant to Section 502, to surcharge the secured party on behalf of the estate under Section 506(c), and to recover property of the estate under Section 542's turnover powers, as well as all of the avoidance powers discussed in Chapter 9 of this book.

	Debtor-in-Possession's Rights and Powers, and the Bankruptcy Code Authority for Each
Section 1107(a)	Rights and duties that a trustee would have
Section 1108	Right to operate the business
Section 363	Power to use, sell, and lease property of the estate
Section 364	Power to borrow money and obtain credit on behalf of the estate
Section 365	Power to assume, assume and assign, or reject executory contracts and unexpired leases
Section 502	Power to object to claims on behalf of the estate
Section 506(c)	Power to surcharge secured parties
Section 542	Power to recover property of the estate — "turnover powers"
Section 547	Avoidance powers (see Chapter 9)

Pre-petition management is permitted to stay in place under CHAPTER 11. This is done to encourage management to file a CHAPTER 11 case — appointing a trustee immediately would dissuade current management from filing — and to preserve the institutional knowledge that the management team has regarding the debtor company and its industry. However, if existing management was really bad or unethical, they can be replaced.

F   A   Q

Q: Why do we trust the company's management and allow them to become the debtor-in-possession? Aren't these the guys who ran the company into the ground in the first place?

A: The idea is that at least existing management knows the industry and understands the business of the company ("institutional knowledge"). If we brought in a trustee from outside, she would have to learn on the job, and she would face a steep learning curve. So keeping existing management is usually the lesser of two evils.

In theory, the debtor-in-possession is supervised by the U.S. Trustee's Office, as well as the unsecured creditors' committee to prevent abuses. The bankruptcy court also can hold status conferences to monitor the debtor's activities. Practically speaking, however, the debtor-in-possession has wide latitude to run the company.

During a CHAPTER 11 case, the debtor is permitted to do what ever needs to be done to run the business, as long as the activity is within the **ordinary course of business**. 11 U.S.C. §363(c). Naturally, the debtor's counsel must determine which activities fit within the ordinary course of business. For example, selling inventory is usually within the ordinary course of business for retailers. Selling off equipment or entire inventory stocks, however, is outside the ordinary course of business because the debtor doesn't typically sell its equipment (or its entire inventory) during normal operations. Buying inventory on credit, just like the debtor did pre-petition, is also typically ordinary course activity. But courts are split over whether a national retailer or a service provider with numerous locations can enter into new leases post-petition without exceeding the ordinary course of business. Some bankruptcy courts dislike new leases because even though it is ordinary for the debtor to lease new space, the post-petition leases will become post-petition obligations that must be paid in full.

B. The Appointment of a Trustee

Although the debtor's management team usually continues to operate the business, Section 1104(a)(1) permits the court to appoint a trustee or an examiner where doing so is "in the best interest of creditors, equity security holders, or other interests of the estate."

A trustee *may* also be appointed in a case for cause, where current management has committed fraud, dishonesty, incompetence, or gross mismanagement of the affairs of the debtor, either before or after commencement of the case. 11 U.S.C. §1104(a)(2). Indeed, the 2005 amendments *require* the court to convert or dismiss any CHAPTER 11 case for "cause," including "substantial or continuing loss to or diminution of the estate and absence of a reasonable likelihood of rehabilitation," gross mismanagement of the estate, failure to maintain insurance, unauthorized use of cash collateral, failure to comply with the Code's reporting requirements, failure to timely pay post-petition taxes, failure to timely file a plan, and several other grounds. 11 U.S.C. §1112(b).

In addition to operating the business and taking on all the rights and responsibilities of managing the estate, a trustee who is appointed in a Chapter 11 case is also required to conduct an investigation of the debtor's financial condition and operation.

C. The Appointment of an Examiner

If the court determines that appointing a Chapter 11 trustee would be too disruptive to the debtor's business, Section 1104 allows the court to appoint an **examiner** instead. Appointing an examiner is less drastic and often preferable to appointing a trustee because the examiner's job is merely to investigate the debtor's affairs while debtor's management continues to operate the company. Interestingly, Section 1104 makes the appointment of an examiner *mandatory* upon a party's request, if the debtor's fixed, liquidated, unsecured debts and other debts exceed $5 million. Otherwise, the court has the *discretion* to appoint an examiner for "cause" if any party-in-interest or the U.S. Trustee's Office requests an investigation into fraud, dishonesty, incompetence, misconduct, mismanagement, or irregularity in the management of the affairs of the debtor.

In deciding whether the best interests of creditors are served by appointing a trustee or an examiner, the court has discretion. Sometimes the "cause" standard becomes a head count, with the court looking at the number of creditors that want a trustee, compared to the number that prefer the debtor-in-possession, or, in the case of an examiner, how many creditors want to augment the debtor's operation with an examiner *and* are willing to pay the costs of the examiner. Both trustees and examiners add costs to the estate, and thus reduce the ultimate payout to creditors. From a practical perspective, unless there is a reason to think the trustee or examiner will locate more assets for creditors, it's usually not worth it.

D. Maintaining the Debtor's Operations and Structuring a Successful Chapter 11 Case: The Debtor-in-Possession's Basic Goals and Requirements

To make any Chapter 11 case successful, the debtor-in-possession must accomplish several things. First, the debtor must keep the business operating by finding cash and taking advantage of the automatic stay once the Chapter 11 plan is confirmed. Second, the debtor must be able to turn the business around by developing a successful business strategy. Third, the debtor must determine which claims are being asserted against it and find a way to pay valid claims. Finally, the debtor must use the Code and any other available law to restructure its debts.

First, let's talk about keeping the business afloat. Money, of course, is the most urgent need, as discussed in Chapter 16. So the debtor-in-possession will request permission (through a cash collateral order) to use cash that has been pledged to secured parties as collateral. 11 U.S.C. §363(c)(2). In addition, the cash that the debtor has on hand will go further because the debtor will not be paying pre-petition claims (except perhaps adequate protection payments to secured creditors and pre-petition payroll). Another way for the debtor to find money for its current operations is to get court approval for post-petition loans. 11 U.S.C. §364.

The automatic stay is the key legal weapon, as discussed in Chapter 17. Section 362(a)(3) and (4) keep creditors from repossessing or executing on assets in which creditors have a lien. Section 363(a)(1) stops ongoing litigation that would otherwise funnel assets away from the debtor. Although the automatic stay does not force a supplier to continue doing business with the debtor, if the debtor has a contract with the supplier, the debtor may be able to force the supplier to continue doing business. 11 U.S.C. §365.

Drawing by Shawn Wamsley.

FIGURE 18.1 Chapter 11 GOAL # 1: KEEP THE COMPANY AFLOAT

The second thing the debtor-in-possession must do to succeed in Chapter 11 is develop a strategy to turn its business around. This part of Chapter 11 is the most exciting for lawyers. Here are some common strategies for setting a business back on course: building inventory; cutting costs or changing the way money is spent; purchasing new and more efficient equipment; rejecting existing equipment leases; selling assets; reducing labor costs; closing locations and taking advantage of special provisions in the Bankruptcy Code dealing with landlord claims; taking advantage of the automatic stay to prevent termination of contracts and leases that are in default; and assigning executory contracts and leases, which may currently be leased to the debtor at below-market rates, and which the debtor can sell for a profit to third parties. 11 U.S.C. §365.

> ## STRATEGIES FOR STABILIZING A BUSINESS
> ### IN Chapter 11
>
> - Find additional cash
> - Stop paying general unsecured creditors
> - Take advantage of automatic stay
> - Develop a successful business strategy
> - Close some locations or operations
> - Enter new markets
> - Reject contracts
> - Assume and assign contracts
> - Sell assets and divisions
> - Buy more efficient equipment

The third thing the debtor-in-possession must do is assess the claims against it. Claims are discussed in detail in Chapter 7. Creditors seeking payment from a Chapter 11 debtor will have filed a proof of claim with the court. In addition to straightforward debts for sums certain, there may be unliquidated claims — for instance, the plaintiff in a tort action against the debtor has a claim, but how much money the plaintiff is going to get is unknown. In that case, the plaintiff files a proof of claim as a creditor in the bankruptcy case, and the claim gets adjudicated by the bankruptcy court. Similarly, if the debtor rejects unexpired leases or contracts, the non-debtor party has an unsecured claim for breach of contract damages. These contract damages are also adjudicated by the court. 11 U.S.C. §§501, 502. In some cases, where the value of a claim is uncertain because it will accrue in the distant future, the court estimates the claim for the purposes of claim allowance. 11 U.S.C. §502(c). Finally, the debtor can seek to **equitably subordinate** certain claims, meaning to take them out of their normal priority status and turn them into lower status claims. 11 U.S.C. §510.

SUMMARY

- The debtor-in-possession has the right to operate the business; to use, sell, and lease property of the estate; to borrow money and use credit; and other powers listed in the chart in Section A of this chapter.

- The debtor-in-possession represents the estate and has fiduciary duties to the creditors.

- In Chapter 11, a trustee is usually only appointed if management has committed fraud, dishonesty, incompetence, or gross mismanagement of the company.

- If replacing management with a trustee would be too disruptive, another option is to appoint an examiner to investigate the company's affairs.

- The appointment of a trustee or examiner costs money, so unless it's likely that they would find more assets for the creditors, it's usually not worth it.

- The handy chart in Section D above summarizes common strategies for successfully restructuring a business in Chapter 11 so that it can return to viability.

CONNECTIONS

The Chapter 11 Plan

Restructuring the debtor's operations is the last big task before drafting and circulating the reorganization plan. The plan process is overviewed in Chapter 14 and explained in detail in Chapter 15. In order to do a good job restructuring the company's operations, attorneys should understand the scope of the debtor-in-possession's authority.

The Debtor's Cash Flow

The debtor-in-possession will want to use the Code to maximize the debtor's cash flow and restructuring options. We explain these legal and business issues in Chapter 16 and Chapter 19.

Restructuring Options

Chapter 19 takes a detailed look at two of the most important Code provisions that facilitate the restructuring process. First, the Code allows the debtor very favorable treatment of pre-petition leases and contracts. Second, the Code helps debtors get the highest price possible for any assets they sell, by cleansing those assets of liens and claims (successor liability) before transferring them to third parties.

Claims

As you think through the need to assess claims against the debtor's estate, including unliquidated claims, you might want to turn to Chapter 7 of this book to review what qualifies as a claim and how claims are filed.

Reshaping the Debtor's Financial Landscape: Assumption or Rejection of Executory Contracts and Unexpired Leases, and Asset Sales

19

The Bankruptcy Code contains an amazing benefit to debtors in dealing with contracts and leases that have not expired or been legally terminated as of the bankruptcy filing. In a nutshell, if a contract is still executory (performance is still due by each party to the contract) or a lease is unexpired, the debtor can choose whether or not to perform the contract (to "assume" the contract or "reject" the contract). In addition, the debtor can sometimes stay in leased premises after rejection, at a reduced rental rate. Moreover, the debtor can sometimes assign a profitable lease to another tenant, even if the landlord objects to the assignee's type of business. Special rules apply to real estate leases — some must be assumed more quickly than other contracts and leases, and some are entitled to other protections.

> **O V E R V I E W**

The debtor also has the ability to sell assets free and clear of liens, with the liens to attach to the proceeds of the sale. This can greatly increase the price of the assets and thus benefit creditors by bringing more money into the estate.

A. ASSUMPTION OR REJECTION OF EXECUTORY CONTRACTS AND UNEXPIRED LEASES PURSUANT TO SECTION 365

1. What Are Executory Contracts and Unexpired Leases?
2. Ipso Facto Clauses

3. Rejection of Executory Contracts and Unexpired Leases
4. Assumption of Executory Contracts and Unexpired Leases
5. Assuming and Assigning Executory Contracts and Unexpired Leases
6. Adequate Protection in Shopping Center Leases

B. SALES OF ASSETS PURSUANT TO SECTION 363(b)

C. SALE OF PROPERTY FROM A DEBTOR'S ESTATE FREE AND CLEAR OF LIENS

D. THE SECTION 363(b) SALES PROCESS: SEEKING OUT HIGHEST AND BEST BIDS

E. SUCCESSOR LIABILITY IN SECTION 363 SALES

A. Assumption or Rejection of Executory Contracts and Unexpired Leases Pursuant to Section 365

If a debtor would like to continue to perform a pre-petition contract or lease, we call that assumption of the contract. If a debtor assumes a contract, the debtor is agreeing to perform it in full, just as if there had been no bankruptcy. 11 U.S.C. §365. In contrast, if the debtor does not wish to perform the contract or lease, the debtor can choose to reject the contract or lease, both sides will be freed from their obligations, and the other party to the contract (the non-debtor party) will receive a general unsecured claim for rejection damages. 11 U.S.C. §502(g). As is the case with all general unsecured claims, the debtor is free to pay only a portion of this claim. Those are the basic principles.

Given that much of our country's wealth is now held in the form of contract and lease rights, it is unsurprising that this Code section has become quite complex. This is the meat and potatoes of CHAPTER 11 practice.

(1) What Are Executory Contracts and Unexpired Leases?

The special rights in Section 365 only apply to leases that have not expired prior to the filing, and to contracts that are still executory. If a contract is no longer executory, the non-debtor party is simply an unsecured creditor for whatever damages he or she may have incurred, meaning that the debtor need not do anything and the creditor must simply file a claim. Practically speaking, this means that there is no chance that the debtor will assume the contract and perform it, and virtually no chance that the non-debtor party will be made whole.

But what does it mean for a contract to be executory? Many decades ago, Professor Vern Countryman articulated a now-ubiquitous test for when a contract is executory. Under the Countryman test, a contract remains executory and thus subject to possible assumption if it is

> a contract under which the obligations of both the bankrupt and the counterparty to the contract are so far unperformed that the failure of either to complete performance would constitute a material breach excusing performance of the other.

Vern Countryman, *Executory Contracts in Bankruptcy: Part I*, 57 Minn. L. Rev. 439, 460 (1973). While this test may seem straightforward, it is not always easy to apply. The test requires that some performance be due by each party to the contract. While the performance by the debtor can be merely the payment of money, the other party must have something left to do under the contract.

(2) Ipso Facto Clauses

Once a debtor files for bankruptcy, the non-debtor party (the debtor's counterpart) must honor an executory contract or unexpired lease. During the initial stages of the case, while the debtor is deciding whether to stay in the contract or to be excused from it, the debtor also must honor the contract. The non-debtor party cannot get out of the contract merely because the debtor has filed for bankruptcy and is in financial difficulty. For example, when Kmart filed for bankruptcy, Martha Stewart attempted to use the bankruptcy filing to back out of her contractual obligations to Kmart. She was unsuccessful, because the rule is that so long as Kmart continues to perform the contract post-petition, Kmart's bankruptcy is no excuse for Martha Stewart to dishonor her side of the deal.

A standard contract clause, the ipso facto clause provides that if one party files for bankruptcy or becomes insolvent, the other party can cancel the contract. Another variation of the clause provides that, upon one party's bankruptcy, the contract terminates automatically. But the Bankruptcy Code invalidates ipso facto clauses in order to preserve the debtor's assets. 11 U.S.C. §365(e). This section strikes ipso facto provisions right out of the contract, as if they were never in the contract at all.

The only exceptions, where the ipso facto clause is valid, are personal service contracts that the debtor wishes to assign to a third party (11 U.S.C. §365(e)(2)(A)), and contracts to make loans or extend financial accommodations to the debtor. In these limited circumstances, ipso facto clauses are enforceable.

Sidebar

BULLYING NON-DEBTORS INTO PERFORMING THEIR END OF THE BARGAIN

The debtor company can use a contract to force the supplier to continue supplying, even though the debtor has breached the contract by not paying. While the debtor is deciding whether to assume or reject the contract, both the debtor and the non-debtor party must continue to perform all of the *post-petition* contractual obligations. This sounds fair. However, if the debtor owes the non-debtor party for money it was supposed to pay *pre-petition*, the debtor need not cure the default until it assumes the contract. In this way these provisions are unfair to the non-debtor party, who must continue to perform post-petition despite being unpaid for pre-petition performance.

(3) Rejection of Executory Contracts and Unexpired Leases

Like all parties to executory contracts and leases, the debtor can choose whether to perform its obligations, or to breach. This is an economic decision that the debtor makes by weighing the cost of performance versus the cost of damages for breach, perhaps taking into account the damage to the relationship with the other party. What matters to the court is what is best for the debtor. What is best for the other party is almost completely irrelevant. If the debtor does not want to perform an executory contract or unexpired lease, it will simply move to reject the contract or lease. 11 U.S.C. §365(a).

A debtor's decision to reject a contract or lease is covered by the **business judgment rule**, under which officers and directors of a company (here the debtor) are free to use their business judgment in making decisions about how to run the company. A court will not second-guess those decisions so long as they are reasonable. The standard is low and easy to meet. Consequently, there is really no defense to rejection. If the debtor chooses to reject, the contract or lease is rejected.

In a sense, rejecting a contract or lease can be the more conservative or cost-saving way to handle a contract or lease. Remember, when a debtor rejects an executory contract or an unexpired lease, the non-debtor party receives an unsecured claim for breach of contract (**rejection damages**). 11 U.S.C. §502(g). This claim usually amounts to **actual damages**, but damages for rejection of a real estate lease are capped at the greater of one year's worth of rent under the lease *or* 15% of the remaining term rent, whichever is larger (but not more than three year's worth of rent). 11 U.S.C. §502(b)(6)(A).

Special Rules for Breach of Lease	
Type of Agreement Breached	Damages
Ordinary contract	Actual damages
Real estate lease	One year's rent or 15% of the remaining term (capped at three year's worth of rent), whichever is greater

(4) Assumption of Executory Contracts and Unexpired Leases

Compared to rejection, the decision to assume a contract is a very serious matter in a CHAPTER 11. When the debtor decides to assume an executory contract or an unexpired lease, the debtor is agreeing to pay or perform the entire contract or lease as it was originally written. Moreover, because assumption of the contract or lease occurs post-petition, and the promise to continue performing the contract is made post-petition, if the debtor later liquidates, all of the obligations under the contract become administrative claims with first priority in the case. Therefore the contract claims must be paid in full (11 U.S.C. §503(b)), rather than partially paid, as general unsecured claims, with whatever money is left over after everyone else gets paid.

For these reasons, the easy standard of the business judgment rule does not apply to the decision to assume a contract or lease. Instead, the court carefully scrutinizes each and every assumption decision. Moreover, because the debtor has until confirmation to assume or reject most leases and contracts,[1] the court normally frowns upon attempts to assume contracts or leases prior to confirmation. The court wants to know exactly what the debtor's reorganization plan is before allowing the debtor to incur extensive and expensive post-petition obligations.

---

[1]The exception is real estate leases, which must be assumed within seven months. 11 U.S.C. §365(d)(4). This could be too short a time for a large retailer to decide which premises to keep and which to abandon.

F   A   Q

Q: Why can't contracts simply be renegotiated?

A: They could be if the creditor agreed. The advantage of assumption, from the debtor's point of view, is that you don't need the creditor's consent. Of course, creditors will be hesitant to give favorable terms to companies that are already in bankruptcy — they'll be suspicious and fearful that a company in bankruptcy won't be able to perform its end of the bargain.

What is the standard for assumption of an executory contract or unexpired lease where the non-debtor party objects? If the debtor is not in default, all that's needed is court approval of the assumption. But if the debtor is in default, the Code imposes additional limitations: The debtor must provide the landlord or other party with adequate assurance of future performance, plus show that it has the funds to promptly cure the existing defaults. See 11 U.S.C. §365(b)(1).

Most disputes revolve around whether the debtor can provide adequate assurance of future performance, which is a test designed to protect the non-debtor party and the estate from future defaults under the lease or contract. While the test sounds complex, it boils down to a common-sense, fact-based decision about whether the debtor can make future payments under the contract or lease. See *In re Superior Toy and Manufacturing Co.*, 78 F.3d 1169 (7th Cir. 1996).

(5) Assuming and Assigning Executory Contracts and Unexpired Leases

Not only can a debtor assume or reject executory contracts and unexpired leases, it can also assume and then assign the contract or lease to a third party. 11 U.S.C. §365(f). The reason to do this is that the market value of the lease, for instance, may be a lot higher than what the debtor is currently paying.

For example, suppose the debtor has a ten-year lease to rent a retail space for yearly rent of $10 per square foot on a 5,000 square foot building ($50,000 in rent per year). There are six years left on the lease, but during the first four years, the real estate market has increased such that the going rate for retail space has gone from $10 a square foot to $20 a square foot (now the market value to rent the building is $100,000 per year). In a market like this, the debtor can sell ("assign") its interest in the lease for $100,000 per year for the next six years, or $600,000 total. Therefore the debtor can make a quick $300,000 profit, just by using Section 365(f) to assign the lease.

What a valuable asset! If that asset were being sold along with other assets, like store fixtures, inventory, goodwill, and so on, the debtor's profit might be even higher.

What must the debtor show in order to take advantage of this Code provision? The debtor must prove adequate assurance of future performance by proving that the new tenant will be able to pay the rent into the future. While the landlord does not have veto power over who the new tenant will be, the landlord can contest the new tenant's ability to pay the rent. Alternatively, the landlord can pay the difference in market value to the debtor, essentially buying back the lease from the debtor, to avoid losing control over who the tenant will be.

(6) Adequate Protection in Shopping Center Leases

Special rules apply when the lease is a shopping center lease, particularly if the debtor plans to assume the lease and assign it to a new tenant. 11 U.S.C. §365(b)(3). Shopping center lease legislation is more than just meaningless special interest legislation. Tenants in a shopping center often depend on one another to survive, and also depend upon a certain tenant mix within the center.

The tricky question under Section 365(b)(3) is what constitutes a shopping center. The determination is factual, focusing on the interdependence of the tenants and the perceived intent of the landlord in developing a particular tenant mix. In conducting this analysis, courts consider whether the following facts are present:

Sidebar

TENANT MIX AND SHOPPING CENTER LEASES

Shopping center leases almost always contain clauses limiting the types of stores that can be tenants, in order to avoid direct competition. This is why you rarely see Marshalls, Ross, and T.J. Maxx in the same shopping center, or Borders and Barnes and Noble, Home Depot and Lowe's, Costco and Sam's Club, or Wal-Mart and Kmart.

1. There is a combination of leases.
2. All leases are held by a single landlord.
3. All tenants are engaged in the commercial retail distribution of goods.
4. There is a common parking area.
5. The premises were purposefully developed as a shopping center.
6. There is a master lease in existence.
7. There are fixed hours during which all stores are to remain open.
8. The stores share in joint advertising.
9. There is interdependence between the tenants, evidenced by restrictive use provisions in their leases.
10. There are percentage-rent provisions in the leases.
11. Tenants have the right to terminate their leases if the anchor tenant terminates its lease.
12. The tenants participate in joint trash removal or other maintenance arrangements.
13. There is an existing tenant mix.
14. The stores are contiguous.

In re Joshua Slocum Ltd., 922 F.2d 1081, 1088 (3d Cir. 1990). As you can see, this test is flexible enough to work well in the context of strip malls, indoor malls, and mixed-use outdoor lifestyle shopping centers.

The most significant factor in deciding whether to allow a lease assignment within a shopping center is whether the new tenant will interfere with the tenant mix of the shopping center. In other words, if the debtor is Home Depot, it could not assume and assign its lease to Wal-Mart if there is already a Kmart in the shopping center. However, in a recent case, the court was faced with whether a debtor-tenant could assume and assign its lease to a Michael's craft store, when the shopping center already contained a JoAnn Fabrics Store. *Weingarten Nostat, Inc. v. Service Merchandise Co.*, 396 F.3d 737 (6th Cir. 2005). Although the stores both sell arts and crafts, the court found no interference with tenant mix, thus allowing the debtor to assume and assign the lease. This case shows that the bankruptcy court's loyalties often lie with the debtor, not the landlord or other tenants.

B. Sales of Assets Pursuant to Section 363(b)

Another area where the Code is very useful to many CHAPTER 11 debtors is asset sales. In general, the debtor-in-possession must get court approval to sell property of the estate *outside* of the ordinary course of business (11 U.S.C. §363(b)), in contrast to the sale of property *in* the ordinary course of business, allowed under Section 363(c)(1).

Logically, then, we are focused here on the sale of property that would ordinarily be used by the debtor in its long-term operations. You can think of **Section 363(b) sales** as a natural part of the downsizing process. Sometimes the downsizing efforts are so pronounced that the debtor is attempting to use Section 363(b) to sell its entire operation. This is sometimes seen as a problem because it circumvents the CHAPTER 11 plan process without giving creditors as much information as they would get if a plan were proposed. 11 U.S.C. §363(b).

In addition to Section 363(b) sales, the debtor can sell all of its assets pursuant to a court-approved CHAPTER 11 **liquidating plan**. While selling all the assets is not the model of CHAPTER 11 that we think of (we think of CHAPTER 11 as the process by which the company continues with the same management and remains operational), sales of all of a CHAPTER 11 debtor's assets have become more and more common. Some scholars even believe that liquidation is the most common use of CHAPTER 11 today, rather than rehabilitating the business using the traditional pay-over-time method.

C. Sale of Property from a Debtor's Estate Free and Clear of Liens

If the property to be sold is encumbered with liens or other security interests, a bankruptcy court can order that the assets be sold "free and clear of any interest in such property." This is a big deal. Purchasers can buy assets without worrying about the liens on, or claims against, the assets. Assets stripped of their encumbrances are worth more.

A court can order this type of sale if one of the five conditions found in Section 363(f)(1)-(5) is met. In practical terms, this means the debtor can sell property out from under the claims and liens of secured creditors and judgment creditors, with the claims and liens attaching instead to the proceeds of the sale. This avoids valuation and priority disputes, which could otherwise delay the proceeding and cause the debtor to lose a once-in-a-lifetime chance to sell (at a great price) for the benefit of creditors.

The ability to sell free and clear of claims — such as successor liability claims — allows the debtor, and thus the creditors, to get a higher price for the assets than could be achieved outside of bankruptcy because the assets are cleansed of future liabilities that reduce their value.

The debtor may sell assets free and clear of all liens and claims if applicable non-bankruptcy law would permit a sale of such property free of the interest, 11 U.S.C. §363(f)(1), and also if the creditors holding such liens and claims consent to the sale. 11 U.S.C. §363(f)(2). If the claim in question is a secured claim, the debtor may also sell free and clear of the secured creditor's lien, if the property's sale price *exceeds* "the aggregate value of all liens" on the property. 11 U.S.C. §363(f)(3). Thus the court can approve a sale over a secured party's objection so long as the property's sale price *exceeds* all the liens.

Although this sounds straightforward, courts are divided about what it means. Does the "aggregate value of all liens" on a debtor's property mean the *face value* of the secured creditors' claims or does it mean the 506(a) value of those claims, i.e., the value of the claims after they have been *stripped down*? Under the **economic value** theory, courts focus on the fair market value of the property (the stripped down value). Under the **face value** theory, courts instead focus on the amount of the claim secured by the liens. Most recent cases apply the face value theory, rather than the more debtor-friendly economic value theory.

D. The Section 363(b) Sales Process: Seeking out Highest and Best Bids

In a Section 363(b) sale, the debtor's goal is to get the best price possible for the assets, so as to maximize the money that goes into the estate. The dollar amount of a bid is not the only factor used to determine the "highest and best offer", however. The trustee or debtor-in-possession has discretion to determine what constitutes the **highest and best offer**. *In re Gucci*, 126 F.3d 380 (2d Cir. 1997); *In re After Six, Inc.*, 154 B.R. 876, 881 (Bankr. E.D. Pa. 1993). Courts have recognized, particularly in connection with negotiated bids, that a lower bid can be accepted when legitimate business reasons exist, such as more favorable payment terms, shorter time frame to complete the sale, fewer contingencies, or doubt as to the ability of the highest bidder to complete the purchase. In sum, the highest bid is not always the *highest and best* bid.

In large sales, there is often a starting bid that is then tested in the market through advertising or auction. This first bidder is called the **stalking horse**. The debtor and all the creditors hope that there will be a bidding war in response to the stalking horse bid. However, because the stalking horse has often incurred substantial costs in reviewing the debtor's business assets in order to make the initial bid, it is not uncommon for the stalking horse to ask for bid protection.

One common form of bid protection is called **overbid protection**, which requires that any higher bid must be a given amount higher than the first bid in order to be accepted. When a court is asked to approve a motion for overbid protection, it must decide whether the amount is so large that it will chill bidding rather than encourage bidding. Another form of bid protection is the **break-up fee**, a fee paid to the first bidder in the event that another bidder outbids the stalking horse (to compensate the stalking horse bidder for the cost of doing the research, analysis, and due diligence necessary to put together the first bid). When a court is asked to approve a break-up fee, it must decide whether the break-up fee is worth the cost. A reasonable break-up fee should reflect the amount of time and money the stalking horse invested in making the initial bid.

E. Successor Liability in Section 363 Sales

An obvious advantage of Section 363(b) sales is that the buyer is assured that the assets are free from secured creditor liens and the claims of general unsecured creditors. 11 U.S.C. §363(f). While existing general unsecured creditors have *no* claims in specific property of the debtor, any time a person purchases assets from an ongoing operation there is a possibility that these assets will cause injury in the future. Under successor liability, a successor-in-interest to a corporation may be liable for the product liability claims of its predecessor where the sale is a consolidation, merger, or restructuring of the two corporations, the purchasing corporation is a "mere continuation" of the seller, or the new buyer continues the same product line. *Fairchild Aircraft, Inc. v. Campbell (In re Fairchild Aircraft, Inc.)*, 184 B.R. 910, 920 (Bankr. W.D. Tex. 1995).

The basic principle behind successor liability is that a *plaintiff* in a product liability suit should not be deprived of a remedy just because the company (the defendant) that made the product has merged, reorganized, or sold its assets and gone out of business. If it were that easy to avoid product liability claims, companies would restructure all the time!

Outside bankruptcy, successor liability claims are frequently and successfully asserted against purchaser companies where one of the categories above is met. CHAPTER 11 debtors, however, have been permitted to sell assets free of successor liability claims under Section 363(f). The argument here is that successor liability claims create an "interest in property" that can be eliminated under Section 363(f), and that successor liability claimants can be "compelled, in a legal or equitable proceeding, to accept a money satisfaction of such interest." 11 U.S.C. §363(f)(5). Because tort claims are always paid through a money judgment, many courts have found this argument persuasive.

The big problem, however, is due process. How can a future plaintiff be given due process in adjudicating a claim arising from an accident that has not even happened yet? Like any other claim against the debtor, successor liability claims must be adjudicated and treated (paid) in the bankruptcy case, which may result in the creation of a fund to pay future plaintiffs. If no fund is created during the bankruptcy, the successor may well end up being liable to the successor liability claimant.

F   A   Q

Q: If successor liability is eliminated in bankruptcy, what remedy will plaintiffs have if they are harmed in the future?

A: That is the heart of the due process issue. Where successor liability claims are likely, such as in a mass tort context like asbestos, the debtor can set aside a fund with which to pay claimants as they become ill in the future. In fact, this solution arose in the asbestos cases, and is now memorialized in the Code in Section 524(g). Depending how the due process issue is adjudicated, plaintiffs may be left with no remedy, just as if their defendant had gone out of business, or they may be allowed to pursue the successor to press their liability claims.

SUMMARY

- An executory contract is simply a contract in which both parties still have to perform their side of the deal. If only one side has to perform, it's no longer executory.

- The Code allows the debtor to back out of executory contracts ("reject" them). Thus the debtor can cherry-pick good contracts ("assume" them), while breaking free from contracts with unfavorable terms.

- Once a contract is rejected, the other side gets a general unsecured claim for rejection damages.

- The Code also allows the debtor to assume or reject leases that have not yet expired.

- A standard provision in commercial contracts, the ipso facto clause, says that if one party declares bankruptcy, the other side can cancel the contract. But the Code invalidates ipso facto clauses, striking them from the contract, so that parties cannot cancel contracts with companies that declare bankruptcy.

- The decision to assume a contract or lease requires the debtor to perform completely. It is a very serious matter because it occurs post-petition and thus must be paid in full in the event of liquidation, rather than being partially paid as a general unsecured claim.

- The debtor may also assume and assign (sell to a third party) an executory contract or lease, which is advantageous where the market value of the contract or lease is higher than what the debtor is currently paying.

- Under Section 363(b), the debtor can get court approval to downsize by selling property that would normally be used for long-term operations, such as heavy equipment and facilities. These sales are outside the course of ordinary business.

- The Code allows debtors to sell encumbered assets free and clear of liens and claims, thereby increasing their value and bringing more money into the estate. The liens then attach to the proceeds of the sale.

CONNECTIONS

CHAPTER 11 — Important Issues

We have now covered the most common and important CHAPTER 11 issues. Chapters 16, 17, 18 and 19 walk you through the issues in chronological order, as they arise in a real case — first day orders, the automatic stay, adequate protection, the debtor-in-possession's scope of authority, and restructuring.

The CHAPTER 11 Plan Process

We broke out of chronological order in Chapter 15 to give you the overall plan process up front, even though in real life the proposed plan, circulation, voting, and confirmation come at the end of the CHAPTER 11 case.

Small Businesses

In the next brief chapter, we discuss some special CHAPTER 11 issues that apply to small businesses.

Small Business Cases Under CHAPTER 11

20

Businesses that fit within the definition of small business under Section 101(51D) are subject to slightly different rules and procedures in CHAPTER 11 than other debtors. They must make more disclosures to the court and to creditors and also meet shorter deadlines. If they fail to do these things, they are at risk of conversion or dismissal. On the upside, small business debtors are allowed to follow a cheaper and more simplified plan and disclosure statement process.

O V E R V I E W

A. **DEFINITION MAKES SMALL BUSINESS STATUS MANDATORY, SORT OF**

B. **SHORTER DEADLINES FOR SMALL BUSINESS DEBTORS**

C. **ADDITIONAL REPORTING REQUIREMENTS AND OVERSIGHT**

D. **SIMPLIFICATION OF THE PLAN PROCESS**

E. **HIGHER RISK OF CONVERSION OR DISMISSAL**

A. Definition Makes Small Business Status Mandatory, Sort of

Chapter 16 covered the Chapter 11 plan process for typical Chapter 11 debtors. But if a debtor qualifies as a small business, the rules on filing the plan, the disclosure statement, and a few other matters are different. A **small business debtor** is defined by the Bankruptcy Code as a person engaged in commercial or business activities (not including a person that primarily owns or operates real property) that has aggregate noncontingent, liquidated, secured, and unsecured debts of not more than $2 million, for which the court has not appointed a committee of unsecured creditors or where the court has determined that the committee of unsecured creditors that has been appointed is not sufficiently active and representative to provide effective oversight of the debtor. 11 U.S.C. §101(51C). The nub of the definition is that a business that owes less than $2 million is defined as a small business.

Congress made the small business changes thinking that few debtors would be affected. Research suggests, however, that with the new debt limits, the new small business provisions could affect the vast majority of Chapter 11 debtors, thus changing the entire face of Chapter 11 practice in most parts of the country, at least outside New York, Los Angeles, and Delaware. This could have a negative effect on many small businesses.

The Code has included a definition of small business debtors for quite some time, but in the past, a business *elected* to become a small business debtor, and if a business made this election, its case was put on a faster track, often to the detriment (or at least perceived detriment) of the reorganizing debtor. As a result, very few debtors elected to be small business debtors.

The 2005 amendments changed the position of small businesses by making small business status mandatory for those that fit within the definition. This is significant because small business cases make up over 80% of the Chapter 11 cases filed in this country.

But small business debtors can get around being classified as a small business by making sure that a creditors' committee is formed. If a creditors' committee is appointed, and the committee is active, the case does not fall within the definition of a small business debtor.

B. Shorter Deadlines for Small Business Debtors

In the past, every Chapter 11 debtor had the exclusive right to file a plan for the first 120 days of the bankruptcy case, and another 60 days to confirm a plan and get out of bankruptcy. Creditors could shorten these time limits, debtors could extend them, and extensions could be granted for an unlimited amount of time, for as long as necessary.[1] There was no limit to the number of extensions a debtor could obtain.

Under the 2005 amendments, *non–small business debtors* can request and obtain an **extension of exclusivity** (the exclusive right to file a plan) for just 18 months after the case is filed. After that anyone can file a plan. Obviously, the debtor wants to avoid

---

[1]Some creditors said the extensions were granted far too freely and long past the time necessary to reorganize, upsetting the negotiating balance between debtors and creditors.

a creditor-filed plan, because creditors often file liquidating plans. Regular (non–small business) debtors get two additional months (20 months total) to get the plan confirmed and get out of bankruptcy.[2]

However, *small business debtors* must file a plan within 300 days (10 months). After that, the debtor risks having the case converted or dismissed. This 10-month deadline is not for exclusivity (again, the debtor's exclusive right to file a plan in its case), but is designed to be an absolute deadline for filing the plan.[3]

F A Q

Q: Why are small businesses given so much less time?

A: The reasoning is that their cases should be less complicated and that they should be able to resolve things quicker. The problem with this notion is that all cases, big and small, raise the same issues — there are just more zeros in the bigger cases. The rub is that in big cases there is usually more money to pay lawyers. On the other hand, shorter cases are cheaper, so maybe it's desirable to put pressure on attorneys to get small businesses in and out of CHAPTER 11 quickly.

C. Additional Reporting Requirements and Oversight

One of the central assumptions underlying the new small business provisions is that small CHAPTER 11 cases often do not have active creditors' committees. In fact, only about 15% of all CHAPTER 11 cases have creditors' committees. Creditors' committees provide oversight in cases and also pressure debtors to finish the case and pay creditors. Given the lack of creditors' committees in so many cases, the 2005 amendments pertaining to small businesses require small business debtors to file a much longer list of documents with the court. This was purportedly designed to further the dual objectives of weeding out cases that had little likelihood of success and also to help smaller debtors reorganize by helping them gather and share basic financial information about their own operations. The idea was that small businesses needed the discipline to do this and such discipline would help the debtor reorganize. It's a good example of tough love at work in social engineering.

Counterintuitively, the new law imposes far greater financial reporting requirements on small businesses than on non–small businesses. 11 U.S.C. §1116. These additional debtor requirements include filing the most recent balance sheet, statement of operations, cash-flow statements, and federal tax return (if the debtor has these documents); attending extra meetings with the U.S. Trustee's Office; filing

---

[2]11 U.S.C. §1121(d)(1) & (2).

[3]In reality, the court can extend this deadline, but only if the debtor demonstrates by a preponderance of evidence that it is more likely than not to be able to confirm a plan within a reasonable period of time. This is tantamount to requiring the debtor to prove feasibility for a plan that has not yet been filed. In other words, this extension comes with a tough standard to meet. See 11 U.S.C. §1121(d)(3).

bankruptcy schedules within 45 days of the filing (even though bigger companies usually get a longer extension); and preparing and filing reports regarding the debtor's operations that disclose whether the debtor is operating at a profit, describe the debtor's cash flow, and state whether the debtor is current in filing tax returns and paying post-petition taxes and operating expenses. Small business debtors also must deposit all withholding taxes ("trust fund taxes") in a separate bank account.

While it makes some sense to require a little extra information from small businesses, this is a lot of extra paperwork, particularly given that small companies have scarce resources to gather all the information and produce all the required disclosures. Some scholars suggest these provisions will quietly overhaul the Chapter 11 system, killing rather than saving many small companies in the process.

Under the new law, the statutory duties of the U.S. Trustee are also expanded in small business cases to include these added tasks:

1. conduct an "initial debtor interview," at which the debtor is advised of its obligations under Chapter 11 and the U.S. Trustee begins "to examine the debtor's viability [and] business plan";
2. visit the debtor's business premises and "ascertain the state of the debtor's books and records" when appropriate;
3. review the debtor's activities to determine whether the debtor is likely to be able to confirm a plan within a reasonable time; and
4. file motions to convert or dismiss when appropriate.

Despite these additional tasks, it does not appear that more assistant U.S. Trustees are being appointed to do the extra work. From a practical point of view, this may strain the system and leave the statutory mandates unimplemented.

D. Simplification of the Plan Process

The small business Code provisions attempt to simplify the confirmation process by allowing the debtor to use a standard form plan and disclosure documents, and combining the hearings on disclosure and plan confirmation so as to reduce cost and delay.

E. Higher Risk of Conversion or Dismissal

Finally, the new law requires the court to convert or dismiss any Chapter 11 case for "cause," which now includes "substantial or continuing loss to or diminution of the estate and absence of a reasonable likelihood of rehabilitation," gross mismanagement of the estate, failure to maintain insurance, unauthorized use of cash collateral, failure to comply with any of the reporting requirements of the Code, failure to timely pay post-petition taxes, failure to file a plan within the time limits set out in the Code, and several other grounds. 11 U.S.C. §1112.

This adds a level of specificity that was absent before, and takes away the court's equitable leeway to choose whether to convert or dismiss the case, based upon the importance of the infraction in the overall scheme of the case. Congress's intent in tightening the rules for small business debtors was to provide for quicker action to prevent losses to the estate, and to shift to the debtor the burden of proof regarding the likelihood of reorganization once such losses are shown. While Congress's goals are laudable, the jury is still out on whether the rule changes will do more harm than good.

SUMMARY

■ Small businesses are generally those that owe less than $2 million.

■ Small businesses that don't want to follow the special rules for small businesses in CHAPTER 11 can get out of them if they can get a creditors' committee formed.

■ Small businesses have 300 days to file a plan—roughly 10 months. The deadline normally cannot be extended.

■ Small businesses have more burdensome financial reporting requirements—they must produce a balance sheet, statement of operations, cash-flow statement, and federal tax returns. They also must deposit withholding taxes ("trust fund taxes") in a separate bank account.

■ Small businesses are allowed to use a standard form for plan and disclosure statements, and to combine disclosure and plan confirmation hearings, in an attempt to streamline the process.

■ Small businesses face an enumerated list of infractions that, even if small or technical, will result in conversion or dismissal of their case.

CONNECTIONS

Unsecured Creditors—State Court Collection Process

Once again, don't forget state collection law—obtaining a judgment, taking a writ to the sheriff, and directing the sheriff to execute or levy by exercising dominion and control over the debtor's property. This costly, inconvenient, time-consuming process may be the best option for keeping unsecured creditors at bay.

Secured Creditors—Negotiation

The best option for a small business dealing with secured creditors may simply be to negotiate for more time, or a reduced interest rate, or a refinancing plan. This may be significantly cheaper and less burdensome than the disclosure and oversight required for small businesses under CHAPTER 11.

Basic Bankruptcy Principles

If bankruptcy does turn out to be the right decision for a small business, remember that the same principles we learned about in the first half of the book still apply—the automatic stay, the debtor's estate, claims, treatment of secured claims, and the avoiding powers.

Exemption Law Does Not Apply

Keep in mind that exemptions do not apply in the business context. Both state law and federal exemption schemes only apply to individuals.

Index